Exploring Poetry

Writing and Thinking About Poetry

Frank Madden
SUNY Westchester Community College

Longman

New York   San Francisco   Boston
London   Toronto   Sydney   Tokyo   Singapore   Madrid
Mexico City   Munich   Paris   Cape Town   Hong Kong   Montreal

Vice President and Editor-in-Chief: Joseph Terry
Acquisitions Editor: Erika Berg
Development Manager: Janet Lanphier
Development Editor: Adam Beroud
Marketing Manager: Melanie Craig
Production Manager: Donna DeBenedictis
Project Coordination, Text Design, Art, and Electronic
    Page Makeup: Elm Street Publishing Services, Inc.
Cover Designer/Manager: John Callahan
Cover Illustration: "Flying People Holding Up Book" by Janet Atkinson, courtesy of
    The Stock Illustration Source, Inc.
Photo Researcher: Photosearch, Inc.
Senior Manufacturing Buyer: Dennis J. Para
Printer and Binder: Quebecor World–Taunton
Cover Printer: Phoenix Color Corp.

For permission to use copyrighted material, grateful acknowledgement is made to the
copyright holders on pp. 328–333, which are hereby made part of this copyright page.

Library of Congress Cataloging-in-Publication Data

Madden, Frank
    Exploring poetry: writing and thinking about poetry / Frank Madden.
        p. cm.
    Includes index.
    ISBN 0-321-08894-8 (alk. paper)
    1. English language—Rhetoric—Problems, exercises, etc. 2. Poetry—History and crit-
icism—Problems, exercises, etc. 3. Criticism—Authorship—Problems, exercises, etc. 4.
College readers. I. Title.

PE1479.C7 M35 2002
808.1—dc21

                                                        2001038640

Please visit our website at http://www.ablongman.com/madden

ISBN 0-321-08894-8

1 2 3 4 5 6 7 8 9 10—QWT—04 03 02 01

For my brother, John: teacher, mentor, poet

CONTENTS

CHAPTER 4
Argumentation: Interpreting and Evaluating Poetry   82

PART III   *An Anthology of Poems   115*

Case Study on Poems and Painting   279

Thinking About Interpretation, Poetry, and Painting

PREFACE

We can ask of every assignment or method or text, no matter what its short term effectiveness: Does it get in the way of the live sense of literature? Does it make literature something to be regurgitated, analyzed, categorized, or is it a means toward making literature a more personally meaningful and self-disciplined activity?
— *Louise Rosenblatt,* Literature as Exploration

At the heart of *Exploring Poetry* is the belief that literature can have an important impact on students' lives, but that this impact will be felt only when students experience the "live sense of literature"—the joy, the sorrow, the comfort, and the wisdom that literature offers. Coupled with this belief is an acknowledgment that most students taking literature courses at colleges and universities in this country are not English majors. If asked why they are taking a literature course, they are likely to respond, "Because it's required." Or, "It fit my schedule." It is not evident to many students why literature is important. Other than completing the requirements for a course or curriculum, they don't know *why* they are reading it. Instruction in textual analysis and literary theory alone does not solve this problem. Students must have a stake in the process—a reason to care about literature. And they need the kind of support that will help them read with more confidence. It is the intention of this text to provide this support.

By encouraging students to see their reading in the light of their own experiences, the commentary, questions, and prompts in this book acknowledge the importance of their personal responses and authorize the "meaning making" role students play in the literary experience. The case study in this text expands this role further by helping students understand the relationship between the poems they read and the larger historical and cultural contexts from which these poems spring. Realizing their active role in this process gets students personally involved and gives them a reason to care about literature. Chapters on writing about poetry, critical thinking, and argumentation complete this experience by helping students understand that the construction of a coherent response is a process that changes with rereading and reflection—and that the quality of their interpretations is measured by the strength of the evidence they bring to support them.

Exploring Poetry is designed for instructors who believe, as I do, that a successful experience with poetry requires students' engagement as well as analysis—not only as motivation to complete the requirements of a course but as a prelude to a lifelong relationship with literature.

KEY FEATURES

The key features of this text are intended to support an expansive process of engaging students in the literary experience. By exploring poetry as an "experience" within a world of personal responses and contextual influences, these features encourage students to invest their emotions, to build on their knowledge and experience, and to think critically—to be fully involved with the live sense of literature.

Making Connections

Confident, experienced readers tap their storehouse of emotional and intellectual knowledge naturally, and, when they draw a blank, feel confident that other elements of the work will help them to make sense of it. Less experienced readers, however, need support and guidance to become confident readers. Questions and exercises in Part I, "Making Connections," are designed to "sensitize" students to the emotional context of poetry by encouraging them to recall their own experiences and to read poems "impressionistically" and with more confidence. This process does not guarantee a masterful analysis, but it does help students acknowledge and build on what they know and feel when they read, enabling them to connect with poems more easily. Acknowledging, reviewing, and thinking critically about the responses students make as they read may provide them with valuable insights into poetry and themselves. These early chapters focus on the process of personal response as a starting point in a recursive sequence leading from engagement and reflection to formal critical tasks and literary interpretation—a journey from participating to observing responses.

Writing About Poetry

From journals to formal critical and research essays, students use writing to learn about poetry. The use of writing as the most important instructional tool in literature classes is well documented. Students who examine their own practices in reading and writing become more self-aware, more independent, and stronger readers and writers.

Critical Thinking

Whether they are reviewing their own judgments or citing evidence to support a critical essay, students are encouraged to think critically about their responses throughout this book. Of special note is Chapter 4, "Argumentation: Interpreting and Evaluating Poetry," which focuses directly on the processes of critical thinking and argumentation. Explanations, examples, and exercises guide students through the processes of inductive reasoning and substantiation, interpretation and evaluation, and planning and supporting an argument. Issues of purpose, audience, and evidence are central to this discussion, which culminates in the writing of a critical essay.

Two Readers, Two Choices

Langston Hughes's poem "Theme for English B" is highlighted and followed by two sample student essays written from different perspectives. These essays illustrate diversity of opinion, exemplify ways in which the poem might be read, and demonstrate how students' own experiences, behaviors, values, and opinions are tools for deepening their understanding and appreciation of poetry.

Samples of Student Writing

There are five student essays and many other samples of students' writing throughout the text.

The Poems

The poems in this book, a broad selection of both classic and contemporary pieces, have been chosen for their quality, diversity, and appeal to students.

A Case Study on Poems and Painting

A case study, **"Thinking About Interpretation, Poetry and Painting,"** includes nine famous paintings and poems written about them. This casebook concludes with a process, a student's journal responses and semantic maps, and product, the final draft of her essay that compares Vincent van Gogh's *Starry Night* and Anne Sexton's poem about it.

Questions and Prompts

Questions throughout this book tap students' responses without implying right or wrong answers. They encourage students to reflect and evaluate. Prompts in this book help students flesh out, clarify, and support their responses. They encourage students to ask their own questions—questions that open up, not shut down, additional possibilities. They respect the reader's role and encourage divergent response, but emphasize that the value of an assertion lies not in itself but in the nature of its supporting evidence.

Voice

The narrative "voice" of *Exploring Poetry* is informal and conversational. This book is intended to be read by students—to be accessible, friendly, and informative.

ORGANIZATION: USING THIS TEXT

Exploring Poetry can be used in many different ways. Its explanations, prompts, and poems are resources to be chosen by instructors and students as needed, in or out of sequence, with maximum flexibility. Although the reading and writing activities in this book are organized in a sequence of increasing complexity, the recursive nature of both writing and responding to poetry is emphasized throughout.

For instructors who want to emphasize a reader-response approach and ask their students to keep journals or write response essays about the poems they read, **Part I, "Making Connections,"** provides a rich source of material. These chapters are more than an exploration of poetry. They are an exploration of the students who read and write about it. Students are encouraged to think about the ways that their own backgrounds and personalities, their understanding of others, their knowledge of texts and contexts—their "meaning making" processes—influence their responses to poetry. Questions that accompany the poems help students clarify their responses and develop them into text-supportable hypotheses and essays. **Chapter 1, "Participation: Personal Response and Critical Thinking,"** helps students develop connections to poetry through their own backgrounds and experiences. **Chapter 2, "Communication: Writing About Poetry,"** introduces students to aspects of literary craft through discussions of voice, description, and comparison—fostering the sensitivity to language necessary for a complete experience with literature. The chapter concludes with a discussion of the writing process, samples of drafts, and a final response essay.

Instructors who favor a more text-based approach may choose to skip Part 1 and move directly to **Part II, "Analysis and Argumentation." Chapter 3, "Exploration and Analysis: The Elements of Poetry,"** emphasizes the importance of close reading and analysis. A general introduction to poetry is followed by a comprehensive explanation of the elements that make poetry a distinct form. Carefully chosen selections illustrate and support these explanations. Wherever possible, explanations of the elements are illustrated with reference to students' experiences and are accompanied by specific examples from poems in the text.

Chapter 4, "Argumentation: Interpreting and Evaluating Poetry," guides students through the processes of critical thinking, reading, writing, and research. Students are reminded of the ways in which they use critical thinking in their own lives, and how similar methods of analysis and support can be used to interpret and evaluate poetry. Inductive thinking, substantiation, interpretation, and evaluation are explained and discussed. The use of argumentation to develop critical essays is presented and supported by student entries, giving students insights into how to develop their own ideas. Based on the elements discussed in Chapter 3, students are provided with questions, prompts, and checklists to help them develop standards. A comprehensive discussion of argumentation helps students see the difference between response and critical essays and suggests specific questions to ask when constructing an effective argument. The chapter concludes with a student's critical essay.

Part III, Alphabetically Arranged Anthology The readings cover a broad selection of classic and contemporary pieces, each chosen for its quality, diversity, and appeal to students.

Appendix A, "Critical Approaches to Literature," is a succinct discussion of major critical theories.

Appendix B, "Research and Documentation—Some Basics," explains what must be documented to evaluate Internet sources, plagiarism, the physical layout of a research essay, and the correct format for MLA documentation.

The **Glossary** provides a useful reference tool.

SUPPLEMENTS

A Workshop Guide for Creative Writing This laminated reference tool offers suggestions for students to keep in mind in a workshop situation—both as a participant and presenter. Blank space is provided for students to record additional guidelines provided by their instructor. Available FREE when value-packed with *Exploring Poetry*. Ask your Longman representative for details. ISBN 0-321-09539-1

The Longman Journal for Creative Writing This journal is designed to help students explore and discover their own writing habits and styles. Various features are provided that will incite students to practice many forms of writing such as: freewriting, concrete and abstract description, exploring the past, and exploring dreams. In addition, there are numerous exercises and activities on a variety of topics including: poetic and prose forms, image, voice, character, plot, setting, sound and rhythm, and theme. A great deal of space is also provided for students to record their thoughts and ideas whenever the urge strikes. Available FREE when value-packed with *Exploring Poetry*. Ask your Longman representative for details. ISBN 0-321-09540-5

Responding to Literature: A Writer's Journal This writer's journal provides students with their own personal space for writing. Writing prompts for responding to fiction, poetry, and drama are included. Available FREE when value-packed with *Exploring Poetry*. Ask your Longman representative for details. ISBN 0-321-09541-1

The Longman Guide to Columbia Online Style This 32-page booklet includes an overview of Columbia Online Style (COS), guidelines for finding and evaluating electronic sources, and examples for citing electronic sources. COS is a documentation style developed specifically for citing electronic sources. Available FREE when value-packed with *Exploring Poetry*. Ask your Longman representative for details. ISBN 0-321-06745-2

Researching On-line, Fifth Edition This supplement shows students how to do research on the Internet in an easy-to-follow, step-by-step format. Internet resources, such as the Internet, e-mail, and "real-time discussion," are explained with straightforward language and clear examples. ISBN 0-321-09277-5

Course Compass Course Compass combines the strength of Longman content with state-of-the-art Learning tools. Course Compass is a nationally hosted, dynamic, interactive online course management system powered by Blackboard, leaders in the development of Internet-based learning tools. This easy-to-use and customizable program enables professors to tailor content and functionality to meet individual course needs. For more information, or to see a demo, visit www.coursecompass.com, or contact your local Longman sales representative.

Penguin Program In cooperation with Penguin Putnam Inc., one of Longman's sibling companies, we are proud to offer a variety of Penguin paperbacks at a significant discount when packaged with any Longman title. Excellent additions to any literature course, Penguin titles give students the opportunity to explore contemporary and classic works.

Analyzing Literature, Second Edition This brief supplement provides critical reading strategies, writing advice, and sample student papers to help students interpret and discuss literary works in a variety of genres. Suggestions for collaborative activities and online research on literary topics are also featured, as are numerous exercises and writing assignments. ISBN 0-321-05504-7

Audio- and Videotapes For qualified adoptors, an impressive selection of videotapes and Longman audiotapes is available to enrich students' experience of poetry.

Exploring Literature **Web site** The *Exploring Literature* Web site can be found at http://www.ablongman.com/madden. This site includes in-depth information about featured authors, activities for writing about poetry, and helpful links to poetry and research sites.

English Pages (http://www.ablongman.com/englishpages) This Web site provides professors and students with continuously updated resources for reading, writing, and research practice in four areas: composition, literature, technical writing, and basic skills. Features include simulated searches, where students simulate the process of finding and evaluating information on the World Wide Web, and first-person essays that show students how everyday men and women have applied what they have learned in composition to a wide variety of writing issues and research topics.

ACKNOWLEDGMENTS

I am indebted to many people over the years who have had a direct and indirect influence on my teaching philosophy—and on the writing of this book. Most notable among these teacher-scholars is Louise Rosenblatt, my teacher at NYU nearly 30 years ago. In addition, John Clifford, Alan Purves, Peter Elbow, Wayne Booth, Robert Scholes, Ann Berthoff, Toby Fulwiler, Robert Berlin, Carl Schmidt, Cindy Onore, John Mayher, Dawn Rodrigues, Judith Stanford, Kathi Blake Yancey, and others have influenced and inspired my work. I am grateful to my generous and caring colleagues at WCC: Bill Costanzo, Joanne Falinski, Richard Courage, Mira Sakrajda, and others who read the manuscript, tried out the materials, contributed ideas, and/or submitted student samples—and to Alan Devenish, Elizabeth Gaffney, and Mary Ellen LeClair who contributed their work to this volume. I am thankful to my students who have taught me so much about teaching and this book, especially those students who contributed their work to this text: Dierdre Curran, Mark Strumke, Barbara Pfister, William Winters, Jennifer Stelz, and others. I am indebted to President Joseph Hankin for fostering an atmosphere at WCC that made this work possible. And I am especially grateful to my brother John, who early in my life gave me a reason to care about literature, and to my wife, Sharon, my most discerning reader and loving supporter.

For their thoughtful and insightful comments about the manuscript, I wish to thank the following reviewers: Beth Ellen Anstandig, San Jose State University; Brian Daldorph, University of Kansas; Carol Ann Davis, College of Charleston; Jackie Donaldson-Pippins, George Mason University; Danielle Dubrasky, Southern Utah University; Annie Finch, Miami University (Ohio); Saundra Morris, Bucknell University; and Porter Shreve, University of Michigan.

At Longman, I am grateful to Erika Berg and Joe Terry whose vision, support, and friendship made this book possible, and to Adam Beroud whose skill, patience, and advice were much appreciated during the process. I am indebted to Katharine Glynn whose guidance on a previous text continued to inform my work on this one. I wish to thank Melanie Craig for getting the word out so effectively, and Donna DeBenedictis, Abby Westapher, and Ann Bailey for their dedication, fine work, and patience while turning a manuscript into a book.

Frank Madden
SUNY Westchester Community College

◆ ABOUT THE AUTHOR ◆

FRANK MADDEN

Frank Madden is Professor and Chair of the English Department at SUNY Westchester Community College. His undergraduate degree is from St. John's University, where he played baseball, and his Ph.D. is from New York University. He has taught in graduate programs at CCNY, Iona College, and the New School for Social Research, and in 1998 was Chair of the NCTE College Section Institute on the Teaching of Literature. He is a recipient of the SUNY Chancellor's Award for Excellence in Teaching, the Foundation for Westchester Community College Faculty Award for Excellence in Scholarship, and the Phi Delta Kappan Educator of the Year Award from Iona College. He was Chair of the College Section of the NCTE from 1995–1998 and has served on the Executive Committees of the NCTE, the MLA-ADE, the SUNY Council on Writing, and as Chair of the MLA ad hoc Committee on Teaching. He is currently Chair of TYCA and serves on the CCCC and NCTE Executive Committees. His articles and chapters about the teaching of literature have appeared in a variety of books and journals, including College English, College Literature, English Journal, Computers and Composition, Computers and the Humanities, *and the* ADE Bulletin. *He is author of* Exploring Literature *(Longman, 2001) and* Exploring Fiction *(Longman, 2002). He lives in Brewster, New York, with his wife, Sharon, and they have two daughters, Michelle and Suzanne.*

PART I

Making
Connections

CHAPTER 1

Participation
Personal Response and Critical Thinking

We begin our exploration of poetry with you, the reader. Your engagement creates the literary experience. By themselves, the poems in this book, as brilliantly crafted or as famous or critically acclaimed as they may be, are just words on a page. It is your reading of these words through the lenses of your own experiences and beliefs that brings them to life and gives them meaning, a meaning ultimately as unique as you are.

Literature reveals a possible world to us. Our engagement and involvement are the keys to enter this world and to imagine its possibilities. Our backgrounds and personalities, our understanding of others, our prior experience with literature, our knowledge of the world—our sources for making meaning—are important factors in this process. And unlike our busy lives, which sometimes race forward with little time for reflection, literature awaits our examination. We can participate in it as we experience it, and analyze it as we step back and observe it.

THE PERSONAL DIMENSION OF READING POETRY

Most poems do not intend to convey a moral or lesson. At their best, they reveal as life reveals. But like life, our *reading* of poetry evokes our emotion and judgment. The speakers in poems express their beliefs in what they say or do, and as we read, we respond to their words and actions through our own beliefs—comparing their choices with our own, and approving or disapproving as they meet or fail to meet our expectations. While most good literature does not teach or preach, it does explore and reveal what it means to be human and provides us with a substantial opportunity for learning and self-understanding.

Later on in this chapter, and throughout the book, you are asked to think about your responses and to consider how your own experiences and beliefs influence them. Acknowledging, reviewing, and thinking critically about the judgments you make as you read may provide you with valuable insights into poetry and yourself.

PERSONAL RESPONSE AND CRITICAL THINKING

Thinking critically about literature is an outgrowth of our personal responses. It is natural for us to want to comprehend what moves us or has meaning to us. As children, we may have tried to make sense of what we read by making connections with other things we had read or experienced. We might have remembered reading something similar or believed that a particular author would keep us engaged. We knew what we liked to read, and even if we didn't analyze our reading systematically, we may have wondered what made it appealing to us.

When we think critically about poetry we build on our personal responses—recording them, reviewing them, discussing them, and supporting them. Being engaged is a crucial initial component of a poetic experience. But once we experience this engagement and believe that the poem has something to offer us, it follows that we want to know more about it, to see how it triggers our responses and judgments, to understand the skill with which it was created, and to articulate what it means to us.

Critical thinking does not mean searching for one right answer. There may be as many answers as there are readers. *Your* best answers are those that analyze and articulate your responses in the light of supporting evidence. This is critical thinking, a process that can make your opinions about poetry well-informed ones.

WRITING TO LEARN

Writing is an excellent way to learn about poetry. Whether you are jotting down notes, writing in a journal, or constructing a formal essay, you're learning. You're learning when you struggle to choose the right words to describe your impressions, and when you revise those words because they are not quite what you mean. And you are learning when you "get it just right" and see your words match what you want to say. In short, writing your responses down helps you learn and articulate what you think and feel more clearly.

Keeping a Journal or Reading Log

One of the best tools for exploring and thinking about your experiences in writing is a journal or reading log, and you may find it helpful to keep one in which to record your responses to the poems in this book. Journals and reading logs can help you view and review your ideas. Writing and reading your words on paper may help you articulate, clarify, and expand your ideas. Use your journal to identify and express your reactions, what moves or bothers you, or what seems intriguing or confusing. Write in your most natural voice and don't worry about sounding wise. Take chances and try out ideas. Unless you decide to share them, you are the only one who will see these entries.

If you use your journal to keep a record of your responses, you can look back for connections later on. These responses, along with subsequent reading and the comments of classmates, can help you develop ideas as you write the essays required by your instructor. If you are conscientious about keeping your journal, your entries will evolve naturally into a statement of the meaning you've constructed from the work. In the long run, the most important ingredient in your essays will not be the position you take, but the support you derive from the literature and your experience with it. Recording these observations in your journal now may provide you with some of this support later.

What you write in your journal or log is your choice. It should be as unique as your experience with the literature itself. You may or may not like what you read. You may find it engaging or filled with meaning. You may find it confusing or boring. Whatever your response, you'll benefit most from keeping a journal or log if your entries honestly reflect your experience.

A variation of the journal is a **literature response sheet**. Like the journal, each response sheet accounts for your first impressions during and after your reading. Your instructor may collect them and use them to initiate class discussion.

There is no one correct way of keeping a journal or log. The student samples that follow are all different, but each is a start and might be built upon to develop a more formal essay. ("Love Is Not All" appears on p. 73 and "There's a Certain Slant of Light" on p. 154.) Even if you are not familiar with these pieces, these samples reflect the kinds of issues that might be addressed in response to any work of literature.

From confusion:

During my reading, I thought the author was saying that love was not important to physically survive. But halfway through she states that people are dying for lack of love alone. After reading this poem, I'm still confused about the meaning.

To an appreciation of the author's artistry:

I really like his poem. The poet says that although love isn't a biological need (food, shelter, safety), you really can't live without it. People can die of a broken heart or of loneliness. It can't physically save your life, but it can in a way--by giving you a will to live. The poet says she wouldn't sell her love or memories for food if she was starving. I don't think I would either. There's really no other feeling like knowing you are unconditionally loved. It can overcome anything. The title of the poem itself seems strange--instead of saying all the great things love is, she described what it isn't, which makes the poem that much more powerful.

From identification:

The first time I read the lines "There's a certain slant of light, / Winter Afternoons-- / That oppresses, like the Heft / of Cathedral Tunes--" I had an immediate picture of grayish-white skies and cold, bare ground. It was almost frightening. The first stanza expresses a feeling I've had for a lifetime <u>of hideous, anxiety-filled, depressing Sunday winter afternoons</u>. From childhood, with homework unfinished and school rearing its terrifying Monday-morning head, through adulthood and its end-of-the-weekend, back to work dread, I've experienced that "Seal Despair--."

To complete frustration:

I've read this poem over and over, repeatedly, non-stop, until I finally collapsed from total exhaustion. This must be the most confusing poem I've had the misfortune of stumbling upon.

WHAT DOES IT MEAN!? What light? The winter afternoon light? As heavy as cathedral tunes? Find a scar from what? Internal difference? Meanings? Aggggh!

Help. Could the author be talking about the sun? All I have are questions when it comes to this poem. I do like the choice of words, though. They sounded grand, royal, imperial, and made me feel like there was something to grab from them. I am disappointed in myself, and the people around me, who also couldn't make sense of it.

Double-Entry Journals and Logs

Because you may be asked to read and write comments about your journal or log entries from time to time, an especially effective format is the double-entry journal. By writing on only the front side of each page (or on the right half of each page), you will leave the back of the previous page (or the left half of each page) free for subsequent commentary (new ideas, revisions, summation, etc.) while rereading and reflecting. Leaving this space, you may go back later, read through your comments, circle and make notes about entries you've made, or add additional comments based on subsequent readings or class discussion.

After talking it over with my group, I see that this is not "beautiful and bright" sunlight but the dim and pale (and depressing) sunlight of winter.

Interesting punctuation! Not really punctuation but capitalization. At first glance the poem appears to be about the beauty of a ray of sunlight shooting through the clouds. Could "slant of light" be a symbolic way of thinking? Maybe this is about falling out of love-- winter afternoons or dead afternoons. This love oppresses me. I'm not sure about the second or third lines but the fourth or fifth could fit the love analogy.

The Social Nature of Learning: Collaboration

Writing ideas down is one effective way to learn, but so much of what we learn is also learned through conversation. Sharing our responses with others, and listening to their feedback and ideas, helps us build and clarify our own ideas.

By articulating what you think you know and what you need to know through conversation, you may develop a clearer understanding of the poem. Throughout this text you'll be encouraged to share and exchange your ideas and collaborate with your classmates in pairs and small groups.

Personal, Not Private

Many of the questions that follow in this chapter prompt you to write about personal issues. These questions are not an attempt to invade your privacy or encourage you to write about aspects of your life or experience that may embarrass you or make you feel uncomfortable. What is personal or private is very different for each of us. You may choose to write some responses for your eyes only, some to share, or some not at all. That choice is always yours.

OURSELVES AS READERS

Our early experiences with books may have a significant influence on how we feel about reading. For many of us who enjoy reading, this joy was discovered outside the classroom. We felt free to experience the books we read without fear of having our responses judged as right or wrong. For many who do not like to read, however, reading was often a painful chore, usually an assignment for the classroom with all the accompanying pressures of being evaluated. How often we read now and whether we see ourselves as good readers may have much to do with these earlier experiences.

You might find it worthwhile to write about some of these reading experiences in your journal or share them with others. It may be illuminating to see how much you have in common as a reader with other members of the class.

Different Kinds of Reading

Unfortunately, for many of us, the different types of reading we were given in school were often treated the same way. Reading assignments that primarily dealt with content or factual information were often not distinguished from imaginative literature. We know, however, that different types of reading material require very different kinds of involvement. Reading a science text, for example, requires that we focus on acquiring information for future use, whereas a poem, while requiring our understanding of the facts, seeks to involve us personally in the moment—to have us share an experience, to evoke our feelings.

Read the following paragraph.

> CAUTION—NOT FOR PERSONAL USE—If splashed on skin or in eyes, rinse immediately. If accidentally taken internally give large amounts of milk or water. Call a physician. Point mouth of container away from you when removing cap. AVOID TRANSFER TO FOOD OR BEVERAGE CONTAINERS—KEEP CONTAINER UPRIGHT IN A COOL PLACE TIGHTLY CAPPED.

▶ GETTING STARTED—YOUR FIRST RESPONSE

1. What is your response to the paragraph above?
2. Of what use is the information in this statement?

Read the following poem.

PETER MEINKE (b.1932)

ADVICE TO MY SON   [1981]

— for Tim

The trick is, to live your days
as if each one may be your last
(for they go fast, and young men lose their lives
in strange and unimaginable ways)
but at the same time, plan long range   5
(for they go slow: if you survive
the shattered windshield and the bursting shell
you will arrive
at our approximation here below
of heaven or hell).   10

To be specific, between the peony and the rose
plant squash and spinach, turnips and tomatoes;
beauty is nectar
and nectar, in a desert, saves—
but the stomach craves stronger sustenance   15
than the honied vine.
Therefore, marry a pretty girl
after seeing her mother;
speak truth to one man,
work with another;   20
and always serve bread with your wine.

But, son,
always serve wine.

➤ GETTING STARTED—YOUR FIRST RESPONSE

1. What is your reaction to this poem?
2. What advice do you think is being given?
3. Do you agree or disagree with this advice?
4. Of what use is the information in this poem?

➤ QUESTIONS FOR READING AND WRITING

Compare your response to the warning label paragraph with your response to the poem "Advice to My Son."

1. Both the poem and the warning label give advice. In what way was your reading experience with each different?
2. Did the physical appearance of each influence *how* you read it? If the warning label were written in verse form would you have read it with different expectations?
3. To what extent can you connect the advice given in the poem to your own background or experience? To what extent can you connect the advice given in the warning label?
4. Did you learn anything from the poem? From the warning label? If so, did the *nature* of what you learned differ in each case? Explain.

Asking Your Own Questions

The process of reading often raises more questions than it answers. After reading, some of the most important questions to address are the ones you have raised yourself. So before you answer the questions that follow each selection in this chapter, you may want to write down your first impressions and any questions that came to mind during and after your reading.

MAKING CONNECTIONS

Among the many factors that influence our responses to literature is identification with characters, circumstances, and issues. Our personalities, backgrounds, and experiences can have a strong impact on these connections.

We may identify with the speakers or characters because we see aspects of our own personalities in them or admire aspects of their personalities and wish we had them ourselves. We might respond negatively to them because aspects of their personalities are different from ours or similar to ones we don't like in ourselves. We may agree or disagree with what they say or do, or ask ourselves if we would have behaved the same way.

Conversely, by showing us a view of life that is different from our own, literature might influence our beliefs and behavior. We may learn from literature as we learn from life itself.

Images of Ourselves

How we view ourselves in relation to the world around us is very complex. We probably have an image of who we are that we carry within ourselves most of the time. That image may have been formed when we were children, but we still carry it with us today. And we are likely to project a different personality according to the situations (home, work, school, etc.) in which we find ourselves. Depending on our relationships with them, the people we know are also likely to describe us very differently. Our families, friends, casual acquaintances, employers, and teachers may experience who we are in very different ways.

MAKING CONNECTIONS—"Zimmer in Grade School"

The self-images we carry with us into adulthood may be formed during childhood. Try to remember how you felt about yourself as a child and compare that self-image with how you see yourself now.

PAUL ZIMMER (b. 1934)

ZIMMER IN GRADE SCHOOL   [1983]

In grade school I wondered
Why I had been born
To wrestle in the ashy puddles,
With my square nose
Streaming mucus and blood.   5
My knuckles puffed from combat
And the old nun's ruler,
I feared everything: God,

Learning and my schoolmates.
I could not count, spell or read.
My report card proclaimed   10
These scarlet failures.
My parents wrang their loving hands.
My guardian angel wept constantly.

But I could never hide anything.   15
If I peed my pants in class
The puddle was always quickly evident.
My worst mistakes were at
The blackboard for Jesus and all
The saints to see.   20
          Even now
When I hide behind an elaborate mask
It is always known that I am Zimmer,
The one who does the messy papers
And fractures all his crayons,   25
Who spits upon the radiators
And sits all day in shame
Outside the office of the principal.

▶ QUESTIONS FOR READING AND WRITING

1. What did you wonder about yourself in grade school? To what extent do you still wonder the same things?
2. What does the speaker mean by "When I hide behind an elaborate mask / It is always known that I am Zimmer"? Who is Zimmer?

▶ MAKING CONNECTIONS—"Not Waving but Drowning"

Many of us have had the experience of being told by people that once they got to know us they discovered we differed greatly from their earlier impression of us. Can you recall an experience like that in your own life? If so, try to remember how it made you feel to hear that.

STEVIE SMITH (1902–1971)

NOT WAVING BUT DROWNING   [1957]

Nobody heard him, the dead man,
But still he lay moaning:
I was much further out than you thought
And not waving but drowning.

Poor chap, he always loved larking   5
And now he's dead
It must have been too cold for him his heart gave way,
They said.

Oh, no no no, it was too cold always
(Still the dead one lay moaning)   10
I was much too far out all my life
And not waving but drowning.

➤ QUESTIONS FOR READING AND WRITING

1. What do you think is happening in the poem? Who is drowning?
2. There is more than one speaker in this poem. Who are these speakers?
3. To what extent is your response to this poem affected by your own experience?

Culture, Experience, and Values

Who we are and how we respond to literature is also influenced by many other factors. Family, religion, race, gender, friends, other influential people in our lives, and our experiences shape our views in significant ways.

We may come from a family that is strongly connected to its ethnic roots, religious or not religious at all, closely knit or disconnected, warm and welcoming, suffocating, or cold and impersonal. Or we may not have a family at all. Our friends, too, may affect who we are, what we believe, and how we act.

We may be strongly influenced by our race, ethnic background, or gender. If we have never experienced or witnessed discrimination, we might not be able to understand its significance. If we have witnessed prejudice or had it directed against us, we know how devastating it can be. Our gender may affect the expectations others have for us, the encouragement we receive for education and career goals, marriage and family, even our involvement in sports. And it certainly influences our view of the opposite sex.

If we are deeply religious, it might be at the heart of everything we value. If we are not, our religious backgrounds may still exert a strong influence on our lives. What we do for a living, how old we are, our sexual orientation, our disabilities, or other factors may also affect how we see the world—and the literature we read.

➤ MAKING CONNECTIONS—"Incident"

If you have ever been called a derogatory name because of your race, ethnic background, gender, or other factor, you know how disturbing that experience can be. If you have ever been in this position or witnessed it happening to someone else, try to recall your reaction. If you've never been in this position, try to imagine how it might make someone feel.

COUNTEE CULLEN (1903–1946)

INCIDENT   [1925]

Once riding in old Baltimore,
    Heart-filled, head-filled with glee,
I saw a Baltimorean
    Keep looking straight at me.

Now I was eight and very small,   5
    And he was no whit bigger,
And so I smiled, but he poked out
    His tongue, and called me, "Nigger."

I saw the whole of Baltimore
    From May until December;   10
Of all the things that happened there
    That's all that I remember.

➤ QUESTIONS FOR READING AND WRITING

1. Can you describe an event in your life that made such a lasting impression
   on you?
2. If you have experienced or observed an event like the one described in
   "Incident," how does this influence your response? If you have not experienced or observed an event like this, how does this affect your response to
   the poem?
3. If the speaker were describing a racist incident he experienced as an adult,
   how do you think the poem would be different? Why does the speaker say,
   "That's all that I remember"?
4. In what way does the title of the poem fit the poem's content?
5. How does the rhyme scheme of the poem affect your response to the
   poem's content?

➤ MAKING CONNECTIONS—"Those Winter Sundays"

Most of us can probably identify a person who was "always there" for us and
who seemed to do the things that really mattered without being asked and who
may often have been taken for granted.

   Before you read the following poem, try to recall someone like that in your
own life.

ROBERT HAYDEN (1913–1980)

THOSE WINTER SUNDAYS   [1962]

Sundays too my father got up early
and put his clothes on in the blueblack cold,
then with cracked hands that ached
from labor in the weekday weather made
banked fires blaze. No one ever thanked him.   5

I'd wake and hear the cold splintering, breaking.
When the rooms were warm, he'd call,
and slowly I would rise and dress,
fearing the chronic angers of that house,

Speaking indifferently to him,   10
who had driven out the cold
and polished my good shoes as well.
What did I know, what did I know
of love's austere and lonely offices?

➤ QUESTIONS FOR READING AND WRITING

1. Describe the situation in the poem. Who is the speaker?
2. How does the speaker feel? Have you ever had similar feelings?
3. If you could identify a person who was "always there" for you, how does this remembrance influence your understanding of the poem?
4. What does the speaker mean by "love's austere and lonely offices"?
5. What other words, phrases, or parts of the poem had an impact on you? How so?

➤ MAKING CONNECTIONS—"Barbie Doll"

In a world that bombards us with images from television, films, and magazines, many of us feel great pressure to look or behave in particular ways. Sometimes this pressure may even make us value our own individual strengths less favorably than what is simply more popular. See if you can recall a time when you felt pressured this way and how you reacted to that pressure.

MARGE PIERCY (b. 1936)

BARBIE DOLL   [1969]

This girlchild was born as usual
and presented dolls that did pee-pee
and miniature GE stoves and irons
and wee lipsticks the color of cherry candy.
Then in the magic of puberty, a classmate said: 5
You have a great big nose and fat legs.

She was healthy, tested intelligent,
possessed strong arms and back,
abundant sexual drive and manual dexterity.
She went to and fro apologizing.   10
Everyone saw a fat nose on thick legs.

She was advised to play coy,
exhorted to come on hearty,
exercise, diet, smile and wheedle.
Her good nature wore out   15
Like a fan belt.
So she cut off her nose and her legs
and offered them up.
In the casket displayed on satin she lay
with the undertaker's cosmetics painted on,   20
a turned-up putty nose,
dressed in a pink and white nightie.
Doesn't she look pretty? everyone said.

Consummation at last.
To every woman a happy ending.   25

➤ QUESTIONS FOR READING AND WRITING

1. To what extent is your response influenced by your own experience?
   Could you identify with the feelings of the "girlchild" in this poem?
2. The media bombard all of us with images that pressure us to act or look in
   a certain way. How does your experience with advertisements, television,
   movies, magazines, or newspapers influence your response to the poem?
3. Do you think a female reader is likely to respond differently to this poem
   than a male reader? Explain.
4. Do you think the "girlchild" is literally dead at the end of the poem?
   Explain.
5. What do you think "Consummation at last. / To every woman a happy
   ending" means?
6. What other words, phrases, or parts of the poem affected you? How so?

7. Compare this poem with "Advice to My Son" (p. 7). If Meinke's poem were called "Advice to My Daughter," do you think the advice would be the same?

Being in the Moment

We can't get at the heart of our experience with literature by summarizing it. We might account for all that matters on the "Caution" label on the bleach bottle (p. 7) by saying, "This is a very caustic liquid and you could hurt yourself by coming in contact with it." But we couldn't get at the essence of the poem "Incident" by saying, "A kid went to Baltimore, someone called him a name, and he's never forgotten it." We read the warning label for the information we take away with us; the label seeks to inform us. Literature seeks to involve us.

A newspaper article, for example, might relate the "who, what, when, where, and why" of an event, but literature must do much more than that. It may even move us to question events in our own lives and influence us as we make our own decisions. The following newspaper account appeared in the *New York Times* the day after the racially motivated bombing of a church in Birmingham, Alabama, in 1963.

BIRMINGHAM BOMB KILLS 4 NEGRO GIRLS IN CHURCH; RIOTS FLARE; 2 BOYS SLAIN

GUARD SUMMONED

Wallace Acts on City Plea for Help as 20 Are Injured

By CLAUDE SITTON
Special to *The New York Times*
BIRMINGHAM, Ala., Sept. 15—[1963]

A bomb severely damaged a Negro church today during Sunday school services, killing four Negro girls and setting off racial rioting and other rioting in which two Negro boys were shot to death.

Fourteen Negroes were injured in the explosion. One Negro and five whites were hurt in the disorders that followed.

Some 500 National Guardsmen in battle dress stood by at armories here tonight on orders of Gov. George C. Wallace. And 300 state troopers joined the Birmingham police, Jefferson County sheriff's deputies and other law-enforcement units in efforts to restore peace.

Governor Wallace sent the guardsmen and the troopers in response to requests from local authorities.

(continued)

Sporadic gunfire sounded in Negro neighborhoods tonight, and small bands of residents roamed the streets. Aside from the patrols that cruised the city armed with riot guns, carbines and shotguns, few whites were seen.

Fire Bomb Hurled

At one point, three fires burned simultaneously in Negro sections, one at a broom and mop factory, one at a roofing company and a third in another building. An incendiary bomb was tossed into a supermarket, but the flames were extinguished swiftly. Fire marshals investigated blazes at two vacant houses to see if arson was involved.

The explosion at the 16th Street Baptist Church this morning brought hundreds of angry Negroes pouring into the streets. Some attacked the police with stones. The police dispersed them by firing shotguns over their heads. Johnny Robinson, a 16-year-old Negro was shot in the back by a policeman with a shotgun this afternoon. Officers said the victim was among a group that hurled stones at white youths driving through the area in cars flying Confederate battle flags.

When the police arrived, the youths fled, and one policeman said he had fired low but that some of the shot had struck the Robinson youth in the back.

Virgil Wade, a 13-year-old Negro, was shot and killed just outside Birmingham while riding a bicycle. The Jefferson County sheriff's office said "there apparently was no reason at all" for the killing, but indicated that it was related to the general racial disorders.

Wallace Offers Reward

Governor Wallace, at the request of city officials, offered a $5,000 reward for the arrest and conviction of the bombers.

None of the 50 bombings of Negro property here since World War II have been solved.

The four girls killed in the blast had just heard Mrs. Ellis C. Demand, their teacher, complete the Sunday School lesson for the day. The subject was "The Love That Forgives."

The blast occurred at about 10:25 A.M. (12:25 P.M. New York time).

Church members said they found the girls huddled together beneath a pile of masonry debris.

Parents of 3 Are Teachers

Both parents of each of the victims teach in the city's schools. The dead were identified by University Hospital officials as:

Cynthia Wesley, 14, the only child of Claude A. Wesley, principal of the Lewis Elementary School, and Mrs. Wesley, a teacher there.

Denise McNair, 11, also an only child, whose parents are teachers.

Carol Robertson, 14, whose parents are teachers and whose grandmother, Mrs. Sallie Anderson, is one of the Negro members of a biracial committee established by Mayor Boutwell to deal with racial problems.

Adie Mae Collins, 14, about whom no information was immediately available.

The blast blew gaping holes through walls in the church basement. Floors of offices in the rear of the sanctuary appeared near collapse. Stairways were blocked by splintered window frames, glass, and timbers.

Chief Police Inspector W. J. Haley said the impact of the blast indicated that at least 15 sticks of dynamite might have caused it. He said the police had talked to two witnesses who reported having seen a car drive by the church, slow down and then speed away before the blast.

Read the following poem about the same event.

DUDLEY RANDALL (b. 1914)

BALLAD OF BIRMINGHAM   [1964]

"Mother dear, may I go downtown
Instead of out to play,
And march the streets of Birmingham
In a Freedom March today?"

"No, baby, no, you may not go,   5
For the dogs are fierce and wild,
And clubs and hoses, guns and jails
Aren't good for a little child."

"But, mother, I won't be alone.
Other children will go with me,   10
And march the streets of Birmingham
To make our country free."

"No, baby, no, you may not go,
For I fear those guns will fire.
But you may go to church instead   15
And sing in the children's choir."

She has combed and brushed her night-dark hair,
And bathed rose petal sweet,
And drawn white gloves on her small brown hands,
And white shoes on her feet.   20

The mother smiled to know her child
Was in that sacred place,
But that smile was the last smile
To come upon her face.

For when she heard the explosion,   25
Her eyes grew wet and wild.
She raced through the streets of Birmingham
Calling for her child.

She clawed through bits of glass and brick,
Then lifted out a shoe.   30
"O, here's the shoe my baby wore,
But, baby, where are you?"

➤ GETTING STARTED—YOUR FIRST RESPONSE

1. What is your response to this poem?
2. Of what use is the information in the poem?
3. If you were the mother in this poem, how would you have responded to
   the daughter's request?

➤ *QUESTIONS FOR READING AND WRITING*

1. Both the newspaper article and the poem recount the bombing. What makes the poem different from the newspaper account?
2. What did you learn from the newspaper account? What did you learn from the poem? How was the *nature* of what you learned different?
3. To what extent is your response to "Ballad of Birmingham" influenced by your own experience?
4. How does the rhyme scheme affect your response to the poem's content? The second and fourth lines of each stanza rhyme. How does this rhyme scheme and the rhythm of the poem affect you? How might it change your response if the first and third lines rhymed instead—or as well?

THE WHOLE AND ITS PARTS

You've probably come across the statement "The whole is equal to the sum of its parts." Seems to make sense, doesn't it? Well, in some areas of study it does, but it cannot account for our response to literature. In poetry and other artistic expressions, there is a whole that is greater than the sum of its parts, a whole that blossoms as the parts come together in our imaginations.

We don't like our favorite music because we identify the parts and add them up to a whole experience; we like it because we experience the sound of the instruments, the rhythms, the voices, the lyrics, all together and all at once. For all of us that means more than the sum of the notes or words we hear, and to each of us that means something different.

Like music, poetry cannot be reduced to its parts to account for its meaning. But like music there are parts, and as we become more experienced listeners or readers we want to know how those parts work together. Later on in this book, we will try to comprehend the craft with which the parts are assembled. However, not until we believe the experience of poetry has something to offer us will we care about the skill with which it was created, so for now, let's continue to explore how and what it means to us.

Participating, Not Solving

It's essential that we are *active* participants when we read or listen to poetry. But if we look for the parts of a poem before we have experienced the whole, we may shut down the emotions we need to experience it—and miss the *life* of the poem. Placing ourselves *emotionally* inside the poem, rather than examining it *rationally* from the outside, enables us to feel and sense the words and images and lets these impressions wash over us. Poetry sometimes involves an imagining that is like our dreams and reveals things to us that are not always understood in rational ways.

However, like much of the "academic" reading we do, reading poetry occurs most often in school. And school, with its right and wrong answers, has a way of making us tense and rigid (and very rational). If you had heard (studied) some of your favorite songs and music for the first time in school, you might never have loosened up enough to like them at all. Poems are not math problems—they don't have one "correct" answer. They might not even "add up." The right answer is the one that makes the most sense to you, a "sense" supported by your own imagination and the text of the poem itself. Being confused and making mistakes along the way is part of the process of finding your own right answer.

RESPONDING TO LANGUAGE: WORD PLAY

A word is dead
When it is said,
Some say.
I say it just
Begins to live
That day.
    —Emily Dickinson

Denotation and Connotation

Faced with an unfamiliar word—dictionary in hand—you might look up its definition and be reasonably satisfied with what you find. But if you are already familiar with that word, a dictionary definition is not likely to account for everything the word means to you. While you might not disagree with the dictionary definition, or **denotation**, of the word, you probably won't be entirely satisfied with it, either. Your own definitions, or **connotations**, for familiar words are flavored with personal associations. Dictionary definitions alone cannot account for this complex response to language.

The compressed nature of language and meaning in poetry makes word choice crucial. Poets are very conscious of the effect that connotations, or suggested meanings, have on readers. Synonyms for the word *thin,* for example, include *slim, slender, lean, skinny,* and *trim*—words that mean almost the same thing. But each of these words has a different connotation and slightly different meaning for each of us—and a different effect on us when we read it. Being conscious of word choices and patterns of language may tell us a great deal about what makes a poem effective and how it triggers our responses.

You might find it illuminating to pick a few words at random and write down the first thing that comes to mind when you hear or see the word. Where do you think these associations come from? If you looked the words up in a dictionary, would the definitions or denotations match your associations or connotations? If not, how can you account for the difference? Where did your "meanings" come from?

Read the following poem:

ROBERT GRAVES (1895–1985)

THE NAKED AND THE NUDE

For me, the naked and the nude
(By lexicographers° construed
As synonyms that should express
The same deficiency of dress
Or shelter) stand as wide apart   5
As love from lies, or truth from art.

Lovers without reproach will gaze
On bodies naked and ablaze;
The Hippocratic eye° will see
In nakedness, anatomy;   10
naked shines the Goddess when
She mounts her lion among men.

The nude are bold, the nude are sly
To hold each treasonable eye.
While draping, by a showman's trick,   15
Their dishabille° in rhetoric,
They grin a mock-religious grin
Of scorn at those of naked skin.

The naked, therefore, who compete
Against the nude may know defeat,   20
Yet when they both together tread
The briary pastures of the dead,
By Gorgons° with long whips pursued,
How naked go the sometime nude!

² **lexicographers** dictionary makers   ⁹ **Hippocratic eye** medical doctor's
¹⁶ **dishabille** undressed state   ²³ **Gorgons** snake-haired women

➤ QUESTIONS FOR READING AND WRITING

1. Is your response to the words *naked* and *nude* different? If so, how so?
2. What's your response to the description of their differences in this poem?
3. Think of other words that have the same denotation but have different connotations for you.

Using Our Imaginations

When we read, the strength of our emotional involvement is based on our ability to experience language and the images it creates as if we were there. If we "surrender" ourselves, we not only imagine the details provided, we create ones that are not. We may occasionally say, or hear people say, "I liked the book better than the movie" or "I can't believe so and so was cast in that role." We probably mean, "I liked the movie of the book in my mind better than the movie on the screen" or "That actor is nothing like the character I created in my mind." Unless we complete the picture in our minds by filling in the details, we may not have a satisfying experience with poetry.

Where do we get these details? Some of what we imagine is shared and comes from our cultural backgrounds. And some of what we imagine is personal and familiar and is fueled by our own experiences—the people, places, or events in our own lives. For example, it doesn't have to be summer for us to imagine the sun and heat on the beach—or winter for us to imagine snow. Through our "sense" memories, we can "recall" now what we felt and saw in previous experiences. What we see in our "mind's eye" may also derive from music, television, film, and other forms of media, and other things we have read.

▶ QUESTIONS FOR READING AND WRITING

1. How did you picture the house in Robert Hayden's poem "Those Winter Sundays"? What did the mother and the little girl look like in "Ballad of Birmingham"? Think about the pictures in your mind from other poems or stories you have read.
2. Where do your pictures come from?
3. How much of what you picture in each of these scenes comes from detail that the author provided and how much completely from your imagination?

Writing to Imagine: Creating Images Through Comparison

One of the best ways to get a feel for how language can evoke images is to use your own language to create some. It can be difficult at times to describe anything without resorting to comparison somewhere along the way. Comparison is at the core of "figures of speech," or figurative language. We use what is already familiar to describe something new, or we describe something familiar in a new way. Used in tandem with concrete language, similes and metaphors can lead to very striking images.

One of the most common ways of making comparisons is to use *like* or *as* to point out similarities (similes). For a formal definition of simile see page 63.

Try to complete the following phrases as imaginatively as you can.

He/she is as (happy, hot , pleased, etc.) as . . .
They are as (happy, hot, pleased, etc.) as . . .
He/she (walks, talks, sounds, etc.) like . . .
They (get along, fight, dance, etc.) like . . .

We also frequently compare one thing with another by giving the first the characteristics of the second or by equating the first with the second (metaphor). For a formal definition of metaphor and personification see page 65.

Pick out something in your life (a car, a room, a piece of equipment, a person, etc.) and compare it to something else by giving it the name or characteristics of this other thing or creature (e.g., "She's a fish out of water." "He's a snake in the grass." "He shot a brick from the foul line."). And then explain how or why this comparison works.

NIKKI GIOVANNI (b. 1943)

WOMAN
[1978]

she wanted to be a blade
of grass amid the fields
but he wouldn't agree
to be the dandelion

she wanted to be a robin singing
through the leaves
but he refused to be
her tree

5

she spun herself into a web
and looking for a place to rest
turned to him
but he stood straight
declining to be her corner

10

she tried to be a book
but he wouldn't read

15

she turned herself into a bulb
but he wouldn't let her grow

she decided to become
a woman
and though he still refused
to be a man
she decided it was all
right.

20

➤ QUESTIONS FOR READING AND WRITING

1. How well did the comparisons in this poem work for you?
2. When we "personify" objects or animals we give them human characteristics. How did this "reversal" of personification affect you?
3. See if you can write some verse lines like this yourself.

Creating Images Through Concrete Sensory Descriptions

Sense Impressions
1. Think back over the past day or so and recall an experience. Focus on the particular sense impressions you felt.
2. Describe as clearly and concretely as you can what you saw, felt, tasted, smelled, or heard during that experience.
3. Read your descriptions back to yourself. Do they capture your experience?
4. Share them. Ask others if they "felt" your experience. Could they picture these moments through your words?

Retrospective
Take a look back at some of the poems you've read.
1. Pick out the phrases that brought the strongest sensory impressions or images to your mind.
2. Why did you like them? What made them effective? What did you see in your "mind's eye" when you read them?

From Sense Impression to Poetry
1. Take a look at the sense impressions you recorded. Do they sound like a poem?
2. Can you turn them into one?

Sound and Sense

Sounds and combinations of sounds can have an appeal and a meaning in themselves—apart from what they mean as symbols or defined terms. Music, for example, can convey powerful meaning—without words. And an example of a poem that relies heavily on our response to the *sound* of "madeup" words is Lewis Carroll's "Jabberwocky" (p. 143).

We may even "find" meaning in seemingly unrelated sounds and words—and have fun doing it in the process.

As fast as you can, write a nonsense poem with the following requirements:

1. Each word in each line must begin with the same letter and consonant sound (e. g. "ants and andean angels anger animals/broken bricks brew bread breaking brooms/etc.). For a definition of *alliteration* see page 70.
2. Write 10 lines—all the words in each line beginning with the same letter and sound.
3. Read your "poem" out loud. Does it, can it, mean anything?

Simple Truths

Poetry often finds the extraordinary in the ordinary—and can slow us down to notice what has always been there but is usually overlooked. There are so many things around us that we take for granted, which we regularly use but never wonder about. And we are much more likely to stop and smell the roses than . . . well, onions.

NAOMI SHIHAB NYE (b. 1952)

THE TRAVELING ONION   [1986]

"It is believed that the onion originally came from India. In Egypt, it was an object of worship — why I haven't been able to find out. From Egypt the onion entered Greece and on to Italy, thence into all of Europe."

—BETTER LIVING COOKBOOK

When I think how far the onion has traveled
just to enter my stew today, I could kneel and praise
all small forgotten miracles,
crackly paper peeling on the drainboard,
pearly layers in smooth agreement,   5
the way knife enters onion
and onion falls apart on the chopping block,
a history revealed.

And I would never scold the onion
for causing tears.   10
It is right that tears fall
for something small and forgotten.
How at meals, we sit to eat,
commenting on texture of meat or herbal aroma
but never on the translucence of onion,   15
now limp, now divided,
or its traditionally honorable career:
For the sake of others,
disappear.

QUESTIONS FOR READING AND WRITING

1. This poem doesn't have the rhyme and tight rhythm of most of the poems we've read in this chapter. How were you affected by that?
2. Did the personification work for you? Did you feel that an onion was worthy of a poem? Explain.
3. Pick out an object from your own experience. See if you can tell its story by bringing it to life like "The Traveling Onion" above.
4. Find an old photograph or postcard and see if you can bring the picture alive by using comparisons and/or concrete sensory descriptions to re-create the image you see in words.

➤ RESPONSE REVIEW

If you've been keeping a journal or writing down other initial reactions, take a look back at your entries up to this point. Identify the factors that seem most important in your responses. Add any insights that may have occurred since writing or reading these entries.

CHAPTER 2

Communication
Writing About Poetry

The goal in this chapter is to develop your initial responses into an essay about poetry. We begin by emphasizing the response essay, but the habits of thinking and writing stressed in this chapter apply equally well to the critical essay explored later. Finding our writing voices; developing a clear thesis statement; showing what we mean through detail, illustration, and comparison; and citing evidence from the text are also core principles for writing a critical essay. Our emphasis on analysis and argumentation in Chapters 3 and 4 will complement and build on our discussion in this chapter.

THE RESPONSE ESSAY

In many ways, writing a response essay is like the journal writing described earlier. You can write in a conversational tone and explore personal connections and associations. You don't have to prove anything, but you do want to say something important enough to share with others.

Why would we want to share our experiences with literature? Perhaps the most compelling reason is the same one we have for communicating any other important event. Why do we discuss our experiences of movies, games, concerts, exhibits, or parties? Why do we chat about dates, meaningful events in our lives, or interesting people we have met?

Although some people need to impress others with their knowledge, accomplishments, or "important" acquaintances, many of us share because we have a need to "review" or "reexperience" with others, to have them say, "I see what you mean" or "I understand why you were affected that way." We don't want advice; we want caring listeners. This kind of sharing has a give-and-take to it. We give a rendering of our experience, and we receive other people's understanding, affirmation, and appreciation—their participation. It's not "scoring points" or *proving* we are right; it's an experience in itself.

The purpose of a response essay is to invite readers into our experience with poetry—not to win an argument. If the voice in our writing, the reader's sense of who we are, is that of a "sharer," not a prosecuting attorney, the essay will feel like a welcome invitation, not a summons. Readers are better able to see when we *show,* not *show off.* The strength of their involvement is based on how much they care about what we share. Our voice in presenting that experience strongly influences their level of interest. For readers who accept our invitation, "I see what you mean" takes on a literal dimension. The clarity and thoughtfulness with which we write will determine how glad they are that they came.

Voice and Writing

Finding Our Voices Few would question the importance of voice in the realm of speaking and listening. Accurately or not, we often make judgments about people's personalities by the sounds of their voices. It would not be unusual to hear someone say, "She sounds like someone I can trust" or "He sounds like a phony." On the other hand, when we speak to a friend, we know that our own voices will usually sound (and feel) more comfortable and confident than when we inquire about a job, ask someone for a date, or speak to a large audience. The sound of our voices and the style with which we speak are bound to be influenced by our level of comfort, to whom we are speaking, and what we want from the communication. It is not surprising, then, that we give so much attention to how we sound and the words we use when we are concerned about making an impression.

For example, leaving a message for incoming calls on a phone answering machine seems like a very simple procedure. But if you have ever recorded or witnessed someone recording a message of this kind, you know that it usually takes more than one try to "get it right." Getting it right, of course, has a lot to do with our situations and who we think will be calling. The kind of message we might leave to amuse our friends is likely to be very different from the one we would want a prospective employer to hear as we await the results of a job interview.

Voice in Writing We know that the tone of voice we use when speaking is likely to make an impression—that *how* we say the words out loud can convey as much meaning as the words themselves. But speech and writing are different. We can think about and revise most writing, but speech is usually spontaneous, and we don't revise what we say in normal conversation. Spontaneous speech contains lots of stops and false starts and sound fillers that would look silly in writing. Unless we say something especially memorable or inflammatory, we're confident these words won't be heard (or read) over and over again. So, what does voice have to do with writing?

Virtually all of us learned to speak before we learned to read. Throughout our lives, we've been conditioned to hear the words we read. As children, many of us said the words out loud as we read to ourselves. Even if we don't move our lips or say the words out loud now, it's difficult to read them without triggering the nerves that activate speech and help us to "sub-vocalize" and hear the words voiced in our minds.

So, too, readers of our writing want to hear our voices—to get a sense of who we are. As writers we are conscious of this. For example, when writing a letter or an e-mail message our voices may change according to whom we send it, what we want, and how we want to be perceived. In a personal letter to an old friend we are probably free "to be ourselves." Our friends know us, and usually we're not anxious about the impression we will make. We are confident they will recognize our voices in the words. However, when writing a letter "To the Editor," flirting with a new romantic interest, or applying for a job, our voices are likely to be quite different. We may want to convey a sense of responsibility, wisdom, wit, or whatever else we can demonstrate to make a positive impression.

What we write about may also have a strong influence on how we are heard. As you might imagine, we write with more feeling and a clearer, stronger voice about issues that move us. Here too, we write with more confidence when we are sure of our audience. Those entries that are private (and for our eyes only) are likely to be different from those we know will be read by others. Those entries written for our friends or agreeable classmates will probably be different from those written for an unknown audience.

Voice and Response to Poetry

Showing and Telling Most of us are best convinced when we see for ourselves. It would certainly seem risky to buy a car "sight unseen." We would probably insist on seeing it, trying it out, getting the "feel" of it before we decided to buy. When we talk with friends about a concert, game, or party, we probably wouldn't settle for "It was great." Again, we would like to get the "feel" of it, to hear the details, to imagine ourselves there, to share the experience.

As readers, we have a similar need. We are not likely to settle for being told an issue is compelling or trivial; an event exciting, suspenseful, or sad; a character fascinating, dull, or manipulative. We want to be moved by the issue, to be present at the event, to know the character for ourselves. Writers' voices are believable when we experience characters and events with them—when the conclusions ("exciting," " sad," "dull") are ours—when we are shown, not simply told.

The entries that follow were written in response to Countee Cullen's "Incident" (p. 12). It's a short poem, so if you haven't read it you might want to do that now and write your own response before you read the entries below.

Nick's Response:

> I know how the young boy felt. I was made to feel inferior in the school
> I attended as a child because I was Italian and poor. He could no longer see
> the beautiful things in Baltimore. He was hurt so deeply by being called
> "nigger." I'm sure this affected the rest of his life. His ego had to be smashed
> now that the other boy made him conscious of prejudice. He must have been

very angry and would always remember this incident. It must have caused him to see the color of one's skin as being a bad thing and therefore he felt as though he was bad. I could relate to the hurt that he felt. It makes you feel very inferior and blocks your vision from other things in life because you feel as though you must hide somewhere.

Ellen's Response:

I've witnessed this kind of prejudice. When I was a freshman in high school, there was one black student in my homeroom class. His name was Jon. Our school was about 99.9 percent white. Every morning was hell for Jon. The "in-crowd" football-playing heroes would always harass him. Not just the ones who belonged in my homeroom, even seniors would make the trip to our classroom to call Jon names like "licorice," and "boy," and all the other juicy racial slurs. Jon never seemed to be affected by this ignorance, but he was probably dying inside. He would just turn away.

One morning, one of the football heroes got very personal with his attack toward Jon. Jon turned and leered at him. The white football hero yelled at him, "Boy! Did I say you could look at me?" Then he got up and punched Jon. Jon fought back. (The teacher never saw any of the harassment, I don't know why.) Jon and Mr. Football Hero went to the principal's office. Jon got suspended. Mr. Football Hero didn't get in trouble; he went to lunch.

Doris's Response:

My own experience of being a woman had influence over my response. I once asked a contractor to do some renovations on my home. I was asked to make an appointment to discuss the work and was told to make it "only when your husband is home so we can talk to him."

I felt sadness for the child who was so hurt by the word "nigger." To be so cruel to lash out at another person in a sensitive area. Words can cut like a knife. We are all born equal and do not ask for our sex, race, color, or ethnic backgrounds. We are just born into them. Each of us needs to be sensitive to each other.

Trudy's Response:

> I was called a name when I was young at school and didn't know anyone and never spoke to anybody. So a group of girls decided to call me a "Jamaican body scratcher." I knew how he felt and what he was experiencing at the time. At the time he was small and traveling to Baltimore for the first time. He was looking out the window, seeing all kinds of sights, but it so happened that he tried to be friendly and was called a "nigger."
>
> No matter what color or what race you are, you cut a white man, he bleeds red blood. You cut a black man, he bleeds red blood. So I think it's about time racism should stop.

➤ QUESTIONS FOR READING AND WRITING

1. How were the responses of Nick, Ellen, Doris, and Trudy influenced by their experiences?
2. Consider your response to the poem. How does it compare to theirs? Does reading their responses affect your own response to the poem? If so, how?
3. To what extent have they "shown" what they've told?
4. Which entries seem most effective to you? What factors seem to make them effective?
5. Read your own response to the poem. How does the voice in your response compare with those you've just read?
6. How would you describe the voice in Countee Cullen's poem "Incident"? What factors make it effective?
7. In what way is "showing" a factor in both the poem and the responses to it? What scenes, details, words, or phrases had the biggest impact on you?

WRITING TO DESCRIBE

An effective description is much more than a summary. A summary has no voice. An engaging description has our voice, impressions, and feelings, as well as relevant details. When someone asks us to describe a person we know very well (a friend, lover, spouse, parent) or a place with which we are very familiar (our home, bedroom, car, or a favorite hangout), we're not likely to respond with factual information alone. A summary of facts (dimensions, features, or colors) will not adequately convey what we feel is most important. Those details support our impression but do not replace it. Important details, however, do help the reader picture what we are describing and clarify *why* we feel the way we do.

Choosing Details

Which details we choose when describing and supporting our responses can make a big difference. Writing, "Tanya makes me feel very comfortable" by itself will not be as clear as combining it with examples or details of what she does that shows it is true: "She's very soft-spoken, smiles a lot, and is a good listener." We would not include every detail ("She wants to graduate next year") unless it's relevant ("So she knows the kind of pressure I'm feeling"). Including details not important to our impression will not support, and may even dilute, the impact of ones that are.

Choosing Details from Poetry

So, too, the details we choose to clarify and support our responses to poetry have an important impact on readers. To describe the young boy's pain in "Incident" without reference to the joyful anticipation he felt about his visit before being called the name is to leave out an important part of his subsequent disillusionment. When describing "Those Winter Sundays," leaving out the powerful images of the father warming up the cold house is to ignore an esential component of the speaker's sense of regret for not having thanked him. Those details, those parts, capture the whole of the work in miniature.

▶ QUESTIONS FOR READING AND WRITING

1. How do you respond when someone asks you to describe a poem that you've read? To what extent does a summary convey what you've experienced—what you feel is most important? To what extent does it seem inadequate? The following exercise may provide some insight:
   a. Choose a favorite poem (either from these first two chapters or from past reading).
   b. Summarize it.
   c. Write down your strongest impressions of that work. Write down the details—from your experience and the poem—that support or clarify those impressions.
   d. What is the difference between the summary and your impressions?
   e. Which parts of the summary support your impression? Which do not?

WRITING TO COMPARE

How many times are we asked to describe something, and our first reaction is "Well, it's like . . ." or "It reminds me of . . ."? In fact it seems hard to describe anything without resorting to comparison somewhere along the way. When we think about our friends, we may compare and contrast them consciously and unconsciously with each other. When we take part in important events, we may compare them to similar events in our past: "This reminds me of the wedding I went to last year" or "My brother's graduation was done very differently."

Comparing and contrasting are also natural ways to describe our responses to poetry. We might compare ourselves or others with the characters, or our own experiences with those in a poem. We may compare the choices made by various characters with the choices we would make. We might even be reminded of previous reading experiences and compare the poem—or elements of the poem—we are reading with one we've read before. We might even compare the poem with a work from another form of art, like painting. A good example of both process and product is the student sample of Barbara Pfister (see p. 300) who compares van Gogh's *Starry Night* with Anne Sexton's poem about the painting.

Comparing and Contrasting Using a Venn Diagram

One effective technique for generating and organizing ideas when writing to compare is a Venn diagram (Figure 2.1). This technique works equally well when comparing personal experience with the poem (Figure 2.2) or comparing poems or characters with one another (Figure 2.3).

1. Draw two interconnecting circles. Identify each circle.
2. In the common, interconnecting area write down what the subjects have in common.
3. In the separate sections, write down what is different.

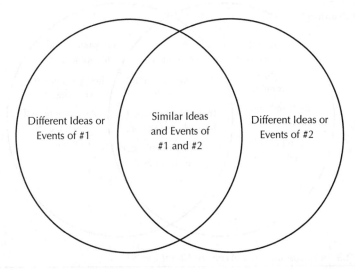

FIGURE 2.1

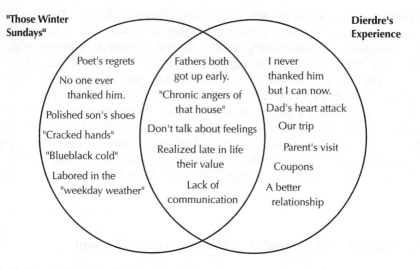

"Those Winter Sundays"

Poet's regrets

No one ever thanked him.

Polished son's shoes

"Cracked hands"

"Blueblack cold"

Labored in the "weekday weather"

Fathers both got up early.

"Chronic angers of that house"

Don't talk about feelings

Realized late in life their value

Lack of communication

Dierdre's Experience

I never thanked him but I can now.

Dad's heart attack

Our trip

Parent's visit

Coupons

A better relationship

FIGURE 2.2 *Comparing Experience with Literature*

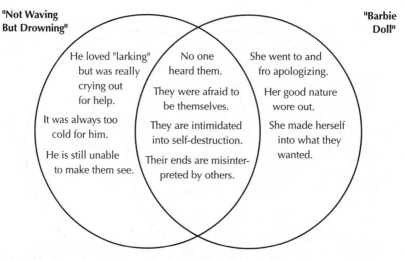

"Not Waving But Drowning"

He loved "larking" but was really crying out for help.

It was always too cold for him.

He is still unable to make them see.

No one heard them.

They were afraid to be themselves.

They are intimidated into self-destruction.

Their ends are misinterpreted by others.

"Barbie Doll"

She went to and fro apologizing.

Her good nature wore out.

She made herself into what they wanted.

FIGURE 2.3 *Comparing Two Works of Literature*

➤ *QUESTIONS FOR READING AND WRITING*

1. If you are jotting down responses to your reading, take a look back through your entries. How many times did a work remind you of someone or something in your own life? If none did at the time you wrote your response, are there entries that bring a comparison to mind now?
2. Can you compare any of the works you've read in Chapters 1 and 2? Do any of these works remind you of other works of literature you've read in the past? If so, how are they alike? How different? Can you construct a Venn diagram to compare them?

Possible Worlds

The frequent comments and questions about "identifying with" or "connecting your experience" in the first two chapters of this text are not suggesting that it is necessary to have had similar experiences or to identify with the speaker in a poem to have a fulfilling experience. In fact, connecting a poem too closely with our own lives—so closely that we can't distinguish one from the other—can interfere with our ability to understand and appreciate the work.

When taking us where we have never been, poetry has the power to increase the breadth and depth of our vision—to help us learn and grow in the way that all new experiences can. Poems take us to a possible world. Ultimately, it is our intelligence and sensitivity to the human condition, not simply a shared experience, that helps us imagine the possibilities and become engaged with the poem.

RESPONSE TO POETRY: DESCRIBING AND COMPARING

You are likely to write with more feeling and a clearer, stronger voice about issues that move you, so your strongest response or impression may provide the best topic to write about, but selecting relevant details to support that response is equally important. You are not only describing how you felt, but what prompted you to feel this way.

Staying Anchored in the Poem

Remember, this is an essay in response to poetry. When sharing personal responses, it can be very easy to see the work simply as a prompt to tell our own stories. Seeing and sharing the parallels between our own experiences and those in a work may strengthen our voices and clarify our responses, but the work on the page must remain prominent in the presentation. To write an effective response essay, it is essential to stay "anchored" in the work and balance references to personal experience with references to the poetry itself.

➤ *QUESTIONS FOR READING AND WRITING*

In this exercise, you may find it illuminating to share your work with a partner or a small group.

1. Take a look back through your responses and select some of your strongest reactions or impressions.
2. If you wrote down details to support your response, do those details adequately convey it? Do those details include specific references to the text?
3. Are there places where you might have clarified your response through a comparison (with other poems, people you know, other students' responses)?
4. If you did not write down supporting details or if you did not cite the text for support, go back to the poem and see if you can.

The entries that follow were written in response to Robert Hayden's "Those Winter Sundays" on page 13. Read (or reread) the poem and write your response before you read the following entries.

LeaAnne's Response:

"Those Winter Sundays" brought to mind my brother Joey. Growing up in a severely dysfunctional home, he always seemed to be the one to have my best interests at heart. He did things for me, and with me without ever being asked, even when he had so many problems of his own to contend with. The poem touched upon the fact that the writer never got around to thanking his father for all he had done, and I was able to relate to that emotion because at the time the age difference between my brother and I made me too young to be able to acknowledge all his efforts and thank him for them. Of course, as an adult I've tried to thank him on many occasions, but the right words never seem to emerge.

Michael's Response:

When I read the poem "Those Winter Sundays" I could not help but think of the relationship I have with my own father. Like the father in the poem, my dad also has "cracked hands that ached from the labor in the weekday." The difference is that my father has a bad back. He injured his back twice in workplace accidents. His second accident forced him to retire.

His job now is taking care of the family. His new role includes driving my younger brother and sister to school, and he also does numerous things around the house. He does all these tasks without complaining about his back. He does so many things for me during the day. When I have class at night, he makes sure that dinner is ready early so I can eat and also make it to school on time. You want to know something? Just like the writer, I have never thanked him once for all the things he has done for me.

Vincent's Response:

Feelings of loneliness and imagery give you a sense of unsaid things, trying to say what the author realizes now and didn't then. I identify with the author very much. It shows a different form of love, that of "austere office" that goes unrecognized and unappreciated. I love the open expression in the imagery--a sense of feeling the scenario from your own experience.

Ken's Response:

This poem made me think of my father. Even though I don't mean to, I never thank my dad. I appreciate him, but I don't really show that. Reading the poem, I could feel the cold floor turn warm as the author's father put the fire on. Then I could feel the icy cold return in the author's words. This poem was personal.

Dierdre's Response:

I love this poem because I am totally able to relate. It brought so many things back to me about my relationship with my father--some painful, some happy. I grew up in a similar situation, and although there was no love ver-bally communicated by my gruff father, he always did little things, like get-ting up early to turn up the heat, digging my car out of the snow and warming it up while I dressed. The day we read this poem in class I got home to find an envelope from my still gruff, uncommunicative father (age has softened him a little). There was no card or letter, just a bunch of coupons, mostly for stuff for my cat, which is his way of sending love. Coupons. It was very nice, and I zipped off a letter of appreciation. I'm glad I still have the opportunity.

➤ *QUESTIONS FOR READING AND WRITING*

1. How were the responses of LeaAnne, Michael, Vincent, Ken, and Dierdre influenced by their backgrounds and experiences?
2. Which entries seem to convey the strongest impressions? How so?
3. Which responses seem more anchored in the poem and which seem to digress more to the reader's own experience?

4. Imagine the entry you like best as the opening of a response essay. Make some suggestions for how it might be supported from the text of "Those Winter Sundays."
5. Consider your own response to the poem and to the questions on page 13. How do your responses compare to theirs? How does reading these journal entries affect your own response to the poem?
6. Take a close look at your own response. What details, quotations, and examples have you used to support your response? To what extent have you anchored your response in the poem itself?

✔ **C H E C K L I S T** • *Developing a Response Essay*

❑ Write down your impressions.

❑ Write down whatever questions come to mind during and after your reading.

❑ What confuses you? What do you want to know more about? How can you find out?

❑ Does the speaker or any of the characters remind you of yourself or people you know? Do any of the events remind you of ones in your own life?

❑ Do these associations with the poem help or interfere with your response? If so, how?

❑ What do you find most interesting or compelling about the poem? Why? How can you "show" what made this issue so compelling for you? What details or passages in the poem illustrate support for your response?

FROM FIRST RESPONSE TO FINAL DRAFT

In the section that follows, we look at Dierdre Curran's response to Robert Hayden's "Those Winter Sundays" on the previous pages and follow its progress through to the final draft of her essay. Though her goal is to write a response essay, the strategies she illustrates work equally well when planning and generating ideas for a critical essay.

The purpose of the strategies that follow is not to move you step-by-step through a rigid sequence. Whether you are composing a response or a critical essay, writing is a continuous process of moving forward and returning and moving forward again. The best way to organize an essay may occur to you early or late in the process. You may get some of your best new ideas just when you thought you were almost finished. Try to let your ideas flow freely throughout the process. Don't close out ideas by imposing a structure that will keep you from expressing what you would really like to say.

Reading literature encourages a variety of responses—and perhaps more questions than answers. Generate and explore as many of your questions and ideas as possible before you decide on one direction. Free your ideas and follow them where they go. You may be surprised by what you find on your journey.

Using First Responses

If you've been keeping a journal or writing other initial responses to your reading, chances are you have already generated some good ideas for writing an essay. After you read your entries and add any comments based on rereading and class discussion, go back and underline or circle what you believe are your strongest impressions.

Let's look at Dierdre's journal response as an example:

> I love this poem because I am totally able to relate. <u>It brought so many things back to me about my relationship with my father--some painful, some happy</u>. I grew up in a similar situation, and although there was no love verbally communicated by my gruff father, he always did little things, like getting up early to turn up the heat, digging my car out of the snow and warming it up while I dressed. The day we read this poem in class I got home to find an envelope from my still gruff, uncommunicative father (age has softened him a little). There was no card or letter, just a bunch of coupons, mostly for stuff for my cat, which is his way of sending love. Coupons. It was very nice, and I zipped off a letter of appreciation. I'm glad I still have the opportunity.

Making Choices When making a choice or choices about which idea(s) to pursue, you may want to answer two essential questions:

1. Do you care enough about this idea to pursue it further?
   You will write with your strongest voice about issues that have the most meaning to you and about which you believe you want to say something that is important for both you and your readers.
2. Is it "do-able"?
   Can you write an essay about this? No matter how compelling your idea is, you won't be able to write an essay about it unless you have enough to say, or you can support it from both your experience and the work (of literature). Remember, if the point you are trying to make is obvious, abstract, or very general, it may be impossible to develop it into an appealing essay in a reasonable amount of time.

Extending Ideas

Dierdre chose the second sentence (underlined) from the entry above as the core of her response. It's obvious that she cares about this idea very much. And she feels confident that there are many lines in the poem that she can use to support the comparison between her relationship and that in the poem. But a look at her journal entry tells us that she has not identified many of them yet. But her essay seems very "do-able," and her journal entry has given her a start.

Dierdre has already followed her core idea with some specific support from her own experience, but she has not provided much specific support from the text of the poem itself. So if she wants to generate more ideas or extend or expand her support, there are a few other techniques she might use.

Directed Freewriting If you don't have a journal entry or other initial response, or you want to generate more ideas, directed freewriting can be a useful technique. The best time to do this exercise is immediately after you finish reading, while your thoughts and impressions are still fresh. The intention of this exercise is to release what you know without blocking it with pauses for reflection, punctuation, or editing.

1. Write down the name of the topic, phrase, or sentence you want to focus on.
2. Write down (nonstop) everything that comes into your mind for five or ten minutes. If punctuation or capitalization gets in the way, don't even use it.
3. Read what you have written and choose (circle or underline) your strongest responses.

Here is Dierdre Curran's directed freewriting response to Robert Hayden's "Those Winter Sundays" in response to the sentence from her journal entry: It brought so many things back to me about my relationship with my father--some painful, some happy.

> My father does not express his love for us by telling us. He does things instead. Growing up was really hard I wanted him to tell me he loved me. It has taken me years to believe that he really does even though he never says it. Did the poet ever get to tell his own father about these things. I'll bet not. He sounds as if he regrets not understanding that his father was really expressing love in the things he did. I really like Robert Hayden's descriptions of how the house felt. My house felt the same way. Why did he have to be so cold? Could he help it? Did he really love my older brothers more than me? Was I a disappointment to him? But not everything was as bleak as it seems now. There were good times but it just feels not. My father is old now and had a heart attack and only now are we beginning to say what I wish we had said before. I feel much better about now. We seem to have found a way

to express our love now. I love him so much. I only hope I will have the
chance to express that now before he's gone.

Dierdre's freewriting adds more detail to her earlier statement, and she was able
to generate some very compelling ideas about her relationship with her father
and her connections to the poem itself. By asking questions about and listing
details of the selected statements, she may uncover even more specific material.

Asking Questions Having already narrowed her choice to a particular idea, she
might ask as many questions (and subquestions) as she can about some aspect of
that idea. Of course, it's useful to ask only the questions that will provide new
information (and cannot be answered yes or no).

1. Choose an important word, phrase, or sentence from your journal entry and
   write down as many related questions as you can.
2. Choose and answer the questions that will add to or clarify your support.

   My father does not express his love for us by telling us.

   How often do we talk?

   What do we talk about?

   How does he express his love?

   Why doesn't he express his love in words?

   Where is the similarity in the poem?

   I'm glad I still have the opportunity to express appreciation.

   Did the speaker in the poem ever get to tell his father what he felt?

   Why does it feel like he never did?

   How do I/will I express my appreciation?

   I really like Robert Hayden's description of the house.

   What language does he use?

   Why is it effective?

   Following up with detailed answers to these questions is likely to provide
additional specific support for the original core idea.

Listing

1. Choose key words or sentences from your response (the name of a character, an event, an element of literature, etc.).
2. List as many related details under each as you can. By choosing some key
   phrases that apply to her identification with the speaker in the poem,
   Dierdre is able to uncover other specific details.

<u>My father does things for me instead</u>.

He got up early and turned up the heat.

Dug my car out of the snow and warmed it up.

Sent me envelopes with coupons.

Took my sister and me on a trip to Maryland.

On Sundays he always made sure we had the comics and jelly doughnuts.

He comforted me when my dog died.

He sometimes laughed and joked around with me and my sister.

He recently sent me the first letter I have ever received from him.

<u>I really like Robert Hayden's description of the house in the poem</u>.

I could feel the pain of the "blueblack cold."

I could feel and hear the cold "splintering, breaking."

Remembering getting dressed quickly in the cold.

Imagining the rooms getting warm.

The house was like their relationship.

Semantic Mapping, or Clustering

For some of us, it is easier to follow directions by looking at a map than follow-ing directions in a printed sequence. Sometimes we need to see the whole pic-ture. When writing in response to literature, too, sometimes we can understand, see relationships, and generate and extend ideas better spatially than linearly. A technique called **semantic mapping** or **clustering** makes it possible to see ideas and relationships this way (Figure 2.4). This is how it works:

1. Write down a question or statement in the center of a blank page in your journal or on another piece of paper. Put a circle around it.
2. Draw lines out from the circle and write a statement or idea related to that central idea.
3. Continue to draw lines out from the central circle and the subcircles. Those from the central circle are subsets of ideas; each circle farther along each line is a level of greater specificity.

One of the intriguing things about mapping is that once you get going, it's hard to stop. Seeing a picture of the ideas seems to make the relationships among them clearer.

Finding Connections With any of these strategies, an additional step that might be productive, and which emerges naturally from the mapping exercise, is find-ing and describing the relationships between and among the ideas (the circles)

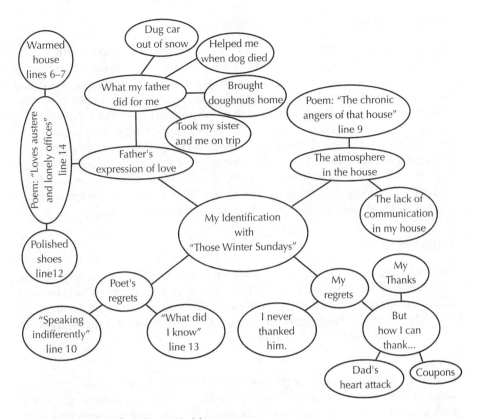

FIGURE 2.4 *Dierdre's Semantic Map*

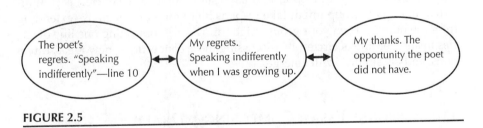

FIGURE 2.5

generated on different lines. When you finish your map, you might draw lines across circles and write statements identifying and examining the relationships. Such statements might go a long way toward answering the central question or identifying a unifying theme for the story. For example, writing a statement about the connection among the circles from Dierdre's map might provide some additional insights (Figure 2.5).

Mix and Match

The strategies above are not an end in themselves, but simply the means to generate and extend ideas, ask questions, and make choices. They should be used in whatever way they work for you. There is no one "right" way to ask questions or list ideas. If a particular method is working, keep using it. If it is not, try something else. For example, you may find that only the first few circles in a mapping exercise are useful. In order to generate details quickly, you may prefer to list them instead of putting circles around them. So you might want to start with a map, get a few ideas, and then make a list to get at the details. Along with keeping a journal, you may want to freewrite as well. Different ways, combinations, and paces of writing may bring different ideas. What matters in this "prewriting" stage is that you feel free to explore in your most productive way.

Collaboration

Sharing Responses If you are keeping a journal or jotting down responses to your reading, you may find it useful to exchange your writing with a classmate. In addition to sharing responses to the work of literature, you might comment on each other's entries. The biggest advantage to sharing this way is that it gives you an audience and immediate feedback.

Combining Questions After generating your own questions about a particular piece of literature, it might be worthwhile to share these questions in pairs or with a small group. Pool everyone's questions, discuss their strengths and weaknesses, and narrow the list down to the strongest ones.

Connecting Cluster Circles You might work collaboratively on a semantic map, or cluster sheet. In response to a question, topic, or character, each individual in a small group might take responsibility for a line of circles extending from the middle. Then your group might draw lines connecting one line of circles to another line of circles. By discussing these connections, new ideas, directions, and possibilities will emerge.

THE RESPONSE ESSAY: COMPOSING A DRAFT

Once you have settled on your topic and gathered supporting ideas and details, you can begin to write a draft of your essay. Even at this stage you may want to avoid forcing your writing into an inflexible outline. There may be possibilities you haven't thought of, so avoid putting walls around your work just yet.

As in earlier stages of the process, what works best for each of us may be different. Some students may work best by writing this first draft as quickly as possible without stopping and then going back to review and revise when finished. Many students (and probably most experienced writers) find that writing more reflectively at this stage works best for them. And if you have already narrowed your focus to a particular idea and generated lots of details to support it, you may want to proceed with more reflection and review what you have written while you write. You may want to read it out loud to hear how the wording sounds and if the ideas are complete and clear. Evaluating your writing may give you valuable insight into where you need to go.

Once you have narrowed your focus to a particular idea and generated lots of details in support of the idea, you are ready to create a thesis statement. Your thesis statement should incorporate all the evidence that you have, but also be specific enough for you to support. Your thesis statement should also reveal what you intend to show in your essay.

Dierdre's Draft

Earlier in this section, we saw Dierdre Curran's journal entry, freewriting, listing, asking questions, and her semantic map in response to Robert Hayden's "Those Winter Sundays." Let's follow up by looking at a draft of her response essay.

Twice on Sunday

The relationship between parent and child is often a significant one in literature. In his poem "Those Winter Sundays," Robert Hayden illustrates the starkness of one such relationship. The author of this poem is left, as an adult, feeling guilt and regret over never being able to communicate understanding and appreciation of the father's limited demonstrative abilities. I found myself being able to fully relate to the emotions of this poem, as I have a strong personal connection with the situation that is detailed.

The author tells of "fearing the chronic angers of that house." The house I grew up in always seemed filled with anger to me, too. The only communication that ever went on between my parents, myself, and all of my brothers and sisters involved displays of anger; we never had conversations, we had arguments and disagreements. No one in my family ever apologized to one another, or told another that they loved them, or expressed sympathy or support when something was wrong. It was a home filled with much bitterness and stress, presumably brought on by constant financial troubles. There was nothing to ever balance it out, no tangible expressions of love from my parents . . . or so I thought until I got a little older and came to understand more.

The author tells of how the father got up early "in the blueblack cold," and then with "cracked hands that ached" from labor in the weekday weather made banked fires blaze. "No one ever thanked him." My Dad has always been a painfully early riser; he would get up hours before the rest of us had to. In the wintertime, he always made sure that he was up and had turned on the heat so that when the rest of us awoke it was to a warm house. In the winters of my late teens, when I needed his car to get to work, he would always go outside to start it and warm it up. Often he dug it out of a night's snowfall for me, too. I was still reeling from the trauma of my teenage years, so, seething with bitterness, I actually resented him doing me a favor. I never once thanked him for it--I was annoyed by it! My obnoxious, sullen, and ungrateful attitude led me to believe that he was only doing something he was expected to do. My behavior is well described when the author tells how he spoke "indifferently to him, who had driven out the cold."

The poem's author realizes, later in life, that although his father never outwardly expressed his love in so many words, it was expressed through a variety of gestures. Something as simple as shining his son's shoes can be interpreted as an open display of affection. When I think back on my child-hood, I realize that although he is a very gruff and restrained man, my father also showed his love in the only ways he knew how. When we were kids, my father spent a lot more time with my brother, throwing the baseball and playing basketball, going to ball games. I think that once we got past a certain age (toddler), he didn't really know what to do with my sister and myself, because we were girls. When I was about six, I remember getting together with my older sister, Lucy, and informing our mother that we resented the fact that Dad always "did stuff with Tighe," but not with us. As a result, we got the treat of spending a weekend with him alone on a road trip (a business trip for him) down to Maryland. He never said, "I love you as much as your brother," or hugged us or kissed us, but he made the effort to spend time with us, and we all enjoyed it (well, I <u>think</u> he did, he seemed to). Upon seeing so many horses on the roadside, I was insistent that I get up close to one. So, intent on getting me to my horses, my Dad came up with a solution . . . he took us to the racetrack!

In retrospect, I realize that my Dad has done many things over the years to convey his affection. When we were very little, I shared a room with my sister Lucy. Sometimes at night if he was in a good mood, right before we went to bed, my Dad would pretend that he was Frankenstein. He would close his eyes and stretch out his arms in front of him, walking like a fictional monster. He would chase us to our beds, approaching slowly, while we shrieked in terrified laughter, running from him. When he finally caught us, we got tickled to the point of hysteria, and then it was time for bed. I also recall how on Sundays (yes, there is a Sunday connection with the poem also), he would go out early to buy the newspapers. On top of making sure that we had the Sunday comics, he always came back with jelly doughnuts from the bakery, too.

The worst day of my life was when I had to put my fifteen-year-old diabetic dog, Freebie, to sleep. The guilt has never left me. No one in my family would go with me to the vet. When my best friend, John, came to the house that morning to drive me and the dog, my mother wouldn't even come downstairs, but at least my father said goodbye to her. He was the only one that was as upset as I was, and I was crushed, only he never showed it. The day I brought her ashes back to throw around the yard, he found me in the house crying hysterically; I was totally heartbroken. When I first came back from the vet on that awful day (when I held her in my arms and watched the life sink from her beautiful brown eyes, then blued by cataracts), no one hugged me, no one said, "I'm sorry." The day I brought Freebie back home for the last time and fell apart in the backyard, my father's only way of acknowledging my grief was to come outside and yell at me. He just stood there and kept yelling, and I just sat there and kept crying. Finally he got quiet and told me that he missed the dog as much as me, and hadn't gone with me because he didn't have the guts to do what I had done. Then he helped me up and walked me up the driveway, hugging me for the very first time in memory.

My parents came out for a visit last summer. They moved to Indiana, and I had not seen them in almost a year. In the parking lot where I met up with them, I gave my father a big hug and told him that I had really missed him. He, of course, did not hug me back, and (surprised by my open display of affection) could only manage the reply, "Yeah, twice on Sunday!" I understood that this was his best effort, and I still laugh about it because it was so typical.

A few weeks later, my oldest sister called to tell me that my father had suffered a heart attack out in Indiana. I was basically floored, and promptly drank a bottle and a half of Merlot. While I was sucking that down, I was crying hysterically. Two very long days later, I was on a plane to see him, even though he tried to tell me it was not necessary because he was doing so well. I had to see for myself. The plane trip was hellacious. It took twelve hours to get there, and the delays were torture. I finally told the airline people that I didn't care about the inclement weather, or the size of the plane. I didn't care if it was a bicycle with wings, they had to fly me to South Bend. I made it to the hospital ten minutes before visiting hours ended on my birthday. As I rushed down the hall frantically toward his room, I heard him call out my name in excited surprise and saw him slowly hurrying toward me, pale, be-tubed and in his hospital gown. I could not believe how happy he was to see me; it made the whole trip worth it. He repeatedly held my hand and offered me his cheek for a kiss, every couple of minutes. When he asked me "what in the hell" I was doing out there, my reply was that I had the day off anyway and decided to come see him for my birthday. He had a good laugh at that one. He was a much less gruff man than the last time I had seen him.

Never in my life has my father verbally expressed his love. In younger years I was blind to the fact that he just doesn't know how, but that he shows it in other ways. That used to make me so mad and frustrated. But he has mellowed with the coming of grandchildren and his own older age, and I have opened my eyes and learned to appreciate the gestures and to interpret their meaning. In "Those Winter Sundays," the author tells of the guilt of his own ignorance of "love's austere and lonely offices." While I can't imagine the day either one of us is ever able to actually say "I love you" to the other one, I am secure in the knowledge that it is mutually understood. I had always planned on naming a child after him, but when my brother named his first son John, I had to settle for naming my cat "Dad." While "Dad the Human" is publicly insulted by the feline's moniker, I suspect inside he is touched.

We still don't talk about personal feelings, although now that his health has dealt him a major wake-up call I see that changing a little. This past month has marked the first letter he ever wrote to me--three pages about the weather, constantly interjected with <u>SO THERE!</u> in large, capital underlined letters. I also received my very first birthday card, which not only did he sign himself, he signed it with "Love." Of course, it doesn't say "Love, Dad," it says "Love, J. C."--his initials. I laughed when I read it, and I was thrilled that he has been able to make so much progress.

The author of this poem conveys some universal feelings of guilty realization that I think all children reach as they become adults. I am just thankful that I have been given the time and opportunity in life to establish a bond with my father that I am not sure any of his other children have the privilege of sharing. I love him very much, and I have a relationship with him that may seem comparatively odd to other people, but that I treasure. Luckily I also have the sense of humor that is necessary to appreciate it.

REVISION

Rethinking, "re-visioning," and rewriting are just as important for a response essay about literature as they are for any other kind of writing. Having discovered what you want to say, you can now focus on how well you have said it. How well is your draft organized? Does it have unnecessary or redundant information? Are there gaps that need to be filled in? Are there enough details? Is there enough support from the work of literature? Have you expressed yourself as clearly as possible?

Organization and Unity

One of the most effective ways of checking the organization of a draft is by doing an **after-draft outline**. Go back to each paragraph and find the controlling idea. List the main ideas they represent, one after the other. This should give you an outline of your draft.

Let's look at an outline of Dierdre's draft:

1. Introduction and Thesis Statement
   The relationship in the poem reminds me of my own.
2. The house I grew up in always seemed filled with anger too.
3, 4. Both my father and his father expressed their love in the same way.
5. My father has done things to express his love.
6. The worst day of my life is also my fondest memory of my father.
7. My parents visited last year.
8. Two weeks ago, my father had a heart attack.
9. I didn't understand when I was younger—now I know.
10. We still don't talk about personal feelings, but our relationship is better.
11. Conclusion (I'm glad I've had the chance the poet missed).

When Dierdre looked at her list, she was concerned that she might have too many paragraphs. For the most part, the organization of her essay followed the pattern of the poem itself. She compared her relationship with her father to that of the poet's with his father. She took lines from the poem and then commented on how each matched her experience. This pattern made sense to her, but it appeared that several of these paragraphs were too long and unwieldy.

Showing Support

The support Dierdre used in this essay came from two sources: the poem and her personal experience. She supported her references to the text by quoting the poem. She supported references to her experience by giving examples. She believed she had enough support in both cases and that her examples firmly established the connection.

Clarity

Dierdre realized that she would have to tighten up her language by deleting unnecessary words, expressions, and sentences. After cutting and combining, she could decide if some of the paragraphs should be combined as well. She also realized that her choice of words did not always express what she meant. In Paragraphs 4 and 5 in particular, she decided that cutting, combining, and reordering some of the examples would strengthen the pace and organization of the essay.

Her most difficult decision was what to cut. She wanted her essay to be clearly expressed and tightly organized, but she didn't want to sacrifice the concrete details and scenes that gave it a strong voice.

Voice

She believed that one of the strengths of this piece was its voice, a voice that "showed" through quotations and examples. Her biggest task was to maintain a strong voice throughout the essay while tightening up her prose overall.

✔CHECKLIST • *Revision*

Organization and Unity
❑ Do all the paragraphs relate to the central thesis?

❑ Is the organization of those paragraphs within the essay clear?

❑ Do each of the sentences within the paragraphs relate to the central idea of the paragraph?

Support
❑ Are there enough details to support or clarify your assertions? Have you "shown" what you've told?

❑ Are there enough quotations from the work of literature to support your assertions?

❑ Are the paragraphs fully developed?

(continued)

❑ Is the essay fully developed? Have you accounted for all aspects of your thesis statement?

Clarity

❑ Is the central thesis of the essay clearly stated?

❑ Does the title of your essay account for your thesis?

❑ Is the language clear?

❑ Are there redundancies, digressions, or meaningless phrases that could be cut?

❑ Is the essay written in the format required by your instructor? Have you documented your references to the text and included a list of works cited?

Voice

❑ Does it sound like you? When you read it out loud, can you hear your voice and emotion?

Editing or proofreading is a crucial final step in the process of producing an essay. In addition to making any changes that did not occur to you earlier and fine tuning your writing, it's essential to check your essays for correct grammar, spelling, punctuation, and typos.

✔ CHECKLIST • *Editing and Proofreading*

❑ Are all of your sentences complete sentences?

❑ Are all of your sentences punctuated appropriately?

❑ Are the words spelled correctly? Have you checked for easily confused words (then/than, your/you're, its/it's, etc.)?

❑ Are you sure of the meaning of all the words you've used?

❑ Are the titles of works underlined or in quotation marks as appropriate?

❑ Is the title and heading on the first page in the correct format?

❑ Have you followed your essay with a works cited list?

❑ Are there particular errors you have a tendency to make? Have you looked for those in this essay?

Remember, computer spell checkers do not make choices about word usage. Confused words (than/then, there/their/they're, etc.) will not be flagged by a spell checker. You will have to use your own eyes and judgment to correct those errors.

Dierdre's Revised Essay

After rewriting her introduction to make it clearer, Dierdre cut many words and phrases, combined many sentences, and shifted some of her examples. After reading this clearer, shorter version, she decided to stay with the same number of paragraphs. She could have combined several of them but decided not to. The resulting paragraphs would have been too long and much more difficult for the reader to absorb.

Dierdre Curran

Dr. Madden

English 102

Fall 200X

Twice on Sunday

In his poem, "Those Winter Sundays," Robert Hayden illustrates the starkness of his relationship with his father. As a child, he was never able to understand or appreciate what his father did for him. As an adult, he feels guilt and regret because it is too late to communicate his appreciation. I have experienced a similar relationship, and I can relate strongly to the emotions expressed in this poem.

The poet tells of "fearing the chronic angers of that house" (9). The house I grew up in always seemed filled with anger to me, too. We never had conversations; we had arguments and disagreements. We never apologized to one another, said "I love you," or expressed sympathy or support when something was wrong. Our home was filled with bitterness and stress. There was nothing to ever balance it out, no tangible expressions of love from my parents . . . or so I thought until I got a little older and came to understand more.

He says his father " . . . got up early / and put his clothes on in the blueblack cold, / then with cracked hands that ached / from labor in the weekday weather made / banked fires blaze. No one ever thanked him" (1–5). In the wintertime, my dad was always up before the rest of us and had turned on the heat so that we awoke to a warm house. When I was older and needed his car to get to work, he would always go outside to start and warm it up. Often he dug it out of a night's snowfall. Reeling from the trauma of my teenage years and seething with bitterness, I actually resented his doing me a favor. I never once thanked him for it. I was annoyed and believed that he was only doing something he was expected to do. My behavior is well described when Hayden tells how he spoke "indifferently to him, / who had driven out the cold" (10–11).

Later in life, the poet realizes that while his father never expressed his love in words, he expressed it through a variety of gestures, like shining his son's shoes. When I recall my childhood, I realize that my father also showed his love in the only ways he knew how. When we were very little, I shared a room with my sister Lucy. Sometimes at night if he was in a good mood, right before we went to bed, my Dad would pretend that he was Frankenstein. He would close his eyes and stretch out his arms in front of him, walking like the fictional monster, approaching slowly, while we shrieked in terrified laughter, running from him. When he finally caught us, we got tickled to the point of hysteria. On Sundays, he would go out early to buy the newspapers and make sure that we had the comics and jelly doughnuts, too.

Once, my older sister and I complained that my father spent much more time with my brother than he did with us, so he took us with him on a business trip to Maryland. He never said, "I love you as much as your brother," or hugged us or kissed us, but he made the effort to spend time with us, and we all enjoyed it (well, I <u>think</u> he did; he seemed to). Seeing many horses on the roadside, I was insistent that I get up close to one. So, intent on getting me to my horses, my dad came up with a solution . . . he took us to the racetrack!

The worst day of my life is also my fondest memory of my father. It was the day I had to put my fifteen-year-old, diabetic dog Freebie to sleep. The guilt has never left me. No one in my family would go with me to the vet. At least my father said goodbye to her. He was the only one who was as upset as I was, and I was crushed. He never showed it. When I brought her ashes back to throw around the yard, he found me in the yard crying hysterically. I was totally heartbroken. No one hugged me, no one said, "I'm sorry." My father's only way of acknowledging my grief was to come outside and yell at me. He just stood there and kept yelling, and I just sat there and kept crying. Finally, he got quiet and told me that he missed the dog as much as I did, and hadn't gone with me because he didn't have the guts to do what I had done. Then he helped me up and walked me up the driveway, hugging me for the first time I can remember.

After I graduated from high school, my parents moved to Indiana. Last summer they came back for a visit. We had not seen each other in almost a year. In the parking lot where I met them, I gave my father a big hug and told him that I really missed him. He, of course, did not hug me back, and (surprised by my open display of affection) could only manage the reply, "Yeah, twice on Sunday!" I understood that this was his best effort, and I still laugh about it because it was so typical.

A few weeks ago, my oldest sister called to tell me that my father had suffered a heart attack. I was floored. I drank a bottle of wine and cried hysterically. Two very long days later, I was on a plane to see him. The plane trip was horrible. It took twelve hours to get there, and the delays were torture. I didn't care about the inclement weather or the size of the plane. I didn't care about anything but getting to South Bend as soon as I could. I made it to the hospital on my birthday, ten minutes before visiting hours ended. As I rushed down the hall looking frantically for his room, I heard him call out my name in excited surprise and saw him slowly hurrying toward me, pale, be-tubed and in his hospital gown. I could not believe how happy he was to see me. It made the whole trip worth it. He repeatedly held my hand and offered me his cheek for a kiss every couple of minutes. When he asked me "what in the hell" I was doing out there, I replied that I had the day off anyway, and decided to come see him for my birthday. He had a good laugh at that one. He seemed much less gruff than the last time I had seen him.

Never in my life has my father verbally expressed his love. In younger years I was blind to the fact that he just didn't know how, but that he showed it in other ways. That used to make me so mad and frustrated. But he has mellowed with the coming of age and grandchildren, and I have opened my eyes and learned to appreciate his gestures, and to interpret their meaning. In "Those Winter Sundays," the poet tells of the guilt of his own ignorance "of love's austere and lonely offices" (14). While I can't imagine the day when we will ever be able to actually say "I love you" to each other, I am secure in the knowledge that it is mutually understood.

We still don't talk about personal feelings, but now that his health has dealt him a major wake-up call, I see that changing a little. This past month has marked the first letter he ever wrote to me--three pages about the weather, constantly interjected with SO THERE! in large, capital underlined letters. I also received my very first birthday card. Not only did he sign it himself, but he signed it with "Love". Of course, it doesn't say "Love, Dad," it says "Love, J. C."--his initials. I laughed when I read it, and I was thrilled that he has been able to make so much progress.

In "Those Winter Sundays," Robert Hayden conveys feelings of guilt that I think most children experience as they become adults. I am just thankful that I have been given the time and the opportunity in life to establish a bond with my father. I love him very much, and I have a relationship with him that may seem comparatively odd to other people, but it's one that I treasure. Luckily, I also have the sense of humor that is necessary to appreciate it.

Work Cited

Hayden, Robert. "Those Winter Sundays." <u>Exploring Poetry</u>. Ed. Frank
    Madden. New York: Longman, 2002, 13.

PART II

Analysis and Argumentation

CHAPTER 3

Exploration and Analysis
The Elements of Poetry

To analyze anything is to look closely at how it works—to examine its parts. Our intention in this chapter, however, is not to reduce poetry to parts. Our goal is to provide you with tools to articulate and develop your responses into effective critical essays. We know that the parts of a poem alone cannot account for its meaning, a meaning that fully blossoms only as the parts work together. But reading a poem carefully and analyzing its parts can tell you a great deal about it—and how it triggered your response. Analysis is an important step in interpreting or evaluating poetry, and it is through this process that you may gather the support to make your opinion an informed one.

YOUR FIRST RESPONSE

When you read a poem for the first time, relax and give yourself enough time to experience it. Don't try too hard to figure it out. Get impressions. Notice words and phrases. Read them out loud. Listen to the rhythms. Follow the personal associations that come up. Let yourself feel the emotions connected to them. Don't be discouraged if you have difficulty understanding every word or line your first time through. Have a dictionary handy and look up unfamiliar words. Let your unanswered questions stick with you. Write them down if you think you won't remember them later.

Immediately after your first reading, jot down your impressions and the questions that came to mind during your reading. Capture your response while it's fresh. If you wait until later, you may forget. In fact, you may come away from your reading with more questions than answers. So a second or third reading with these questions in mind may clarify much that was confusing the first time through. If you were reminded of people or events in your life, try to think about the difference that those associations made in your response. Did they help? Did they interfere? Does the text of the work support your response?

Before you analyze the poem, try to grab hold of what you found most provocative about it. You will write with a stronger voice and more conviction when you write about what interests you most.

✔ CHECKLIST • *Your First Response*

- ❑ Write down your first impressions.
- ❑ Write down the questions that come to mind during and after your reading.
- ❑ What confuses you? What do you want to know more about? How can you find out?
- ❑ What words or phrases affect you most?
- ❑ Do the speaker or character(s) remind you of yourself or people you know?
- ❑ Do any of the events remind you of ones in your own life?
- ❑ Do these associations help or interfere with your response? If so, how?
- ❑ What do you find most interesting or compelling about the poem?

CLOSE READING

Analysis requires close reading. In a way the term *close reading* means the opposite of what it sounds like. When we read closely, we don't get closer to the literature and our experience with it; rather, we step back. We move from being inside the work to looking at it from the outside, from participating to observing. This process requires a careful reading and a conscious examination of the elements of the work and how they contribute to its overall meaning.

A close reading is not a first reading, it is a rereading. When you return to read the work or your notes again after discussion in class, you are doing a close reading. You have already stepped back from your own views to hear the responses of others. You are reading your notes and the literature informed by what you have learned from those discussions.

ANNOTATING THE TEXT

One effective way to do a close reading of a poem is to mark up the text by underlining, circling, highlighting, or making notes in the margins. You may even find it useful to do these annotations in more than one stage. In the first stage you might want to concentrate on your understanding of the poem by summarizing, noting words or passages you don't understand, and asking questions—exploring the text. Later on, as you narrow your focus, you may want to identify elements of the poem, patterns, evidence, or quotations to support your thesis—analyzing the text. If you don't want to mark up the pages of your book, make a copy of the work and do your annotations on this copy. Or write your annotations on Post-it notes and attach them in the margins of the work.

First Annotation: Exploration

PERCY BYSSHE SHELLEY (1792–1822)

OZYMANDIAS [1818]

I met a traveler from an antique land
Who said: "Two vast and trunkless legs of stone   *What does he mean*
Stand in the desert . . . Near them on the sand,   *"trunkless legs"?*
Half-sunk, a shattered visage lies, whose frown   *Look up visage.*
And wrinkled lip, and sneer of <u>cold command</u>,   *"Cold command"—a ruler?*   5
Tell that its sculptor well those passions read   *A sculptor—a statue?*
Which yet survive, stamped on these lifeless things,
The <u>hand that mocked</u> them, and the <u>heart that fed</u>;   *Hand-mocked, heart-fed? How does*
And on the pedestal these words appear: *"hand" differ from "heart"?*
'My name is Ozymandias, king of kings: 10
Look on my works, ye Mighty, and despair!'   *Summary—He met someone from a*
Nothing beside remains. Round the decay   *faraway country who saw an*
Of that colossal wreck, boundless and bare   *ancient, large, broken statue with*
The lone and level sands stretch far away."   *an arrogant statement on it.*

This first annotation is an exploration of your first reading. You may clarify
what you understand and ask questions about what you don't understand, or
indicate what you need to know more about. You might make guesses, note
impressions, summarize, and, in general, give yourself something to think about
when you begin a second reading.

How does this compare with other
Shelley poems I've read?

Second Annotation: Analysis

PERCY BYSSHE SHELLEY (1792–1822)

What was going on in England at
this time? Who was the king?

OZYMANDIAS [1818]

Why "antique" and not just "old" or
"ancient"?
I met a traveler from an <u>antique</u> land
Who said: "Two vast and trunkless legs of stone   *The rhyme scheme: abab—"stone"*
Stand in the desert . . . Near them on the sand,   *and "frown"?*
Half-sunk, a shattered visage lies, whose frown   *Not just grand but arrogant as*
And wrinkled lip, and sneer of cold command,   *well.*   5
Tell that its sculptor well those passions read   *"Read" and "fed" rhyme but not*
Which yet survive, stamped on these lifeless things,   *"command" and "things."*
The <u>hand</u> that mocked them, and the <u>heart</u> that <u>fed</u>;   *The hand of the sculptor / the*
And on the pedestal these words appear: *heart of the king?*
'My name is Ozymandias, king of kings: *A powerful image—decayed and*   10
Look on my works, ye Mighty, and despair!'   *worn-out grandeur and arrogance in*
Nothing beside remains. Round the decay   *a desert.*
Of that colossal wreck, boundless and bare   *Rhymes: despair/bare—decay/away*
The lone and level sands stretch far away."   *What a powerful ironic contrast!*

The second annotation is a closer reading and more analytical. Here you might look for some of the elements of literature we discuss in this chapter, try to find patterns, seek evidence to support your early conclusions, or even place the work within a larger historical, social, or biographical context.

POETRY IN ITS MANY CONTEXTS

Our focus on textual analysis in this chapter—on the elements of poetry—is not an attempt to limit the scope of your writing to the parts of the work alone. Those parts and those works exist in a larger world—a context framed by personal, cultural, historical, biographical, and other influences. Seeing beyond the poem to the contexts that influenced its writing—and your reading—may enliven and enrich your experience of the work and help you produce a more interesting essay.

Your Critical Approach

What you value most about literature, your critical stance, can be an important factor in determining what you analyze and write about when interpreting and evaluating poetry. Critical approaches are broadly classified as reader based (emphasizing the reader's response and the text), text based (emphasizing the text), context based (emphasizing the background of the work), and author based (emphasizing connections to the author's life or intentions). Whatever approach you take may determine the strategy and terms you use in your writing. For a more comprehensive explanation of these approaches see Appendix A (p. 305). Keep in mind that critical approaches may easily overlap, and critics often combine them in their analyses. The difference between one critical stance and another may be more a matter of emphasis than kind, and drawing upon several approaches can yield a rich interpretation.

Interpretive Communities

Stanley Fish, a professor and literary critic, has suggested that groups of readers who value the same approach to analyzing literature belong to "an interpretive community." Although our interpretations are influenced by whatever collaborative group or class we are in at present, we also carry and apply our own individual values and those of the many other communities (family, friends, religion) to which we belong. In this respect, we are members of many interpretive communities, and we are continually refiguring and revising our interpretations and evaluations in the light of our personal beliefs and group discussions. You may find it worthwhile and productive to keep track of this complex mix of personal response and group discussion as you write about the poetry you read and discuss.

READING AND ANALYZING POETRY

The subject of poetry is human experience. We are not likely to say of any event, "You can't write a poem about that." Birth, death, youth, old age, love, jealousy, ambition, loyalty, laughter, triumph, defeat—if we can experience it, we can write poetry about it. The more an experience moves us, the more important it seems to record the emotion, sensation, or memory with a poem. Reading poetry is a personal as well as a social experience. It is personal in the way it offers us a reflection of our own interior lives, our thoughts and emotions expressed in the words of others; and it is social in the way it offers us a glimpse of other people's interior lives, the shared expression of their hearts and minds.

Poems are not written to fill textbooks or create academic exercises. They are written to communicate with us. If we reduce our reading to analysis alone, we may "figure out" the poem's structure, its rhyme scheme and rhythm, or how it might be classified, but we may miss the experience of the poem itself. That experience relies on our ability to imagine—the ability to take the "sleeping" poem from the print on the page and "wake it up" through our imagination, senses, and emotions. This is not the kind of reading we might be used to doing in an academic environment, where we often read for information alone. And it may not be the style of reading we are used to in our everyday lives—in a world that bombards us with the exaggerated language of advertising, TV commercials, and talk shows, or reduces everything to sound bites. Given the lack of meaning in so much of that language, we may speed through it or ignore it altogether. We are not used to paying attention to language with our senses and emotions, to forming images; they are so often formed for us.

Poetry invites your engagement and comprehension. To be engaged by a poem, you need the time to read slowly and participate fully with your mind and senses. Once engaged, you have reason to analyze the poem's language, its structure, its rhymes or rhythms—to comprehend *how* it has prompted your response. Reading a poem this way involves your mind, senses, and emotions—and it has the power to change you the way that all meaningful experiences can.

LANGUAGE AND STYLE

Voice

Be sure to differentiate between the poet and the speaker in a poem. In some poems the poet and the speaker are virtually the same, and we can assume that the thoughts of the speaker are those of the poet as well. In Robert Hayden's poem "Those Winter Sundays" (p. 13), the speaker's remembrance seems to be that of the poet himself. On the other hand, the speaker (the "voice") in a poem may use vocabulary and express attitudes that are not characteristic of the poet. The speaker in Robert Browning's "Porphyria's Lover" (p. 141), a demented, homicidal lover, is clearly not the poet himself. Being able to identify the speaker, the speaker's attitude toward the poem's content, and the speaker's intended audience helps us read the poem more effectively.

Tone

The key to **tone** is voice. When we see or hear a poet speaking, the words, intonations, physical gestures, and facial expressions tell us the attitude of the speaker toward the subject. When we "hear" voice in our reading, we can also sense the intonations. Cues in a printed poem are not always obvious, however, and to sense the tone we must often rely on the pattern and types of words the poet chooses. Sometimes the contradictory nature of the language can give us a strong sense of that tone.

STEPHEN CRANE (1871–1900)

WAR IS KIND   [1899]

Do not weep, maiden, for war is kind.
Because your lover threw wild hands toward the sky
And the affrighted steed ran on alone,
Do not weep.
War is kind.   5

    Hoarse, booming drums of the regiment,
    Little souls who thirst for fight,
    These men were born to drill and die.
    The unexplained glory flies above them,
    Great is the battle god, great, and his kingdom—   10
    A field where a thousand corpses lie.

Do not weep, babe, for war is kind.
Because your father tumbled in the yellow trenches,
Raged at his breast, gulped and died,
Do not weep.   15
War is kind.

    Swift blazing flag of the regiment,
    Eagle with crest of red and gold,
    These men were born to drill and die.
    Point for them the virtue of slaughter,   20
    Make plain to them the excellence of killing
    And a field where a thousand corpses lie.

Mother whose heart hung humble as a button
On the bright splendid shroud of your son,
Do not weep.   25
War is kind.

► *QUESTIONS FOR READING AND WRITING*

1. How did your feelings about war influence your response?
2. What do you think about the choice of words Crane uses to describe war?
3. With many poems, being sensitive to the voice of the speaker is crucial to our response. The tone expressed by that voice may change the meaning. How are you affected by the tone in this poem?
4. What indications of tone are there in the text of the poem? Is there a contradiction between the title "War Is Kind" and the details that Crane uses to support it?
5. How does the poet's tone affect the meaning of "War Is Kind"?

Imagery

An **image** is a mental picture prompted by words. Images result from concrete language that appeals to our senses. "Nice image," we've heard people say about particularly striking words or phrases. But images do not exist in words on a page. They exist in our minds. The words on the page may prompt the images in our minds, but it is our own senses and memories that evoke the pictures. Experiments have shown that we use the same parts of our brains when we see or hear the word for an object as we do when encountering the object itself. It is our sense memories that bring a poet's words to life to form an image. We can see (hear, taste, touch, or smell) them in our mind's eye (ear, tongue, hand, or nose).

HELEN CHASSIN (b. 1938)

THE WORD PLUM

[1986]

The word *plum* is delicious

pout and push, luxury of
self-love, and savoring murmur

full in the mouth and falling
like fruit   5

taut skin
pierced, bitten, provoked into
juice, and tart flesh
question
and reply, lip and tongue   10
of pleasure.

ROBERT BROWNING (1812–1889)

MEETING AT NIGHT   [1845]

The gray sea and the long black land;
And the yellow half-moon large and low;
And the startled little waves that leap
In fiery ringlets from their sleep,
As I gain the cove with pushing prow,   5
And quench its speed in the slushy sand.

Then a mile of warm sea-scented beach;
Three fields to cross till a farm appears;
A tap at the pane, the quick sharp scratch
And blue spurt of a lighted match,   10
And a voice less loud, through its joys and fears,
Than the two hearts beating each to each!

▶ QUESTIONS FOR READING AND WRITING

1. Not all poetry intends to make a serious statement. Some poems simply
    intend to engage us in an aesthetic or sensory experience. Does "The Word
    Plum" have a different effect on you than "Meeting at Night" or "War Is
    Kind"? Explain.
2. To what extent can you connect "The Word *Plum"* and "Meeting at Night"
    to your own experience? How does that connection affect your response to
    the imagery?
3. In "The Word *Plum,"* the senses of taste and touch are primarily the senses
    we rely on to experience the images in the poem. How many senses do
    you use to experience the images in "Meeting at Night"?
4. How do these images add to the overall effect of the poems for you?

Figurative Language: Everyday Poetry

There is nothing unusual about figurative language. In fact, we would have a
hard time communicating with each other without it. Comparison is at the core
of "figures of speech," or figurative language. We use what is already familiar to
describe something new, or we describe something familiar in a new way. Used
in tandem with concrete language, similes and metaphors can lead to very striking images.

A **simile** is an announced comparison. We announce or introduce this comparison by using the words *like* or *as.* For example, "He's as quiet as a church
mouse" or "She swims like a fish." The things compared usually have only one
characteristic in common. Some of the most evocative descriptions in poetry are
similes. Marge Piercy's words, "Her good nature wore out like a fan belt" (see
"Barbie Doll," p. 14) are a vivid example of how simile can evoke lasting images
in our minds.

LANGSTON HUGHES (1902–1967)

A DREAM DEFERRED   [1951]

What happens to a dream deferred?

Does it dry up
like a raisin in the sun?
Or fester like a sore—
And then run?   5
Does it stink like rotten meat?
Or crust and sugar over—
like a syrupy sweet?

Maybe it just sags
like a heavy load.   10

Or does it explode?

N. SCOTT MOMADAY (b. 1934)

SIMILE   [1974]

What did we say to each other
that now we are as the deer
who walk in single file
with heads high
with ears forward   5
with eyes watchful
with hooves always placed on firm ground
in whose limbs there is latent flight.

FRANCES CORNFORD (1886–1960)

THE GUITARIST TUNES UP

With what attentive courtesy he bent
Over his instrument:
Not as a lordly conqueror who could
Command both wire and wood,
But as a man with a loved woman might,   5
Inquiring with delight
What slight essential things she had to say
Before they started, he and she to play.

▶ *QUESTIONS FOR READING AND WRITING*

1. Each of these poems relies on comparison to make its point. To what extent do these comparisons bring personal experiences to mind?
2. There are five announced comparisons (similes) and one implied comparison (metaphor) in "A Dream Deferred." What are they? What images do they prompt in you? What senses do you use to experience them?
3. As its title suggests, there is one announced comparison in "Simile." What is it? What image does it prompt in you?
4. To what extent are you affected differently by the many brief similes of "A Dream Deferred" in comparison to the one extended simile in "Simile"?
5. To what extent does "The Guitarist Tunes Up" differ from either of these poems?
6. What is the point of each poem? In each case, how do the similes present it effectively?

A **metaphor** is a more direct and more complete comparison than a simile. A metaphor does not announce itself; it states that something *is* something else (My love is a red rose) or implies it (My love has red petals and sharp thorns). Our everyday language is filled with metaphors. We call attractive-looking people "hunks" and "foxes." Businesses use implied metaphors to name their products. We buy an antiperspirant named Arrid, soap named Irish Spring, computers named Thinkpads, and cars named Jaguars. Sometimes, however, people get carried away and mix metaphors, with curious results. A baseball manager once remarked about a suspended player that "The ball was in his court now [tennis], so he better not step out of bounds [basketball], or he'd be down for the count [boxing]."

CARL SANDBURG (1878–1967)

FOG [1916]

The fog comes
on little cat feet.
It sits looking
over harbor and city
on silent haunches   5
and then moves on.

H. D. (HILDA DOOLITTLE) (1886–1961)

OREAD° [1924]

Whirl up, sea—
whirl your pointed pines,

°**oread** mountain nymph

splash your great pines
on our rocks,
hurl your green over us,   5
cover us with your pools of fir.

Personification is a frequently used form of metaphor. To personify is to give human characteristics or qualities to something not human. Consider how often you personify objects in your everyday use of language.

JAMES STEPHENS (1882–1950)

THE WIND   [1915]

The wind stood up and gave a shout.
He whistled on his fingers and

Kicked the withered leaves about
And thumped the branches with his hand

And said he'd kill and kill and kill,   5
And so he will and so he will.

▶ QUESTIONS FOR READING AND WRITING

1. To what extent is your response to "Fog," "Oread," or "The Wind" influenced by your own experience? Support your explanation with reference to the poems.
2. What are the metaphors in each poem?
3. What images do they prompt in you?
4. What senses do you use to experience them?
5. How do these images add to the overall effect of the poems?

Symbol

A **symbol** is something that represents more than itself. Every word we speak is a symbol. Government flags, religious objects, and logos on college sweatshirts are all symbols. We have personal symbols (meaningful objects, special songs), public symbols (flags), and conventional symbols (a road as the journey of life, seasons to represent the stages of our lives). Symbols are subject to personal interpretation. A nation's flag may symbolize truth and justice to one person, but deceit and oppression to another.

ROBERT FROST (1874–1963)

THE ROAD NOT TAKEN   [1915]

Two roads diverged in a yellow wood,
And sorry I could not travel both
And be one traveler, long I stood
And looked down one as far as I could
To where it bent in the undergrowth;   5

Then took the other, as just as fair,
And having perhaps the better calm,
Because it was grassy and wanted wear;
Though as for that the passing there
Had worn them really about the same,

And both that morning equally lay   10
In leaves no step had trodden black.
Oh, I kept the first for another day!
Yet knowing how way leads on to way,
I doubted if I should ever come back.

I shall be telling this with a sigh   15
Somewhere ages and ages hence:
Two roads diverged in a wood, and I—
I took the one less traveled by,
And that has made all the difference.

TESS GALLAGHER (b. 1943)

THE HUG   [1987]

A woman is reading a poem on the street
and another woman stops to listen. We stop too,
with our arms around each other. The poem
is being read and listened to out here
in the open. Behind us   5
no one is entering or leaving the houses.

Suddenly a hug comes over me and I'm
giving it to you, like a variable star shooting light
off to make itself comfortable, then
subsiding. I finish but keep on holding   10
you. A man walks up to us and we know he hasn't
come out of nowhere, but if he could, he
would have. He looks homeless because of how
he needs. "Can I have one of those?" he asks you,
and I feel you nod. I'm surprised,   15

surprised you don't tell him how
it is—that I'm yours, only
yours, etc., exclusive as a nose to
its face. Love—that's what we're talking about, love
that nabs you with "for me   20
only" and holds on.

So I walk over to him and put my
arms around him and try to
hug him like I mean it. He's got an overcoat on
so thick I can't feel   25
him past it. I'm starting the hug
and thinking, "How big a hug is this supposed to be?
How long should I hold this hug?" Already
we could be eternal, his arms falling over my
shoulders, my hands not   30
meeting behind his back, he is so big!

I put my head into his chest and snuggle
in. I lean into him. I lean my blood and my wishes
into him. He stands for it. This is his
and he's starting to give it back so well I know he's   35
getting it. This hug. So truly, so tenderly
we stop having arms and I don't know if
my lover has walked away or what, or
if the woman is still reading the poem, or the houses—
what about them?—the houses.   40
Clearly, a little permission is a dangerous thing.
But when you hug someone you want it
to be a masterpiece of connection, the way the button
on his coat will leave the imprint of
a planet in my cheek   45
when I walk away. When I try to find some place
to go back to.

➤ QUESTIONS FOR READING AND WRITING

1. To what extent is your response to "The Road Not Taken" or "The Hug"
   influenced by your own experience?
2. If the road in "The Road Not Taken" is a symbol for the journey of life,
   what is the symbol in "The Hug" and what does it represent?
3. What images do these poems prompt in you?
4. What senses do you use to experience these images?
5. How does the symbolism add to the overall effect of the poem for you?

✔ **CHECKLIST** • *Language and Style*

- ❏ How does the poet's choice of words affect your response?
- ❏ How are you affected by the speaker's voice?
- ❏ What images do you experience?
- ❏ Are there similes or metaphors?
- ❏ Is there symbolism?
- ❏ How do word choice, voice, imagery, figurative language, and/or symbolism affect your response?
- ❏ How can you support your responses from the text?

SOUND AND STRUCTURE

Long before we had the ability to speak, we enjoyed making and listening to sounds. As newcomers to the world, we were probably soothed or frightened by the sound of the adult voices around us. The sounds we made helped us develop our vocal chords, but there was much more to it than that. We listened to the sounds we made and adjusted them until we got them just right. We made the leap from gurgles and hisses to new sounds with real syllables like ba-ba, ma-ma, da-da.

The amazing thing is that all of this happened before we could speak and understand words or sentences from the adult language that surrounded us. Those sounds were a universal language we shared with children all over the world. And those sounds, like music, seemed to have an appeal in and of themselves—an appeal we haven't forgotten. Sometimes we listen to songs and sing along or sing the songs to ourselves—even when we don't know all the words. And sometimes we like the sounds of the words and the rhymes and rhythms of poems just as much as their meanings.

Finding the Beat: Limericks

A light, usually humorous, form of poetry that is helpful for getting the feel of rhyme and rhythm is the **limerick**. Limericks are very common and almost always anonymous (usually for good reason), and we're just as likely to see them scrawled on a wall as on paper.

The limerick packs laughs anatomical
Into space that is quite economical.
   But the good ones I've seen
   So seldom are clean,
And the clean ones so seldom are comical.

Read it out loud several times. Listen to the rhythm. Look at the rhyme pattern or scheme. Which lines rhyme? What is the rhythm like? Can you describe the pattern of a limerick? If you need to, read it out loud again.

Here's another one:

There was a young maid who said, "Why	(*a*)
Can't I look in my ear with my eye?	(*a*)
If I put my mind to it,	(*b*)
I'm sure I can do it.	(*b*)
You never can tell till you try."	(*a*)

Can you figure out the pattern?

Limericks have five lines. The first, second, and fifth lines rhyme (*aaa,* above) and so do the third and fourth (*bb,* above). The first, second, and fifth have approximately the same verbal rhythm (**meter**) and length, and so do the third and fourth.

Sometimes we don't notice what we have until it's gone:

A decrepit old gas man named Peter,
While hunting around for the meter,
   Touched a leak with his light.
   He arose out of sight,
And, as anyone can see by reading this, he also destroyed the meter.

What "destroyed" the meter? Can you fix it by rewriting the fifth line yourself?

Rhyme, Alliteration, Assonance

As kids in school, we may have used rhymes to memorize the number of days in each month or the names of the states or presidents. The most obvious rhymes come at ends of lines when the final vowel and consonant sounds in a word at the end of one line match the vowel and consonant sounds at the end of another (l*and* and s*and,* th*ings* and k*ings,* b*are* and desp*air*).

Less obvious are repeated initial consonant sounds (*d*o or *d*ie, *s*ink or *s*wim, *s*uffering *s*uccotash"), which is called **alliteration**.

Less obvious still are **assonance,** or repeated vowel sounds (t*i*me l*i*ne, fr*ee* and *ea*sy) and **consonance,** or repeated consonant sounds (sho*rt* and sma*rt,* st*ru*ts and f*re*ts).

When we listen to music, we are moved along (in spirit and time) and can anticipate structure by patterns and combinations of repeated tones. If we listen sensitively to rhyme and rhythm in poetry, we are likely to have a similar experience.

Look at the following quatrains (units of four lines) from two different William Blake poems. This quatrain has an *ab, ab* rhyme scheme:

From "London"

In every cry of every Man, (*a*)
In every Infant's cry of fear, (*b*)
In every voice, in every ban, (*a*)
The mind-forg'd manacles I hear. (*b*)

This quatrain has an *aa, bb* rhyme scheme:

From "The Tyger"

In what distant deeps or skies (*a*)
Burnt the fire of thine eyes? (*a*)
On what wings dare he aspire? (*b*)
What the hand dare seize the fire? (*b*)

   Recite each quatrain out loud several times. How does the ordering of rhyme affect your pace? How does it affect the content of the lines and the units of thought you remember?
   Examine other poems in this section. For example, Robert Browning's "Meeting at Night" and Robert Frost's "The Road Not Taken" have very different rhyme schemes. Read them out loud and see how the rhyme scheme affects how you hear and organize the content of the poems.

Meter

Some rhythm in poetry is described by the word *meter*. **Meter** refers to the pattern of stressed (/) and unstressed (˘) syllables in a line. The group of syllables making up one metrical unit is called a **foot**. The metrical feet most commonly used are **iambic** (unstressed, stressed), **trochaic** (stressed, unstressed), **anapestic** (two unstressed, one stressed), and **dactylic** (one stressed, two unstressed).
   The number of feet in each line is described as **monometer** (one foot), **dimeter** (two feet), **trimeter** (three feet), **tetrameter** (four feet), **pentameter** (five feet), **hexameter** (six feet), **heptameter** (seven feet), and **octameter** (eight feet).
   The most common form of meter in poetry written in English is **iambic** (unstressed, stressed) **pentameter** (five feet).
   The pair of lines from two sonnets written over three hundred years apart are examples of iambic pentameter (five feet of iambic per line):

Desir\ing this\ man's art \and that\ man's scope,
With what\ I most\ enjoy\ content\ed least;

—William Shakespeare (1609)

Nŏr yét\ ă floát\ĭng spár\ tŏ mén\ thắt sínk
Añd ríse\ añd sínk\ añd ríse\ añd sínk\ ăgáin;

—Edna St. Vincent Millay (1931)

Formal Verse: The Sonnet

One of the most popular and enduring formal verse structures is the sonnet. Sonnets are 14 lines long and are usually written in iambic pentameter. Rhyme schemes will vary according to type. The oldest form of the sonnet is the Italian, or Petrarchan, sonnet (named for its greatest practitioner, Petrarch). Its rhyme scheme is usually an octave (eight lines) and a sestet (six lines). The octave usually follows a pattern of *abbaabba*. The concluding sestet may be *cdecde, cdcdcd,* or *cdedce*.

In English, the most popular form is the English, or Shakespearean, sonnet (named for its greatest practitioner, William Shakespeare, who wrote 154 of them), so we use it here to illustrate formal verse. The Shakespearean sonnet is a 14-line poem of three quatrains (four-line units) and a final couplet (a two-line unit) in the rhyme scheme *abab cdcd efef gg*. It is a structure that presents the content of the poem in predictable ways. The first two quatrains often present a problem. The third quatrain is often pivotal and begins a reversal. The final couplet most often suggests a solution.

WILLIAM SHAKESPEARE (1564–1616)

SONNET NO. 29   [1609]

When, in disgrace with Fortune and men's eyes, (*a*)
I all alone beweep my outcast state, (*b*)
And trouble deaf heaven with my bootless° cries, (*a*)
And look upon myself and curse my fate, (*b*)
Wishing me like to one more rich in hope, (*c*)   5
Featured like him, like him with friends possessed, (*d*)
Desiring this man's art and that man's scope, (*c*)
With what I most enjoy contented least; (*d*)
Yet in these thoughts myself almost despising, (*e*)
Haply I think on thee, and then my state, (*f*)   10
Like to the lark at break of day arising (*e*)
From sullen earth, sings hymns at heaven's gate; (*f*)
   For thy sweet love remembered such wealth brings (*g*)
   That then I scorn to change my state with kings. (*g*)

³**bootless** useless

EDNA ST. VINCENT MILLAY (1892–1950)

LOVE IS NOT ALL   [1931]

Love is not all: it is not meat nor drink (*a*)
Nor slumber nor a roof against the rain; (*b*)
Nor yet a floating spar to men that sink (*a*)
And rise and sink and rise and sink again; (*b*)
Love cannot fill the thickened lung with breath, (*c*)   5
Nor clean the blood, nor set the fractured bone; (*d*)
Yet many a man is making friends with death (*c*)
Even as I speak, for lack of love alone. (*d*)
It well may be that in a difficult hour, (*e*)
Pinned down by pain and moaning for release, (*f*)   10
Or nagged by want past resolution's power, (*e*)
I might be driven to sell your love for peace, (*f*)
Or trade the memory of this night for food. (*g*)
It well may be. I do not think I would. (*g*)

➤ *QUESTIONS FOR READING AND WRITING*
1. Describe the emotions of the speakers in these poems.
2. Do their circumstances bring to mind any of your own experiences? Would you describe love in these terms? How does that affect your response?
3. In what way does the sonnet structure of each affect your response?
4. Can you find a pattern in the structure of each that is connected to the content?

The Villanelle

Another form of rhyming fixed verse is the *villanelle*, which has 19 lines. It uses only two rhymes and repeats two of its lines according to a set pattern. Line 1 is repeated as lines 6, 12, and 18; and line 3 is repeated as lines 9, 15, and 19. Lines 1 and 3 are repeated as a rhymed couplet at the end of the poem. The villanelle's rhyme scheme is *aba aba aba aba aba abaa*. An excellent example of a villanelle is Dylan Thomas's "Do Not Go Gentle into That Good Night" on page 262.

Blank Verse

An especially popular verse form is **blank verse**. Blank verse is unrhymed but follows a regular verse form, usually iambic pentameter. Some of the greatest epic poems and plays (including Milton's *Paradise Lost* and Shakespeare's plays) have been written in blank verse, and it is still a very popular form today.

Here are the first 11 lines from Robert Frost's "Mending Wall." The entire poem is 45 lines long (see p. 170).

Something there is that doesn't love a wall,
That sends the frozen-ground-swell under it,
And spills the upper boulders in the sun;
And makes gaps even two can pass abreast.
The work of hunters is another thing:
I have come after them and made repair
Where they have left not one stone on a stone,
But they would have the rabbit out of hiding,
To please the yelping dogs. The gaps I mean,
No one has seen them made or heard them made,
But at spring mending-time we find them there.

While it does not rhyme, the iambic pentameter still moves us from line to line in a regular predictable rhythm and influences our "hearing" of the poem. Read it out loud several times and see if you can hear and feel the regular beat.

Iambic pentameter is the dominant pattern in blank verse, but every word and every line may not conform to this pattern. For example, "Something," the first word of Frost's poem above, with its emphasis on the first syllable, is trochaic (stressed, unstressed), not iambic (unstressed, stressed). So, too, while the dominant pattern of Shakespeare's sonnets and plays is blank verse, not every foot is iambic, nor every line pentameter.

Free Verse

As its title implies, this is verse that is not constrained by an imposed form. **Free verse** does not have a rhyme scheme or regular rhythm. It is not formless, however, but relies on its own words and content to determine its best form. The poem that follows was written by Walt Whitman, a celebrated pioneer of free-verse writing.

WALT WHITMAN (1819–1892)

WHEN I HEARD THE LEARN'D ASTRONOMER   [1865]

When I heard the learn'd astronomer,
When the proofs, the figures, were ranged in columns before me,
When I was shown the charts and diagrams, to add, divide, and
    measure them,
When I sitting heard the astronomer where he lectured with much
    applause in the lecture-room,

How soon unaccountable I became tired and sick,   5
Till rising and gliding out I wander'd off by myself,
In the mystical moist night-air, and from time to time,
Look'd up in perfect silence at the stars.

➤ QUESTIONS FOR READING AND WRITING

1. Have you ever been in a situation where the explanation of the experience paled in comparison to the experience itself? Explain.
2. What does the speaker mean when he says, "How soon unaccountable I became tired and sick"?
3. How does the free verse affect your response to the poem?

✔ CHECKLIST • *Sound and Structure*

❑ Is there a rhyme scheme in the poem? If so, what is its pattern? How does the rhyme scheme add to the overall effect of the poem?

❑ Are there other sound devices (alliteration, assonance, consonance)? If so, how do they affect your response?

❑ Is there a regular pattern to the verse? If so, what is it? How does it add to the effect of the poem?

❑ If there is no regular pattern, how does the unique form of the poem match the content? How did it affect your response?

INTERPRETATION: WHAT DOES THE POEM MEAN?

Theme is the meaning we construct from the poem. It is an insight about life that we derive from the poem as a whole. Identifying and articulating this meaning is not an easy task. While our experience of the poem may be holistic or impressionistic, the analysis and support required for its articulation demand a close look at the parts—the language, events, and outcome of the poem.

Explication

An explication involves a line-by-line analysis of a text. Most poem are relatively brief and by their nature "packed with meaning." So they present a good opportunity for a very close reading and examination—an opportunity to look closely at sounds, words, images, lines, and how they all work together to deliver the poem's meaning. An explication is not just a summary or translation of the poet's language into your own; it is a detailed interpretation of *how* and *what* you believe the poem means.

Remember, poems are not problems to be solved. They don't have one correct answer or interpretation. What makes an interpretation convincing or defensible is your ability to support it.

Theme or Moral

Be wary of reducing what the poem means to a moral or lesson. Good poetry reveals a complex world. A moral preaches; it teaches us a lesson or a code of conduct. A theme reveals; it gives us insight into human nature.

✔ CHECKLIST • *Interpretation and Theme*

- ❏ What are the major details (the sounds, words, rhymes, rhythms, etc.) of the poem? What conclusion can you draw from these details?
- ❏ What generalization about life does the conclusion lead to?
- ❏ What does the poem mean? What is the theme of the poem?
- ❏ Is the poem didactic? Does it preach or give a lesson?

TYPES OF POETRY

For the sake of clarification and simplification, poetry may be classified into two types: lyric and narrative. As with other forms of literature, classifications of this kind are not exclusive. There is overlap between the designations of lyric and narrative. Poems in each of these categories may have elements characteristic of the other. And both lyric and narrative poetry have dramatic qualities.

Lyric Poetry

Lyric poetry is the most popular form of poetry written today. Lyric poems are characterized by the expression of the speaker's innermost feelings, thoughts, and imagination. The word *lyric* is taken from a stringed musical instrument called the *lyre*, which was used in classical and medieval times to accompany a singer. In addition to the very subjective stance of the speaker, lyric poems are melodic—a melody not derived from a lyre but from words and their arrangement. It's not mere coincidence that the words that accompany the melody in a song are called *lyrics*. Most of the poetry in this text can be classified as lyric poetry, but a specific example of this type is Edna St. Vincent Millay's "Love Is Not All" (p. 73).

One kind of lyric poetry that deserves special mention is the **dramatic monologue**. In a dramatic monologue, the poet, like an actor in a play, assumes a different persona and speaks to us through the voice and personality of another person. Robert Browning's "Porphyria's Lover" (p. 141) is an example of a dramatic monologue.

Narrative Poetry

A narrative poem tells a story. The poet takes on a role similar to that of a narrator in a work of fiction. The oldest stories were recorded in poetry and recited by "bards" who used the rhythms of the verse to help them memorize their lines. One difference between the narratives of short stories and those of narrative poems is length. With the exception of epic poems—book-length, narrative poems with lots of room for development of conflict and character—the length of most narrative poems limits the development of conflict and character. The brevity of the poems allows little space for exposition, and the poem usually moves quickly to the "chase," or crisis, beginning virtually in the middle of the story (or *in medias res*). Dudley Randall's "Ballad of Birmingham" (p. 17) and Seamus Heaney's "Mid-Term Break" (p. 184) are examples of narrative poems.

✔ C H E C K L I S T • *Types of Poetry*

❑ Is the poem an expression of the poet's thoughts and feelings, or is it telling a story?

❑ Is it a narrative or lyric poem, or a dramatic monologue?

✔ S U M M A R Y   C H E C K L I S T • *Analyzing Poetry*

Language and Style
❑ How does the poet's choice of words affect your response?

❑ How are you affected by the speaker's voice?

❑ What images do you experience?

❑ Are there similes or metaphors?

❑ Is there symbolism?

❑ How do word choice, voice, imagery, figurative language, and/or symbolism affect your response?

❑ How can you support your responses from the text?

Sound and Structure
❑ Is there a rhyme scheme in the poem? If so, what is its pattern?

❑ How does the rhyme scheme add to the overall effect of the poem?

❑ Are there other sound devices (alliteration, assonance, consonance)?

❑ If so, how do they affect your response?

(continued)

❑ Is there a regular pattern to the verse? If so, what is it?

❑ How does it add to the effect of the poem?

❑ If there is no regular pattern, how does the unique form of the poem match the content? How did it affect your response?

Interpretation and Theme

❑ What are the major details (the sounds, words, rhymes, rhythms, etc.) of the poem?

❑ What conclusion can you draw from these details?

❑ What generalization about life does the conclusion lead to?

❑ What does the poem mean? What is its theme?

❑ Is the poem didactic? (Does it preach or give a lesson?)

Types of Poetry

❑ Is the poem an expression of the poet's thoughts and feelings, or is it telling a story? Is it a narrative or lyric poem, or a dramatic monologue?

GETTING IDEAS FOR WRITING ABOUT POETRY

Following "Pigeon Woman," many of the questions from the summary checklist above are applied to the poem, and we consider some of the ways the elements discussed in this section might be used to prompt ideas for an essay.

MAY SWENSON (1919–1989)

PIGEON WOMAN   [1958]

Slate, or dirty-marbled-colored,
or rusty-iron-colored, the pigeons
on the flagstones in front of the
Public Library make a sharp lake

into which the pigeon woman wades   5
at exactly 1:30. She wears a
plastic pink raincoat with a round
collar (looking like a little

girl, so gay) and flat gym shoes,
her hair square-cut, orange.   10
Wide-apart feet carefully enter
the spinning, crooning waves

(as if she'd just learned how
to walk, each step conscious,
an accomplishment); blue knots in the   15
calves of her bare legs (uglied marble),

age in angled cords of jaw
and neck, her pimento-colored hair,
hanging in thin tassels, is gray
around a balding crown.   20

The day-old bread drops down
from her veined hand dipping out
of a paper sack. Choppy, shadowy ripples,
the pigeons strike around her legs.

Sack empty, she squats and seems to rinse   25
her hands in them—the rainy greens and
oily purples of their necks. Almost
they let her wet thirsty fingertips—

but drain away in an untouchable tide.
A make-believe trade   30
she has come to, in her lostness
of illness or age—to treat the motley

city pigeons at 1:30 every day, in all
weathers. It is for them she colors her own
feathers. Ruddy-footed   35
on the lime stained paving,

purling to meet her when she comes,
they are a lake of love. Retreating
from her hands as soon as empty
they are the flints of love.   40

GENERATING IDEAS FOR WRITING

One of the best ways to get ideas for an essay is to ask and answer your own
most compelling questions. Write down whatever questions come to mind
during and after your reading. See if the answers to these questions provide
topics for writing. Or choose a compelling idea from a journal entry, draw a
Venn diagram to compare elements or other works (pp. 31–32), use directed
freewriting (p. 38), ask questions (p.8), list, or draw a cluster, or semantic map (p.
41), to loosen up ideas.

Listed below is a more structured approach based on the elements of poetry
discussed earlier in this section. Applying these questions to "Pigeon Woman"
may demonstrate how the elements might be applied to any poem.

Getting Started—Your First Response

1. What questions came to mind as you read "Pigeon Woman"?

2. What words or expressions are not clear to you?

3. To what extent can you connect "Pigeon Woman" to your own background or experience?

4. What do you find most compelling or provocative about the poem?

Language and Style

1. Who is the speaker in "Pigeon Woman"? What kind of voice does (s)he have? What is the speaker's tone? What is the speaker's attitude toward the woman being described?

2. One image in the poem describes the pigeons as making "a sharp lake into which the pigeon woman wades." Where else in the poem is that image supported?

3. What other images in the poem have an effect on you? To what senses do the images appeal?

4. What similes or metaphors do you find in the poem? How do they contribute to the imagery?

5. How does the figurative language in "Pigeon Woman" help convey its meaning?

6. Is there symbolism in the poem? Explain.

Sound and Structure

1. This poem does not have an obvious rhyme scheme. How does that affect your response?

2. What instances of alliteration or assonance can you identify?

3. To what extent does "Pigeon Woman" have a rhythm or a regular pattern to the verse? How does that influence your reading?

4. How does the form of "Pigeon Woman" match its content? To what extent does it help convey its meaning?

Interpretation and Theme

1. What does the last line, "they are the flints of love," mean?

2. What are the major details of the poem?

3. What conclusion can you draw from the details? What is the poem about?

4. To what extent does this conclusion lead to a generalization about life?

5. What is the theme of "Pigeon Woman"?

Types of Poetry

1. Is "Pigeon Woman" expressing the poet's innermost thoughts and feelings, or is it telling a story? Is it a narrative or lyric poem? Explain.

Topics for Writing

The following list is not exhaustive, but simply illustrative of the kinds of questions that might emerge from the more specific analytical questions (and combinations of questions) like those above. Your responses to these questions might provide worthwhile topics for writing.

1. To what extent is "Pigeon Woman" a love story?

2. Some poems paint pictures; some make statements. In what way does this poem do both?

3. How do the structure, images, and sounds of the poem convey the meaning of "Pigeon Woman"?

4. To what extent is this poem a comment about human relationships?

5. It is not unusual to see lonely old people looking for companionship. In what way does "Pigeon Woman" enable us to "be there" and experience what that means?

6. Many people rely on the company of "nature's creatures" for companionship. To what extent is this a poem about this kind of mutual dependency?

7. How necessary was it to understand the social circumstances of the woman to make sense of the poem?

8. Can you compare this poem or the woman in it to another work or character in that work? Explain.

9. This poem was written in 1958. Does it still make sense today? How so?

10. Are you familiar with other poems of May Swenson? If so, how does this poem compare with them?

CHAPTER 4

Argumentation
Interpreting and Evaluating Poetry

The goal in this chapter is to develop your writing and analysis into a critical essay. Writing a critical essay is a natural extension of your earlier work. At their best, your essays should continue to express, in your strongest voice, what you believe is important. There is no need for you to become completely formal or use complicated terminology. But writing a critical essay does require reading and rereading a poem carefully, gathering textual evidence, building observations into an interpretation or evaluation, and articulating a sound argument. Convincing others requires clear thinking and writing. We may write with a stronger voice when we feel passionate about an issue, but it is our ability to explain *why* with evidence, not just our passion, that gives clarity and credibility to our arguments.

THE CRITICAL ESSAY

The difference between a response essay and a critical essay is more a matter of emphasis than kind. A response essay describes our experience with literature—how we are personally affected by the work. The primary intention of a response essay is to share our personal experience, not to argue for a position.

A critical essay, while motivated by our experience with literature, shifts the emphasis toward the work itself and builds an argument for what the work or some aspect of it means (an interpretation), or its worth (an evaluation), or both. In addition to analyzing or explicating the text of a work, or making comparisons, a critical essay may address the beliefs or actions of the narrator or characters, or view a work or its elements within a variety of historical, cultural, biographical, or other contexts (see Appendix A for an explanation of these approaches).

Writing a critical essay builds on your earlier work. Beyond this work, you must be prepared to offer arguments in support of your views and state them clearly and persuasively. Reading the excerpts below—taken from two student essays later in this chapter— may give you an insight into the difference between a personal and a critical response.

William's Response to Countee Cullen's "Incident":

> I could picture myself in this situation because I have also had the feeling of not being wanted in a new place for racist reasons. My family and I were looking at a college in New Haven last year when something similar to this happened to me.

Jennifer's Response to Countee Cullen's "Incident":

> The theme of both "Theme for English B" by Langston Hughes and "Incident" by Countee Cullen is racism. While the two poems are similar in this way, however, they convey their messages very differently. The speaker in "Theme for English B" comments from the point of view of a young adult, while in "Incident" the narrator's perspective is that of an adult looking back into his childhood.

William writes about how the poem affected him—what emotions he felt and how the poem reminded him of an event in his own life. His intention seems to be to share his personal experience of the poem, not to argue an interpretation or evaluation.

Jennifer, on the other hand, writes about the speaker's perspective in each poem and discusses the way that these different perspectives convey the same essential message. The emphasis of her response and her primary intention in the essay are to write about the speaker's voice and perspective in the poems rather than to share the emotions she felt as she read the poems.

CHOOSING A TOPIC: PROCESS AND PRODUCT

The explanations below identify a number of different approaches you might choose when writing a critical essay.

Writing to Analyze or Explicate

To analyze a poem is to look closely at how it works—to examine its parts or elements as they contribute to the poem's meaning.

An **explication** is a detailed analysis, a line-by-line interpretation of *how* and *what* a poem means. Because they are longer pieces, works of fiction, drama, and essays usually don't lend themselves to such close reading. Most poems, however, are relatively brief, and by their nature packed with meaning. Poetry presents a good opportunity for a very close reading and an examination of sounds, words, images, lines, and how they all work together to deliver the poem's meaning. An explication is not just a summary or translation of the poet's language into your own; it is a detailed explanation of *how* the work conveys meaning. Mark Strumke's essay about Helen Chassin's "The Word <u>Plum</u>" at the end of this chapter is a clear example of explication.

Writing to Compare

In what way is the poem or aspects of it comparable to other poems or aspects of them? The objective of a comparison is not just to list similarities and differences but to reveal something important about whatever is being compared. Which details you choose as the basis of this comparison can make a difference. To give yourself a clear direction, and an overview of what you have, it may be helpful to make separate lists of similarities and differences before you start to write. Ask yourself what's worth comparing and what's not—and how this comparison might yield an effective essay. One useful method of lining up similarities and differences is the Venn diagram, described in Chapter 2 on pages 31–32.

In her essay later in this chapter (p. 90), Jennifer Stelz compares the "young adult" perspective of Langston Hughes's "Theme for English B" with the "adult looking back" perspective of Countee Cullen's "Incident." She concludes that while both poems are about racism, the nature of the speaker in each poem creates a very different impression on the reader.

Writing About the Beliefs or Actions of the Speaker or Characters

Speakers or characters in poems often express their beliefs in what they say or do. It's natural for us to judge their words and actions through our own beliefs, compare their choices with our own, and approve or disapprove as they meet or fail to meet our expectations. This is the kind of topic that lends itself well to a response essay—an essay that describes our experience of the poem and the emotions we felt—the sympathy, frustration, pleasure, or pride we experienced in response to the beliefs expressed. But writing about the beliefs or actions of the speaker can also be a good topic for a critical essay.

Remember, a critical essay shifts the emphasis toward the poem and builds an argument for what the poem or some aspect of it means (an interpretation) or its worth (an evaluation), or both. To write a critical essay about the beliefs or actions of the speaker or other characters, you must clearly identify those beliefs or actions and cite evidence that exemplifies them. Based on your own clearly stated criteria, you might interpret what they mean or build an argument for or against them.

Writing About Poetry in Context

To write about a poem in context is to consider it within a framework of cultural, historical, biographical, or other influences. For a more comprehensive explanation of these approaches (including historical, gender, political-economic, psychoanalytic, archetypal, and biographical criticism), see Appendix A: Critical Approaches to Literature, on page 305.

✔ C H E C K L I S T • *Choosing a Topic for a Critical Essay*

- ❏ What poem or aspect of a poem interests you?
- ❏ Is there a poem that you would like to analyze or explicate?
- ❏ Would it be illuminating to compare this poem or some aspect of it to another poem or poems?
- ❏ Are there beliefs of the speaker or characters that you want to interpret or evaluate?
- ❏ Do you want to interpret or evaluate the poem or aspects of it within a larger historical, cultural, biographical, or other context?

RESPONSE ESSAY OR CRITICAL ESSAY?

TWO READERS ⁓ TWO CHOICES

Following Langston Hughes's "Theme for English B" below, the complete versions of the two student essays excerpted earlier in this chapter illustrate the difference between a Response Essay and a Critical Essay.

Making Connections   The title of Hughes's poem probably strikes a familiar chord. After all, what could be more usual in an English class than being asked to write a theme or an essay? But for the speaker in this poem, the only African-American in his class, the assigned topic, to "let that page come out of you," presents a particular dilemma. He says, "I wonder if it's that simple?" In response to that question, this poem raises a number of compelling issues about racism, commonality, and difference.

Your Experiences and Beliefs   Before you read "Theme for English B" it may be helpful to think about your own beliefs and experiences as they apply to some of the issues that emerge from this poem. If you were asked to write about who you are—your own sense of identity—what would you write? Would your comments include ethnic, cultural, or class differences? When you meet other people for the first time, what do you notice first? What characteristics are most important to you? Have you ever prejudged or felt prejudged by those around you because of ethnic, cultural, or class differences?

LANGSTON HUGHES (1902–1967)
(See biography on p. 188.)

THEME FOR ENGLISH B   [1951]

The instructor said,

> *Go home and write*
> *A page tonight.*
> *And let that page come out of you—*
> *Then, it will be true.*   5

I wonder if it's that simple?

I am twenty-two, colored, born in Winston-Salem.
I went to school there, then Durham, then here
to this college on the hill above Harlem.
I am the only colored student in my class.   10
The steps from the hill lead down into Harlem,
through a park, then I cross St. Nicholas,
Eighth Avenue, Seventh, and I come to the Y,
the Harlem Branch Y, where I take the elevator
up to my room, sit down, and write this page: 15

It's not easy to know what is true for you or me
at twenty-two, my age. But I guess I'm what
I feel and see and hear. Harlem, I hear you:
hear you, hear me—we two—you, me, talk on this page.
(I hear New York, too.) Me—who?   20
Well, I like to eat, sleep, drink, and be in love.
I like to work, read, learn, and understand life.
I like a pipe for a Christmas present,
or records—Bessie, bop, or Bach.

I guess being colored doesn't make me *not* like   25
the same things other folks like who are other races.
So will my page be colored that I write?
Being me, it will not be white.
But it will be
a part of you, instructor.   30
You are white—
yet a part of me, as I am part of you.
That's American.
Sometimes perhaps you don't want to be a part of me.
Nor do I often want to be a part of you.   35
But we are, that's true!

As I learn from you,
I guess you learn from me—
although you're older—and white—
and somewhat more free.   40

This is my page for English B.

➤ *QUESTIONS FOR READING AND WRITING*

1. To what extent does your background or experience influence your response to "Theme for English B"?
2. If you were asked to write an assignment that "let that page come out of you," what would you write about?
3. Has the speaker in the poem "let that page come out of" him? Explain.
4. This poem was first published in 1951. How would it be different if written today?

∿ TWO STUDENT ESSAYS

In the student essays that follow, two students compare Langston Hughes's poem with a poem they have read earlier, Countee Cullen's "Incident" (see p. 12). Both student essays address the issue of race in these poems, but what the students write and the way they organize their comparisons are quite different.

A Response Essay

In his response essay, William Winters writes about one poem and then the other—but compares both poems to his own experience—using his experience with racial prejudice as an entry point and source of identification.

William Winters

Dr. Madden

English 102

November 16, 200X

Black and White

The poems "Incident" and "Theme for English B" provide us with a unique understanding of racism. When someone passes judgment on someone else based on that person's race or ethnicity we call it racism. These two poems by Countee Cullen and Langston Hughes gave me an entirely new perspective on racism. I have been fortunate enough not to be the subject of racist remarks. I never thought about what it would be like to have someone direct racist comments at me--except once, which I will return to later. Even though I feel that we cannot understand how it feels to be a victim of racism unless we experience it in real life, these two poems have given me a small taste of it.

"Incident" is short, simple, and to the point. Here we have an innocent eight-year-old child whose heart and head are "filled with glee" (2) because he is excited about visiting the city of Baltimore. The child sees a man and smiles at him. The man then points to him and calls the child a "nigger." When the speaker describes this happening, I could feel the child's heart sink. And my heart sank too. The child must have felt he was not wanted in this new place. Countee Cullen does an excellent job of letting the reader see the world through the child's eyes.

I could picture myself in this situation because I have also had the feeling of not being wanted in a new place for racist reasons. My family and I were looking at a college in New Haven last year. I was driving around a street outside the campus when a black man casually approached our car. When I slowed down to chat with him, he made an obscene gesture at us. My heart sank, and I was disturbed that this man did this to us for no reason except that we were white. Then, as we were getting on the highway to leave the city, a car with several young black men in it pulled up beside us. One of them rolled down his window and threw a softball at our car. Fortunately, the ball bounced off one of our windows, but any good thoughts I had about the school I had visited or the city of New Haven were shattered. Whenever I hear the words "New Haven" that's all that I remember. This is similar to the child's memory of Baltimore.

I believe that racism is not something we are born with. Instead, it is something we learn from others. The child in the story did not judge the man by the color of his skin. When the child smiled at him, the color of the man's skin did not even cross his young mind. However, the bigot has now made the child aware that people feel strongly about the color of his skin. That bigot was probably not a racist at one time. He learned to hate by observing the behavior of others. This brief, simple poem is very powerful and says a lot with a few words.

"Theme for English B" also deals with the topic of racism. It gets its message across very well, too, but in a slightly different way. Unlike

"Incident," it did not put me in the shoes of the main character. I felt more like I was having a conversation with the speaker in the poem. The message I got from this poem is that people are generally the same, but the color of their skin does separate them.

Evidently the main character is very aware of his ethnicity. He describes himself as "twenty-two, colored, born in Winston-Salem" (7). He also tells us that he is the only "colored" student in his class. This contrasts with the poem "Incident," in which the speaker, who is only eight years old, has not yet learned to see the world in black and white. The speaker says he likes to "eat, sleep, drink, and be in love" (21). He also tells us of other "normal" things that he likes. He does this to show that his interests are the same as white people's. I guess some people might be surprised by this!

He continues, however, by saying, "So will my page be colored that I write? / Being me, it will not be white" (27-28). Here I think he is telling us that even though he enjoys many of the same things that white people enjoy, his paper will be different because he is black. For him, this is an excellent segue into another thought: "Sometimes perhaps you don't want to be a part of me. / Nor do I often want to be a part of you" (34-35). Here, too, he indicates that though we share the same humanity, there are things that make us different. Our ethnic backgrounds, where we grew up, our families, our individual personalities make us different. But this difference is good. It is not something negative. It is good for all of us to have pride in our backgrounds. It gives us the opportunity to learn something from each other. As the speaker in the poem says, "That's American" (33). It is the abuse of these differences that separates ethnicity from racism.

We are all different. We come from different races, cultures, classes, families. These differences, however, are good. They make us unique and give us something to have pride in. Much too often our ethnicity is looked upon as something negative and this results in racism. Unlike our ethnicity, racism is not something we are born with, but something we learn by observing others and living our lives. Racism is not logical; it is stupid. How can we dislike someone just because of the color of their skin? Yes, there are evil people in all races, yet there are good people too. The poems "Incident" and "Theme for English B" are a very good reflection of my own views on this troubling issue.

Works Cited

Cullen, Countee. "Incident." <u>Exploring Poetry</u>. Ed. Frank Madden. New York: Longman, 2002. 12.

Hughes, Langston. "Theme for English B." <u>Exploring Poetry</u>. Ed. Frank Madden. New York: Longman, 2002. 86.

A Critical Essay

Jennifer Stelz discusses the speaker's voice and perspective and compares and contrasts the two poems point by point, finding similarities and differences throughout while explicating the poems' common theme of racism.

Jennifer Stelz

Dr. Madden

English 102

November 15, 200X

Racism

The theme of both "Theme for English B" by Langston Hughes and "Incident" by Countee Cullen is racism. While the two poems are similar in this way, however, they convey their messages very differently. The speaker in "Theme for English B" comments from the point of view of a young adult, while in "Incident" the narrator's perspective is that of an adult looking back into his childhood. Despite this difference, we can see that both speakers are equally affected by the pain that prejudice inflicts. Though the poems were written twenty-six years apart, the strong message about racism in each continues to have a strong impact.

The most obvious difference in the poems is that their speakers are telling their stories from the perspective of very different ages. In "Theme for English B," the speaker is a twenty-two-year-old student who is attending a predominantly white university. "Incident" is told as a memory of a child's visit to Baltimore. In "Theme for English B," the speaker seems reminded every day of the fact that he is "colored" in a "white" university:

I am twenty-two, colored, born in Winston-Salem.

I went to school there, then Durham, then here

to this college on the hill above Harlem.

I am the only colored student in my class. (7-10)

In "Incident," the young boy has only visited Baltimore for a short time, yet racism is branded into his mind forever. The speaker suggests that he does not experience prejudice every day:

I saw the whole of Baltimore

From May until December;

Of all the things that happened there

That's all that I remember. (9-12)

In "Theme for English B," Langston Hughes gives us an image of this twenty-two-year-old slowly and gradually. He describes his similarities, not his differences with whites:

Well, I like to eat, sleep, drink, and be in love.

I like to work, read, learn, and understand life.

I like a pipe for a Christmas present,

or records--Bessie, Bop, or Bach.

I guess being colored doesn't make me <u>not</u> like

the same things other folks like who are other

races. (21-26)

By listening to this young man we get into his mind; we begin to understand who he is. We think of him as being no different than a brother or a best friend. As this image develops in our mind, it helps us identify with the speaker and makes us sympathetic to him. His goal is to convince us not to judge others by the color of their skin.

In the poem "Incident," the poet takes a different route entirely to get his message across to the reader. Countee Cullen uses shocking, hurtful words coming from a child's mouth to show how painful racism is:

Now I was eight and very small,

And he was no whit bigger,

And so I smiled, but he poked out

His tongue, and called me, "Nigger." (5-8)

That one word "nigger" is enough to grab our attention and get a reaction. Not much building up by the speaker is needed to spark strong feelings. That he was only a small boy in particular was enough to make our hearts race with emotion.

The final difference that I noticed between the two poems was the choice of words the poets use. In "Incident" we can see that the speaker has a positive outlook on being an African-American. Although he used the word "nigger" to make his point clear, he also used the word "Baltimorean" rather than the word "white." His word choice shows that he knows there is racism in the world but that he is not going to inflict it upon others even though it has been inflicted on him.

In "Theme for English B," the speaker calls himself "colored" and says that his instructor is white. He is acknowledging their differences yet emphasizing that we are all American, which makes us the same:

So will my page be colored that I write?

Being me, it will not be white.

But it will be

a part of you, instructor.

You are white--

yet a part of me, as I am a part of you.

That's American. (27-33)

He suggests that we not forget our races but learn to accept and appreciate our differences.

While both poems express a similar theme, they deliver their messages in different ways. Both "Theme for English B" and "Incident" emphasize the importance of respecting people of all races, not just blacks and whites. While the poems are different, they have the same purpose--to stop senseless hate.

Works Cited

Cullen, Countee. "Incident." Exploring Poetry. Ed. Frank Madden. New York: Longman, 2002. 12.

Hughes, Langston. "Theme for English B." Exploring Poetry. Ed. Frank Madden. New York: Longman, 2002. 86.

CRITICAL THINKING: INDUCTION AND SUBSTANTIATION

Have you ever watched a toddler discover the world? The child crawls through the grass, stops to examine it blade by blade, picks it up, feels it, shakes it, tastes it. The child explores the surroundings and tests them piece by piece, and after several tries, probably comes to a conclusion: Grass is good for crawling but not so great for eating. When someone offers you a type of food you've never eaten before, how do you respond? How do you discover if you like it or not? Well, you probably ask for a taste. If you like the taste, you might ask for more. If you don't like the taste, you may or may not try more. This kind of examining, testing, making tentative observations, retesting, and concluding is a fairly common process in our lives. It is called **inductive reasoning**.

When you think or write inductively, you move from specific observations to conclusions. If you try a new food and like it, the next time it's offered you can respond with more certainty. You've tested it and can come to a tentative conclusion. Each subsequent tasting gives you more information and solidifies your conclusion: I like sushi; it tastes good.

Once you arrive at your conclusion, you are ready to make a generalization: Sushi tastes good. The process of supporting this generalization is called **substantiation**. When we substantiate, we support our conclusion with specific observations. This brings the process full circle. We discover how much we like sushi through specific tastings; we explain why sushi is good with support from those tastings: This sushi sits lightly on my tongue; it's soft and moist with a full seafood flavor and pleasant smell. We arrive at our conclusion inductively; we support, defend, and explain it through substantiation.

Developing Standards

As we examine our reasons for liking something, we also identify and develop standards. We know how good this food can be; we now have certain expectations. (Standards for sushi: 1. Soft. 2. Moist. 3. Full seafood flavor. 4. Pleasant smell.) When something meets our expectations, we can identify why. When it doesn't, we can say where and perhaps why it falls short.

THINKING CRITICALLY ABOUT POETRY

In many ways, thinking and writing about poetry follow a similar induction and substantiation pattern as that described above. As we initially read, respond, discuss, and write about our experience with a poem, we build on our specific observations of the poem and arrive at our conclusions inductively. With those conclusions in hand, we substantiate them with reference to our specific observations of the text. Writing an effective, convincing essay requires that we have enough evidence to support our conclusions and that we have clearly explained the connection between the two. Finding the evidence and making the connections require a close rereading of the text.

Facts and Opinions

All of us have probably been criticized at some time for not being objective or allowing our personal feelings to influence our judgment. It's not possible, of course, to be entirely objective—to separate the facts from who we are and how we see them. Most of our feelings and prejudgments come from our personalities, backgrounds, and experiences, and they form values we have developed unconsciously over time. In the course of our daily lives, we're not usually required to justify our feelings or our opinions. But writing an effective critical essay requires a rationale for our judgments—reasons derived not only from our feelings and values but from ingredients in the poem that prompt those judgments. Although there is no guarantee that everyone will agree with our conclusions, we can make sure that our evidence is recognized and respected as valid.

▶ GETTING STARTED—YOUR FIRST RESPONSE

1. Read one of your responses to a poem.
2. Which parts are fact, which opinion? How can you tell the difference?
3. To what extent can you support your opinions with facts?
4. To what extent can you explain how the facts support your opinions?

▶ SUPPORTING CONNECTIONS—"EX-BASKETBALL PLAYER"

Remember, "telling" your views alone will not convince readers. Telling what the literature means or declaring its effectiveness is not convincing unless you support those views by *showing* what led to your conclusion. Identifying details, giving examples, making comparisons, and quoting from the text of the work are means to this end.

JOHN UPDIKE (b. 1932)

(See biography on p. 264.)

EX-BASKETBALL PLAYER   [1958]

Pearl Avenue runs past the high-school lot,
Bends with the trolley tracks, and stops, cut off
Before it has a chance to go two blocks,
At Colonel McComsky Plaza. Berth's Garage
Is on the corner facing west, and there,   5
Most days, you'll find Flick Webb, who helps Berth out.

Flick stands tall among the idiot pumps—
Five on a side, the old bubble-head style,
Their rubber elbows hanging loose and low.
One's nostrils are two S's, and his eyes
An E and O.° And one is squat, without   10
A head at all—more of a football type.

Once Flick played for the high-school team, the Wizards.
He was good: in fact, the best. In '46
He bucketed three hundred ninety points,   15
A county record still. The ball loved Flick.
I saw him rack up thirty-eight or forty
In one home game. His hands were like wild birds.

---

[11]**ESSO** brand of gasoline (now called Exxon Mobil)

He never learned a trade, he just sells gas,
Checks oil, and changes flats. Once in a while,   20
As a gag, he dribbles an inner tube,
But most of us remember anyway.
His hands are fine and nervous on the lug wrench.
It makes no difference to the lug wrench, though.

Off work, he hangs around Mae's luncheonette.   25
Grease-gray and kind of coiled, he plays pinball,
Smokes those thin cigars, nurses lemon phosphates.
Flick seldom says a word to Mae, just nods
Beyond her face toward bright applauding tiers
Of Necco Wafers, Nibs, and Juju Beads.   30

➤ QUESTIONS FOR READING AND WRITING

Induction
1. Go back and read "Ex-Basketball Player" again.
2. As you read, write down as many details about Flick Webb as you can.
3. Review what you wrote down as you finished the poem, any questions you jotted down, and your list of details.
4. What conclusion does this information lead you to draw about Flick Webb?

Substantiation
1. Write down your conclusion.
2. Support your conclusion through reference to your details.
3. Are all of these details facts? Would everyone agree that they are facts?
4. Explain how these details support your conclusion.
5. Reread what you've written and answer the following questions:
   a. Do you have enough details to support your conclusion?
   b. Do *all* the details about Flick Webb in the poem support your conclusion?
   c. If not, how can you account for these details?
   d. When you consider *all* the details—all the evidence—does your conclusion still hold up? If not, revise your conclusion to match the evidence.

Conclusion
1. Sometimes what seems self-evident to us is not so evident to our readers. Write a statement that explains *how* the details in the poem support your conclusion about Flick Webb.

INTERPRETATION: WHAT DOES IT MEAN?

The idea of coming up with an interpretation may seem a bit overwhelming, but in our everyday lives we hear and respond to this request regularly. "What do you make of that?" "What was that all about?" and "What's your read on that?"

are among the many ways we might be asked for an interpretation. At the core of all these questions is a basic request for an explanation of "meaning." When we construct and articulate that meaning we are giving our interpretation.

What goes into our explanation of meaning, of course, has a lot to do with who we are. Our interpretations are influenced by many personal factors, but what makes an interpretation convincing or credible is our ability to explain *why*—a why not based on unsupported personal opinion but on support with evidence.

An interpretation may involve almost any aspect of the poem, from the meaning of a single word, image, character, or place to a statement of its overall meaning. It may even involve more than one work, so don't feel that you must limit yourself to choosing from the possibilities discussed here.

A Defensible Interpretation, Not *the* Right Answer

Poems are not problems to be solved. They don't have one correct answer or interpretation. Remember, what makes an interpretation convincing or defensible is the quality of its support. Your belief about what a poem means may change as you move back and forth through the stages of your reading experience. The first time you read a poem you may feel one way, but writing down your reflections, rereading the text, and discussing it with others may lead to a different, better-informed understanding and interpretation.

DEVELOPING AN INTERPRETATION

As you consider the statements and questions that follow, think about the poems you've read and how the language, the speaker's voice and perspective, and the larger context in those pieces influenced your response. Our brief discussion of these elements below is a carryover from a more comprehensive explanation of these terms in Chapter 3. *If you have unanswered questions about these elements, you may find it helpful to refer to that discussion beginning on page 60.*

Language and Form

The diction of the narrator or characters, concrete images, similes, metaphors, and symbols may all contribute in crucial ways to the meaning of poetry.

Think about the impact of the powerful, concrete imagery in Robert Hayden's "Those Winter Sundays" (p. 13) or Marge Piercy's "Barbie Doll" (p. 14) and the effect it has on your reading. Try to imagine less powerful images, vague descriptions, unnatural diction, and how your response to these works might differ.

The sounds and structures of rhyme, rhythm, and verse may also play a vital role in conveying a poem's meaning. Consider the rhymes, rhythms, and verse form in Countee Cullen's "Incident" (p. 12) or Dudley Randall's "Ballad of Birmingham" (p. 17)—and in other poems you've read—and how they influence your response.

The Speaker

The perspective from which the poet addresses us can strongly influence our interpretation. As mentioned in Chapter 3, the speaker in the poem is not necessarily the poet. The speaker's *voice* gives us a personality behind the words, and this speaker's perspective controls what we experience in the poem.

Consider the impact of the speaker in Robert Browning's "Porphyria's Lover" (p. 141), Stephen Crane's "War Is Kind" (p. 61), or Stevie Smith's "Not Waving But Drowning" (p. 10) and the way the speaker or speakers influence your response to the poem. Recall other poems you've read and how the speaker's voice or perspective affect your response to the poem's meaning. Imagine how a shift to a different voice or perspective might change your interpretation.

The Whole: Theme

Theme is the central idea expressed by a poem. Identifying and articulating this idea is not always an easy task. It's true that the whole poem's theme or meaning is greater than the sum of its parts, but the support required for your justification of it still calls for an analysis of the poem's elements—the language, the speaker, and the outcome—and their relationship to the whole.

What conclusion about the poem can you draw from its elements? Try to expand your conclusion about the poem into a generalization or idea that addresses the human condition. What is the poem saying about being human? What is its theme?

Beliefs or Actions Expressed by the Speaker or Characters

It is natural for us to respond to the beliefs and actions of the speaker or characters in a poem through the lenses of our own values, so it's not surprising that this is one of the more popular topics for interpretation. What's your interpretation of the beliefs or actions of the speaker in Peter Meinke's "Advice to My Son" (p. 7) or in Philip Larkin's "This Be the Verse" (p. 198) or in Michael Lassell's "How to Watch Your Brother Die" (p. 200)? Think about the beliefs or actions of other speakers or characters in your reading. What are they? How do you feel about them? How are these beliefs exemplified by what the speaker or characters say or do? How would you interpret them?

The Work in Context

To interpret a work in its context successfully, you must be able to identify the contextual framework that surrounds it and articulate the influence that context has on the work or an element of the work. If you're not very knowledgeable about this background, it may be necessary to do additional reading and research before you begin to write your essay.

What are the cultural imperatives that influence the girl in Marge Piercy's "Barbie Doll," or the historical, cultural, and biographical influences on Robert Hayden's "Those Winter Sundays"?

Think of other poems you've read, and the historical, cultural, biographical, or other contextual factors that influenced them. How do these factors affect or enrich your reading and interpretation of those works?

✔ CHECKLIST • *Developing an Interpretation*

Language and Form

❑ In what ways are diction, imagery, figurative language, or symbolism important to the work and your understanding of it?

❑ What role do rhyme, rhythm, or verse form play in the work?

The Speaker: Voice and Perspective

❑ In what ways do the voice and perspective of the speaker affect what you know in the poem?

❑ How does the speaker influence your understanding of the work's meaning?

❑ How would you interpret the impact of the speaker on the work?

Theme

❑ Describe the elements (language, narration, setting, conflict/plot, characters) of the work.

❑ What conclusion can you draw from these elements?

❑ What comment about the human condition—what generalization about life—does this conclusion lead to?

❑ What is the central idea expressed by the poem? What do you think the poem means?

Interpreting the Beliefs or Actions of the Speaker or Characters

❑ What beliefs are expressed by the speaker or characters in the poem and how does what they say or do exemplify these beliefs or actions?

❑ How would you interpret the effect of these beliefs on the work?

Interpreting a Poem in Context

❑ How is the poem influenced by historical, cultural, biographical, or other contextual factors?

❑ How would you interpret the poem in the light of these contextual factors?

Interpretation or Evaluation?

Like many other classifications in literature, *interpretation* and *evaluation* are not separate and distinct. In our reading, both often occur at the same time. When we write about our reading, however, we can make choices about which to emphasize. Do we want to interpret what the poem or an aspect of it means or its worth? While each is a different emphasis, it may be difficult to separate them, and many critical essays are a combination of both.

EVALUATION: HOW WELL DOES IT WORK?

Throughout this book you have been encouraged to identify and write about what you value. Those values or standards directly influence your response to poetry. Writing an effective evaluative essay requires that you make these standards explicit and account for the ways in which they have led to your evaluation of a work. You become a credible critic by evaluating in the light of these clearly defined standards.

Developing Standards

Each of us has clearly defined standards about some things and not about others. Every day we are bombarded with advertisements that make great claims without support. They assume our lack of standards. They tell us with glitz rather than showing us with facts. Do we always buy products because we know a lot about them? Do we buy cars, stereos, or computers because we know they are quality products or because we like the ads and the attractive people in them? What are our standards for judging?

You've been evaluating poetry ever since you first started reading it. You like it or don't like it, believe it's good or bad. How specific you are about "why" may depend on your experience as a reader. Those of us who read often have probably given some thought to why we like to read some things more than others. Experienced readers are likely to respond to "why" by pointing to particular qualities that are present or absent. Those of us who don't read very much might simply say, "I couldn't get into it" or "It was boring" and leave it at that. Our standards, the principles by which we evaluate poetry, tend to be developed through experience and over time.

► *QUESTIONS FOR THINKING AND WRITING*

Write down your responses to the following questions. You may even find it interesting to share them with other members of the class in pairs or small groups.

1. Choose a topic you know a lot about (music, dance, sports, cars, computers, etc.). How did you learn about it? By yourself? Did someone show you or teach you? Why do you think you know a lot about it?
2. What are your standards or criteria for evaluating the topic you chose in Question 1? See if you can make a list and explain the importance of each standard.
3. Think back to a large purchase you made recently (clothes, computer, stereo, etc.). What were your standards or criteria for evaluation? Make a list and explain the importance of each of these standards.

4. Do you feel as if you know a lot about poetry? How would you feel if someone asked you to evaluate a poem? Explain.
5. What are your standards for evaluating poetry? See if you can make a list of standards and explain the importance of each one. If you can't, what difficulties did you encounter?

Developing Standards for Evaluating Poetry

Our task in this chapter is not only to help you develop new standards but to identify and build on those you already have. You've been developing and applying standards for evaluating poetry throughout your life. They're as familiar to you as your everyday experiences, so familiar you don't usually stop to analyze or spell them out.

We live in the world that poetry reveals. We make judgments about the nature of that world—people's biases, our surroundings, difficult circumstances, and the authenticity of people we meet. We feel pain, joy, pleasure, sorrow, loss—a wide range of human emotion. We know what these moments feel like. In this way we have already experienced and developed standards about the authenticity of what life reveals. What may not be so familiar, however, is a systematic way of applying these standards to poetry.

Your Own Standards: Expectations and Intentions

When we choose entertainment, we usually know what to expect. When we see a fantasy movie like *Alien* or *Star Wars,* we have very different expectations than when we see a realistic film. Listening to a rock song brings different expectations than listening to an opera. We have different expectations for the light, sentimental verse in a greeting card than for a poem like Dudley Randall's "The Ballad of Birmingham."

The standards we have for evaluating poetry are directly affected by our expectations. Is the primary purpose of this poem to bring a smile to our faces? To make a social comment? To reveal something essential about the human condition? All of these? Some of these? It would be unfair to apply the same standards to light, sentimental verse that we would to a serious poem about a tragic event like "Ballad of Birmingham." On the other hand, applying our "smile" standards to a poem that intends to give insight into the human condition seems equally unfair.

Standards for Evaluating Poetry

Of course, we may not always be aware of the type and intentions of the poetry we read until after we begin reading. Many of the pieces in this book may put you in that position. Almost all of these pieces, however, have been chosen because they seek to reveal something important about the human experience.

The expectations and standards discussed below are measured against this intention.

The standards for language, the speaker, theme, or context discussed here are derived from our description of these elements in earlier chapters. The questions and brief explanations that follow are a guide to the kinds of qualities we might look for when evaluating these elements.

Language and Form   When language is effective it prompts our imaginations and provides us with clear images, rhythm, and insight. Form complements content and effectively conveys meaning to us.

The Speaker   When the voice and the perspective is effective, we experience the moment(s) of the poem from a viewpoint that helps us feel the impact the overall meaning of the poem.

Theme   An effective theme gives us an insight into human nature. When poetry preaches or teaches a lesson, it doesn't usually account for the complexities of the real world. An effective theme transcends the time and place of its writing. It has universal qualities that make it applicable to human nature in any time or place.

Beliefs or Actions of the Speaker or Characters   Before you evaluate the beliefs or actions of the speaker or characters, be clear about what they are and be clear about your own standards for judging them. Only when you have clarified both will you be able to evaluate the beliefs in the poem measured against your own criteria, take a position, and build an argument for or against those beliefs.

The Poem in Context   Before you can evaluate the influence of historical, cultural, biographical, or other contextual factors on the poem, you must have knowledge of these areas. If you don't have knowledge of these contexts, you must do research and additional reading to give yourself standards and criteria with which to evaluate.

✔ CHECKLIST • *Developing an Evaluation*

Language and Form

- ❑ How well does the language prompt your imagination and engage your emotions?
- ❑ How effective are the language and form in conveying the poem's meaning?

The Speaker

- ❑ How effective is the speaker's voice and perspective in helping you understand the poem's meaning?

Theme

- ❑ Does the theme *reveal* or *preach*? Is it an insight about life or a lesson?

(continued)

❏ How universal is the theme? Is it limited by time, place, and circumstances?

Beliefs and Actions of the Speaker or Characters

❏ What are the beliefs and actions of the speaker or characters in the poem?

❏ What are your standards for evaluating these beliefs or actions?

❏ Why do you agree or disagree with these beliefs or actions?

The Work in Context

❏ How much do you know about the contextual background of the poem? What do you need to know? How will you find out more?

❏ What are your standards for evaluating this context?

❏ How well does the poem fulfill these standards?

GENERATING IDEAS FOR A CRITICAL ESSAY

The same processes that are so useful in generating ideas for a response essay are just as valuable for giving you ideas and narrowing your topic for a critical essay. Reading poetry encourages a variety of responses—and perhaps raises more questions than answers. It is a good idea to generate and explore as many of your questions and ideas as possible before you decide on a topic. Below is a quick review of strategies to get started. For a detailed explanation of these techniques, with examples, see Chapter 2, pages xxx–xxx.

- *Using directed freewriting* can generate ideas. The best time to do this exercise is immediately after you finish reading, while your thoughts and impressions are still fresh. The intention of this exercise is to release what you know without blocking it with pauses for reflection, punctuation, or editing.
- *Asking questions about a general topic* is likely to provide you with new information. Responding with detailed answers to these questions may provide you with ideas for a narrowed thesis and specific support for that thesis.
- By *choosing a few key words or phrases* that apply to your topic and then *listing* as many related details under each as you can, you should be able to generate many concrete details and much specific support for your ideas.
- *Clustering your ideas* or drawing a semantic map may help you discover and understand relationships, and generate and extend ideas better, by seeing them spatially rather than linearly.

ARGUMENTATION: WRITING A CRITICAL ESSAY

There are many different ways to plan and structure a critical essay. The suggestions that follow represent one approach. The purpose of this discussion is not to move you step-by-step through a rigid sequence. Constructing an argument is a continuous process of moving forward and returning and moving forward again. The strongest thesis, the most convincing evidence, the most effective structure may occur to you early or late. Let your ideas flow freely throughout the process. Some of your best ideas may come to you when you think you're almost finished.

The Shape of an Argument

The subject

The proposition about the subject (the thesis)

The evidence that supports the proposition about the subject

The explanation that connects the evidence to the proposition about the subject

Planning Your Argument

Determine the Argument's Feasibility   Can you write a critical essay about this? No matter how compelling your proposition, you cannot write an essay about it unless you have enough to say and can find enough evidence to support your argument. If the point you want to make is obvious, abstract, or very general, it may be impossible to come up with a solid argument and develop it into a convincing essay in a reasonable amount of time.

Consider Your Own Motivation   How much do you care about the subject? Will it sustain your enthusiasm long enough for you to complete the essay? Can you identify strongly with the situation in the poem? Do you approve or disapprove of the speaker or character's action? Do you believe the poem has helped you understand yourself or inspired you to act in a particular way? Have you learned something about your own life through your experience of the poem? Finally, do you feel strongly about your ability to convince an audience of your argument?

You will work with more enthusiasm and write with a stronger voice when you care about the subject.

Clarify Your Proposition: Write a Thesis Statement   Do you have a clear understanding of the proposition you are trying to prove? If you don't, you won't be able to express it in a form your readers will understand. Try to put your proposition into the form of a complete sentence that connects it to the subject. This thesis statement will sit at the core of your argument. Everything in your argument must relate back to and support this thesis statement. If you've put it in a form that you and your readers clearly understand, you will know if the evidence you've gathered adequately supports it.

If your thesis is an interpretation, define what you mean by the terms of the proposition or thesis. In her essay earlier in this chapter, Jennifer has identified the subject of both "Incident"and "Theme for English B" as racism. Her proposition about this subject, her thesis statement (how the speaker in each poem addresses racism differently), will not be clear unless she spells out what she means by "the speaker's voice" in poetry.

Be careful to distinguish between the *subject* of your essay and your *proposition* about the subject—your thesis statement. Jennifer's subject is the common theme of racism in these poems. What she believes is different about the way each poem addresses racism—her thesis statement—is that the speaker's voice in each case makes our experience of each poem distinct.

As you consider the evidence you have and gather new evidence, you may discover that your thesis statement must be adjusted to accommodate this new information. Be flexible. Match the statement to the evidence, and the evidence to the statement. Until you submit your final draft, it's never too late to make adjustments to strengthen your thesis.

Know Your Readers   What can you assume about your readers? If you're writing this essay to be read by those in your class, you may already have some idea what your classmates and instructor think about your opinion. If so, does your thesis statement agree with the majority of responses you've heard? If not, it's important to "speak to" these contrary views when you present your own view.

No matter how convincing your evidence may be, if you don't address their contrary position, your readers will always wonder, "Yes, but what about? . . ." This doesn't mean you must change their minds, but it does mean that you must account for all the evidence, especially the evidence that may seem (to some) to go against your thesis statement. If you cannot account for it, it may be time to reexamine your original proposition.

Remember, many interpretations of a work may be acceptable. The strength of your thesis is in its support, not the thesis itself. So don't offend your readers by being inflexible and suggesting that anyone holding a different view is ignorant. Feeling strongly about what you want to prove gives you a stronger voice, but insulting or overpowering your readers is not likely to be persuasive.

Supporting Your Argument

Arrange Your Support Effectively   Substantiation and induction (see "Critical Thinking," p. 3) are the two most common approaches to argumentation. In each case, the order in which the proposition, or thesis statement, and the supporting evidence are presented is different.

You substantiate your argument when you place the thesis statement or proposition at the beginning of the essay and lay out evidence in the rest of the essay to support it. You begin with a generalization and support it with specific examples as evidence. You immediately make it clear to your readers what you intend to prove. Your thesis remains in their minds as they encounter each piece of subsequent evidence. In fact, if what you propose at the outset is interesting enough, your thesis statement may act as a "hook" for your readers and pull them into the essay.

Substantiation

$$(a = b + b + b + b + b + b)$$

(Your thesis equals the sum of the evidence.)

This approach may not work well if you are trying to convince skeptical readers, that is, readers who have already made up their minds and hold a contrary view. Encountering a proposition they disagree with at the beginning may interfere with their response through the rest of the essay. Once they know what you want to prove, they may not give you an open-minded reading. They may be predisposed to disagree with you no matter how compelling your evidence.

Inductive argumentation moves from specific examples to a generalization or conclusion. It mimics the process you probably went through when you came up with your proposition to begin with. As the specifics of the work built up in your mind, they moved you toward a conclusion and a proposition. A more effective strategy to convince a skeptical reader may be to withhold your proposition until the end. By first providing support, before readers know what your position is, they may withhold judgment and be more likely to accept your thesis when it comes as the natural conclusion of strong evidence.

Induction

$$(b + b + b + b + b + b = a)$$

(The sum of the evidence equals your thesis.)

And, of course, there are variations of these strategies. For example, if you're stating your thesis up front, you may want to provide background information to "educate" the reader before you present your thesis, and then follow with supporting evidence. If you are using an inductive approach, you may want to build your support to a natural conclusion, and then discuss why this conclusion makes sense. In any case, you should consider your audience and your intentions before you decide which strategy will work best.

Support Your Thesis with Facts from the Text   Earlier, we discussed the difference between facts and opinions (pp. 93–94). Facts are verifiable. You can cite them in the text. They should be the core of the evidence that supports your argument.

For example, it is a fact that in John Updike's poem "Ex-Basketball Player," Flick Webb was a high school basketball star. You can verify this fact by citing the text of the poem:

> Once Flick played for the high-school team, the Wizards.
> He was good: in fact, the best. In '46
> He bucketed three hundred ninety points,
> A county record still. The ball loved Flick.

And you can verify the fact of his current employment by citing the text:

> He never learned a trade, he just sells gas,
> Checks oil, and changes flats.

But if (based on these few facts) you say that Flick is an "unhappy loser," you are expressing an opinion, not a fact. You may hold this opinion for any number of personal reasons, prompted by a few facts in the poem. But if you want to build an argument to support this opinion, you will need to connect most or all the facts in the poem in a convincing way, and logically demonstrate how they lead to this conclusion. A good critical essay requires reasons for your judgments, factual support derived not only from your feelings and values but from ingredients in the text that logically combine to prompt them. There is no guarantee, of course, that everyone will agree with your conclusions, but you should make sure that your evidence is recognized and respected as valid.

Account for All the Evidence   A strong thesis is constructed from all the evidence, not just the parts that agree with your conclusion. A discerning reader sees contrary evidence whether you point it out or not. For example, it is a fact that the speaker in Robert Frost's "The Road Not Taken" (p. 67) has taken the road less traveled, as suggested in the first and third lines of this stanza:

> Then took the other, as just as fair,
> And having perhaps the better claim,
> Because it was grassy and wanted wear;
> Though as for that the passing there
> Had worn them really about the same,

To suggest that one road was very different from the other, though, is to ignore the last two lines.

It is a fact that he says his choice will make a difference in his life:

> I shall be telling this with a sigh
> Somewhere ages and ages hence:
> Two roads diverged in a wood, and I—
> I took the one less traveled by,
> And that has made all the difference.

But suggesting that the speaker knows that this choice was the best one and has made him happiest is to ignore other lines in this last stanza that seem to indicate uncertainty. Do we know that "all the difference" means a positive difference? How would you support that from the text?

None of this is to say that the personal meaning you derive from the poem is not the most important meaning for you—a meaning that is often based on many factors beyond the text. But for the purposes of a critical essay, you must rely heavily on the text and its factual support to make a convincing case for your reader.

Explain the Connections   Sometimes what seems self-evident to us is not so evident to our readers.

In addition to highlighting the facts to support your argument, explain the connections. Explicitly show your readers *how* the chosen evidence supports your conclusion. For example, if your proposition is that "The two poems convey their messages very differently," and your evidence is that the speaker in "Theme for English B" comments from the point of view of a young adult, while in "Incident" the narrator's perspective is that of an adult looking back into his childhood, it is still necessary to explain the connection between the evidence (the different perspectives of the speakers) and the proposition (that these different perspectives change our response).

Consider the explanation: "The negative impressions made on us in the openness and vulnerability of youth can be more devastating than when we are older and know how to protect ourselves emotionally from the bigotry around us." This explanation shows the connection between the proposition and the quoted evidence and makes your logic clear to the reader.

Opening, Closing, and Revising Your Argument

Write Your Introduction After You Know Your Argument   It may seem strange to wait until you're almost finished with the first draft of an essay before writing its introduction. However, introducing an essay is a bit like introducing a person. In both cases, you can make a more effective introduction when you know who or what you are introducing. This does not mean you have to mention everything you know. It means that you know your subject well enough to say the essential things.

Make your introduction interesting. You want the reader to continue reading beyond the first paragraph. Remember what seemed so interesting to you about the work, and try to pass that interest on to the reader. Make sure that what you say flows smoothly and maintains the same voice used in the rest of the essay. If you're developing your argument through substantiation, this is the place to state your thesis as clearly as possible.

Close Your Argument Reasonably   Although there is no need to summarize your essay in the conclusion, it may be helpful to remind the reader of the logic of your argument and explain the basic connections between your support and your thesis. Avoid being too ambitious. Only make claims or take credit for connections you've actually established.

If you've developed your argument inductively, this is the place where you want to state your thesis. Remember not to overstate your case. If you've proved your point, the evidence will carry it.

Revise with a Fresh View   If you really want to "re-vision" your essay, to see it again from a fresh perspective, it's best to let some time pass. Try to place yourself in the position of the reader who is reading your essay for the first time.

As with any other essay, it can be very useful to do an after-draft outline. Go back and identify the point of each paragraph. List those points. This should give you a pretty good overview of your essay. How well is your draft organized?

Does the sequence make sense? Are there gaps that need to be filled? Is there enough support?

Within the body of the essay have you explained the connections between your support and your thesis? Have you expressed those connections as clearly as possible? Have you maintained a consistent voice throughout the essay?

Check Against Your Intentions and Organization

- State your thesis clearly. Support and clarify your thesis with enough details and examples from the text of the poem. *Show* what you have stated.
- Give the essay a title based on your thesis. If you're having trouble thinking of a title, it may be an indication that the thesis itself is not clear.
- Make sure that your essay is fully developed. Account for all aspects of your thesis statement. All your paragraphs must relate to that central thesis, and the organization of those paragraphs within the essay should be clear.
- Each paragraph should be fully developed too; each of the sentences within your paragraphs should relate to the central idea of that paragraph.
- All your statements should add something to the essay. Are there redundancies, digressions, or meaningless phrases that could be cut?

Proofread Carefully

- Proofreading is a crucial final step in the process of producing an essay. In addition to making any changes that did not occur to you earlier and fine-tuning your writing, check your essay for correct grammar, spelling, and punctuation and typos.
- Make sure all your sentences are complete and punctuated appropriately.
- Check to see that all of your words are spelled correctly. Check for easily confused words (then/than, your/you're, its/it's, etc.), which computerized spell checkers do not pick up.
- Check on the meaning of any words you are not sure of. Make sure the titles of works are underlined or in quotation marks, as appropriate.
- If there are types of errors you personally have a tendency to make, look carefully for them.
- Finally, make sure you've followed the *MLA Handbook for Writers of Research Papers* or another documentation format recommended by your instructor. Have you cited and documented your sources correctly? Do you have a "Work(s) Cited" list at the end of your essay?

✔ **C H E C K L I S T** • *Writing a Critical Essay*

Planning Your Argument

Determine Its Feasibility

❏ Can you write a critical essay about this?

❏ Do you have enough to say, and can you find enough evidence to support your case?

(continued)

Consider Your Motivation

❑ Will this topic sustain your interest long enough for you to do a good job?

Clarify Your Thesis

❑ Do you have a clear understanding of the thesis you want to argue? Can you articulate it in a thesis statement?

Know Your Readers

❑ What assumptions can you make about your readers? Are they likely to agree or disagree with your thesis?

Supporting Your Argument

Arrange Your Support Effectively

❑ Is the support for your thesis arranged in the most effective way?

❑ Is it more effective to develop your argument by stating your thesis first and then supporting it with evidence, or by allowing the evidence to build up to your thesis?

Support Your Thesis with Facts from the Text

❑ Is your support based on facts or opinions?

❑ Have you supported your opinions with facts and quotations from the text?

Account for All the Evidence

❑ Have you accounted for *all* the evidence in the text?

❑ Have you accounted for evidence that may not support your thesis?

Explain the Connections

❑ Have you explained *how* the evidence you've chosen supports your thesis?

Opening, Closing, and Revising

Write or Rewrite Your Introduction After Your First Draft

❑ Is your introduction clear, informative, and interesting?

❑ If appropriate, does it map out the journey for the reader?

Close Your Argument Reasonably

❑ Have you explained the connections between the thesis and your support?

❑ Have you claimed anything for which you haven't delivered evidence?

Revise with a Fresh View

❑ Have you reread and reviewed your essay?

❑ How well is your draft organized? Does the sequence make sense?

❑ Are there gaps that need to be filled? Is there enough support?

(continued)

❑ Have you explained the connections between your support and your thesis?

❑ Have you expressed those connections as clearly as possible?

❑ Have you maintained a consistent "voice" throughout the essay?

Review Your Intentions and Organization

❑ Is the central thesis of the essay clearly stated? Does the title account for your thesis?

❑ Is the essay fully developed? Have you accounted for all aspects of your thesis statement?

❑ Are there enough details to support or clarify your thesis? Have you *shown* what you've told?

❑ Are there enough quotations from the work to support your thesis?

❑ Do all the paragraphs relate to your thesis? Is the essay fully developed?

❑ Is the organization of the paragraphs within the essay clear?

❑ Are the paragraphs fully developed?

❑ Do each of the sentences within the paragraphs relate to the paragraph's central ideas?

❑ Is the language clear?

❑ Are there redundancies, digressions, or meaningless phrases that could be cut?

Proofread Carefully

❑ Are all your sentences complete sentences?

❑ Are all your sentences punctuated appropriately?

❑ Have you checked for easily confused words (then/than, your/you're, its/it's, etc)?

❑ Are you sure of the meaning of all the words you've used?

❑ Are the titles of works underlined or in quotation marks, as appropriate?

❑ Are there particular errors that you have a tendency to make? Have you looked for those in this essay?

❑ Is the essay written in the format required by your instructor? Have you documented your references to the text and included a list of works cited?

A Student's Critical Essay: Explication and Evaluation

In the essay that follows, Mark Strumke explicates and evaluates Helen Chassin's poem "The Word *Plum*" (Chapter 3, p. 62). This essay is a good example of the way that interpretation and evaluation can naturally intersect in a critical essay. In the process of analyzing the language Chassin uses in describing the eating of a plum, Mark also describes how well her word choice works, and concludes that this is an excellent poem. He not only makes a convincing argument for what it means to him but has established criteria and demonstrated, based on that criteria, why this is a good poem.

Mark Strumke
English 102
Professor Madden
May 6, 200X

A Plum of a Poem

Poems can take many forms and cover any subject. Some poems try to convey great meaning, some are about love, still others tackle the everyday events of life. A poet has many tools to choose from to engage the reader. Regardless of the style or subject the most important requirement is that the poet choose his or her words carefully.

"The Word <u>Plum</u>" is a very short poem, but one in which the poet carefully chose each word for maximum effect. This poem has much meaning in its few words, and I am reminded of the description of poetry that says poems have "compressed meaning." This poem is like a compressed accordion that can only be stretched out to its full meaning with our interpretation and involvement. The speaker in this poem takes a mundane activity, eating a plum, and imbues it with fresh life. She focuses on the consumption of one fruit, but she could have just as easily been writing about all good tasting food.

Eating a plum is delicious, as anyone who has eaten one knows, but the speaker goes further. She opens the poem with a line noting that "the word <u>plum</u> is delicious"(1) in its own right. The images that she conjures up in the reader's mind about plums make that statement true. Eating is an essential factor of life, but it doesn't have to be a boring, mechanical activity. It can also be a pleasurable experience. The author remarks that eating a plum is the "luxury of self-love"(2–3). Eating a plum is a form of self-indulgence, enjoyment, and treating ourselves to pleasure. The purple plum is a good choice for this theme because purple is the color of royalty. And who knows indulgence better than royalty?

The next line appeals to our sense of hearing as well as touch. She writes, "and savoring murmur full in the mouth"(3–4). The plum, full in the mouth, prevents the speaker from being able to say anything. Unable to articulate any words, because the plum is lodged full in her mouth, she "murmurs" her pleasure instead. Getting the plum into our mouths is only half the job done, however. Once between our teeth, we still need to coax the juice out of it. The author chooses the words, "pierced, bitten, provoked into juice"(7–8), and we can feel the "taut skin" giving way a little bit before it's punctured by sharp teeth. This creates a vivid picture in our minds of the skin being depressed before finally giving way, its juice spraying onto the top of our mouths. We can feel the spray of the plum hitting us. She makes this act of biting into the plum sound almost violent when she writes of it as being "provoked into juice"(7–8), as if the plum were reluctant to give up its sweet nectar. It seems as though the plum is almost being attacked. It conjures up the image in my mind of a poisonous snake backed up into a corner by an attacker and jetting its venom in response. The plum's sweet juice, however, unlike the snake's venom, gives pleasure and life rather than pain and death. But the poet doesn't forget to appeal to our complex sense of taste, and describes the taste of the skin experienced after it is bitten into as "tart flesh."

The last three lines in the poem summarize the experience best. She writes, "question and reply, lip and tongue of pleasure"(9–11). The lips and teeth pose the question of how the plum tastes, and the taste buds on the tongue provide the answer. The question is soundless, unspoken, it is provided not with words but with questing teeth and lips.

If "a picture is worth a thousand words," then this poem is many thousands of words for all the vivid pictures that it creates in our minds. Each word is evocative and helps us experience the plum with all our senses. This poem is very economical with its words--nothing wasted, nothing superfluous. With the words that she does use, though, vivid images are painted in our minds. I can envision the poet laboring carefully over each word, hunched over like a fine watchmaker doing intricate work. Writing like this takes individual craftsmanship, not soulless mass production. It's our responsibility to sense lines, to inject our own meaning and to let our imaginations play with the words on the page. A good poet can engage a reader's imagination in just such a way, and Helen Chassin has accomplished this with this poem.

Work Cited

Chassin, Helen "The Word <u>Plum</u>." <u>Exploring</u> <u>Poetry</u>. Ed. Frank

    Madden. New York: Longman, 2002. 62.

PART III

An Anthology
of Poems

&

SHERMAN ALEXIE (b. 1966)

Sherman Alexie achieved a goal by having ten books of poetry and fiction published before he turned 30. In 2000, he added another two.

His very first book, The Business of Fancydancing *(Hanging Loose Press, 1992), was chosen as a New York Times Notable Book of the Year and reviewer James R. Kincaid wrote, "Mr. Alexie's is one of the major lyric voices of our time." Alexie's latest poetry collection is* One Stick Song *(Hanging Loose) and his latest fiction collection is* The Toughest Indian in the World *(Atlantic Monthly Press). A film,* Smoke Signals, *for which he wrote a script adapted from one of the short stories in his book* The Lone Ranger and Tonto Fistfight in Heaven, *won rave reviews and large audiences. He is presently involved with new film projects and a new novel. He has also written criticism and articles.*

Alexie's poems and stories have appeared very widely, and he has read from his work in virtually every state as well as in several European countries. Among many awards, he has won a Lila Wallace-Reader's Digest Writer's Award, an American Book Award, and a Creative Writing Fellowship from the National Endowment for the Arts.

An enrolled Spokane/Coeur d'Alene Indian, Alexie was born on the Spokane reservation in Wellpinit, Washington. He is very active in the American Indian community and frequently gives workshops. He now lives in Seattle with his wife and infant son.

ON THE AMTRAK FROM BOSTON TO NEW YORK CITY   [1993]

The white woman across the aisle from me says, "Look,
look at all the history, that house
on the hill there is over two hundred years old,"
as she points out the window past me

into what she has been taught. I have learned   5
little more about American history during my few days
back East than what I expected and far less
of what we should all know of the tribal stories

whose architecture is 15,000 years older
than the corners of the house that sits   10
museumed on the hill. "Walden Pond,"°
the woman on the train asks, "Did you see Walden Pond?"

---

[11]**Walden Pond** the place where Henry David Thoreau (1817–1862) lived and about which he wrote his most famous book, *Walden* (1854)

and I don't have a cruel enough heart to break
her own by telling her there are five Walden Ponds
on my little reservation out West   15
and at least a hundred more surrounding Spokane,

the city I pretend to call my home. "Listen,
"I could have told her. "I don't give a shit
about Walden. I know the Indians were living stories
around that pond before Walden's grandparents were born.   20

and before his grandparents' grandparents were born.
I'm tired of hearing about Don-fucking-Henley° saving it too,
because that's redundant. If Don Henley's brothers and sisters
and mothers and fathers hadn't come here in the first place

then nothing would need to be saved."
But I didn't say a word to the woman about Walden   25
Pond because she smiled so much and seemed delighted
that I thought to bring her an orange juice

back from the food car. I respect elders
of every color. All I really did was eat
my tasteless sandwich, drink my Diet Pepsi   30
and nod my head whenever the woman pointed out

another little piece of her country's history
while I, as all Indians have done
since this war began, made plans
for what I would do and say the next time   35

somebody from the enemy thought I was one of their own.

[22]**Don Henley** a rock singer who helped protect Walden from commercial development

► QUESTIONS FOR READING AND WRITING

1. What is the significance of the title? Do you think the Amtrak between Boston and New York is an appropriate setting? Why or why not?
2. In what way is the speaker's Native American heritage a factor in this poem? Why does he refer to the white woman as "the enemy"?

JULIA ALVAREZ (b. 1950)

Though Julia Alvarez was born in New York City, she spent her childhood in the Dominican Republic. When she was 10, she returned with her parents to New York City, where she attended public schools. Confused and lonely (she spoke only Spanish),

*she struggled until high school, where she
encountered an English teacher who encouraged her to write of her experiences as a
stranger to the United States and its language.
This experience was transforming, and she discovered her love of writing. She went on to
study at Middlebury College, where she currently teaches, and later earned a master of fine
arts degree from Syracuse University. She has
published two books of poetry,* Homecoming
(1984) and The Other Side/El Otro Lado
(1995), and four novels: How the Garcia Girls
Lost Their Accents *(1991),* In the Time of the
Butterflies *(1994),* !Yo! *(1996), and* In the
Name of Salome *(2000).*

DUSTING   [1984]

Each morning I wrote my name
on the dusty cabinet, then crossed
the dining table in script, scrawled
in capitals on the backs of chairs,
practicing signatures like scales   5
while Mother followed, squirting
linseed from a burping can
into a crumpled-up flannel.

She erased my fingerprints
from the bookshelf and rocker,   10
polished mirrors on the desk,
scribbled with my alphabets.
My name was swallowed in the towel
with which she jewelled the table tops.
The grain surfaced in the oak   15
and the pine grew luminous.
But I refused with every mark
to be like her, anonymous.

➤ QUESTIONS FOR READING AND WRITING

1. The speaker's attitude toward her mother seems to be revealed in the
   poem's final word. What effect did the speaker's final comment have on
   you? Were you expecting the poem to end this way?
2. In what sense is the mother "anonymous"? Why do you think the speaker
   refuses to be like her?

3. How else might this poem have ended? Generate a list of words that could have been chosen to describe the mother, and consider how each would change the overall effect of the poem.

MAYA ANGELOU (b. 1928)

Maya Angelou was born Marguerite Johnson in St. Louis, Missouri, and lived with her grandmother in Stamps, Arkansas. She studied music, dance, and drama, and also became a writer. She became very involved in the black civil rights movement, and from 1963 to 1966 she lived in Ghana. Angelou is known for her many volumes of autobiographical novels, the first of which is I Know Why the Caged Bird Sings *(1969). Her six works of poetry are* Just Give Me a Cool Drink of Water for I Die *(1971),* Oh Pray My Wings Are Gonna Fit Me Well *(1975),* And Still I Rise *(1978),* Shaker, Why Don't You Sing? *(1983),* Now Sheba Sings the Song *(1987), and* I Shall Not Be Moved *(1990). She read her poem "On the Pulse of Morning" at the inauguration ceremony for President Bill Clinton in 1993. In the same year, a collection of Angelou's essays,* Wouldn't Take Nothing for My Journey, *was published. She teaches at Wake Forest University.*

PHENOMENAL WOMAN   [1978]

Pretty women wonder where my secret lies.
I'm not cute or built to suit a fashion model's size,
But when I start to tell them,
They think I'm telling lies.
I say,   5
It's in the reach of my arms,
The span of my hips,
The stride of my step,
The curl of my lips.
I'm a woman   10
Phenomenally.
Phenomenal woman,
That's me.

I walk into a room
Just as cool as you please,   15
And to a man,
The fellows stand or
Fall down on their knees.

Then they swarm around me,
A hive of honey bees.
I say,   20
It's the fire in my eyes,
And the flash of my teeth,
The swing in my waist,
And the joy in my feet.
I'm a woman   25
Phenomenally.
Phenomenal woman,
That's me.

Men themselves have wondered   30
What they see in me.
They try so much
But they can't touch
My inner mystery.
When I try to show them   35
They say they still can't see.
I say,
It's in the arch of my back,
The sun of my smile,
The ride of my breasts,   40
The grace of my style.
I'm a woman
Phenomenally.
Phenomenal woman,
That's me.   45

Now you understand
Just why my head's not bowed.
I don't shout or jump about
Or have to talk real loud.
When you see me passing,   50
It ought to make you proud.
I say,
It's in the click of my heels,
The bend of my hair,
The palm of my hand,   55
The need for my care.
'Cause I'm a woman
Phenomenally.
Phenomenal woman,
That's me.   60

▶ QUESTIONS FOR READING AND WRITING

1. What is so "phenomenal" about the speaker? What lines in the poem indicate that?

2. Compare this poem with Marge Piercy's "Barbie Doll" on page 14. Do you think the "girlchild" might have become a phenomenal woman? Explain.

GLORIA ANZALDÚA (b. 1942)

Gloria Anzaldúa was born in southern Texas of Mexican, Native American, and Anglo ancestry. Her mixed background has served as the major influence on her writing. She has taught at the University of Texas at Austin, San Francisco State University, the University of California at Santa Cruz, and Vermont College. "To Live in the Borderlands Means You" is taken from her critically acclaimed book Borderlands / La Frontera: The New Mestiza (1997).

TO LIVE IN THE BORDERLANDS MEANS YOU [1987]

[To live in the Borderlands means you]
are neither *hispana india negra española*
ni gabacha,° eres mestiza, *mulata,* half-breed
caught in the crossfire between camps
while carrying all five races on your back   5
not knowing which side to turn to, run from;

To live in the Borderlands means knowing
    that the *india* in you, betrayed for 500 years,
    is no longer speaking to you,
    that *mexicanas* call you *rajetas,°*   10
    that denying the Anglo inside you
    is as bad as having denied the Indian or Black;

Cuando vives en la frontera
    people walk through you, the wind steals your voice,
    you're a *burra, buey,* scapegoat,   15
    forerunner of a new race,
    half and half—both woman and man, neither—
    a new gender;

---

³**gabacha** a white woman   ¹⁰**rejetas** "split"

To live in the Borderlands means to
    put *chile* in the borscht,   20
    eat whole wheat *tortillas,*
    speak Tex-Mex with a Brooklyn accent;
    be stopped by *la migra* at the border checkpoints;

Living in the Borderlands means you fight hard to
    resist the gold elixir beckoning from the bottle,   25
    the pull of the gun barrel,
    the rope crushing the hollow of your throat;

In the Borderlands
    you are the battleground
    where enemies are kin to each other;   30
    you are at home, a stranger,
    the border disputes have been settled
    the volley of shots have shattered the truce
    you are wounded, lost in action
    dead, fighting back;   35

To live in the Borderlands means
    the mill with the razor white teeth wants to shred off
    your olive-red skin, crush out the kernel, your heart
    pound you pinch you roll you out
    smelling like white bread but dead;   40

To survive the Borderlands
    you must live *sin fronteras*
    be a crossroads.

➤ QUESTIONS FOR READING AND WRITING

1. What are the "Borderlands"? Is this solely a geographical location? To what extent do you, your family, or friends live in the Borderlands?
2. In the last stanza, what does the speaker mean by "to survive the Borderlands / you must . . . / be a crossroads"?

MATTHEW ARNOLD (1822–1888)

Poet and critic Matthew Arnold was born in Laleham, a tiny village along the Thames in England. His father, Dr. Thomas Arnold, was a famous headmaster of Rugby, one of England's most prominent schools for boys. Arnold attended Oxford University, where he spent as much time roaming the countryside and writing poems as he did on his formal studies. After working for a time for a member of Parliament, Arnold secured a post as an inspector of schools in 1851, a position he held for most of his life. In addition, he served as a professor of poetry at Oxford for ten years, beginning in 1857. In his old age, Arnold embarked on two lecture tours of the United States (in 1883 and

1886). He died suddenly in 1888, shortly after returning from his second trip. A famous literary critic as well as a poet, Arnold strongly believed that the primary purpose of literature was a moral one—that it should "animate and ennoble" its readers. His first collection of poetry, The Strayed Reveler and Other Poems, *was published in 1849 and was followed by six others including* Poems, Second Series *(1855), in which "Dover Beach" first appeared. His works of literary criticism include two volumes of* Essays in Criticism *(1865 and 1888),* Literature and Dogma *(1873), and* The Study of Poetry *(1880), in which he argued that "most of what now passes for religion and philosophy will be replaced by poetry."*

DOVER BEACH

[1867]

The sea is calm tonight.
The tide is full, the moon lies fair
Upon the straits; on the French coast the light
Gleams and is gone; the cliffs of England stand,
Glimmering and vast, out in the tranquil bay.   5
Come to the window, sweet is the night-air!
Only, from the long line of spray
Where the sea meets the moon-blanched land,
Listen! you hear the grating roar
Of pebbles which the waves draw back, and fling,   10
At their return, up the high strand,
Begin, and cease, and then again begin,
With tremulous cadence slow, and bring
The eternal note of sadness in.

Sophocles long ago   15
Heard it on the Aegean, and it brought
Into his mind the turbid ebb and flow
Of human misery; we
Find also in the sound a thought,
Hearing it by this distant northern sea.   20

The Sea of Faith
Was once, too, at the full, and round earth's shore
Lay like the folds of a bright girdle furled.
But now I only hear
Its melancholy, long, withdrawing roar,   25
Retreating, to the breath

Of the night-wind, down the vast edges drear
And naked shingles of the world.

Ah, love, let us be true
To one another! for the world, which seems   30
To lie before us like a land of dreams,
So various, so beautiful, so new,
Hath really neither joy, nor love, nor light,
Nor certitude, nor peace, nor help for pain;
And we are here as on a darkling plain   35
Swept with confused alarms of struggle and flight,
Where ignorant armies clash by night.

▶ QUESTIONS FOR READING AND WRITING

1. Does this poem seem like a typical love poem to you? If so, how? If not, why not?
2. What is the speaker's attitude toward nature? Compare his attitude to that of the speaker in Stephen Crane's "A Man Said to the Universe" (p.150).
3. How do you think the speaker formed his impression of nature? To what extent is an answer suggested in the poem?
4. In the final image of the poem, the speaker says, "we are here as on a darkling plain / Swept with confused alarms of struggle and flight, / Where ignorant armies clash by night." What do you think he means?
5. According to the speaker, what is the importance of love in this world?

MARGARET ATWOOD (b. 1939)

Margaret Atwood was born in Ottawa, Canada, and took extensive trips during her childhood through the wilds of Canada with her father, an entomologist. In 1962, the same year she graduated from the University of Toronto, she published her first book of poetry, Double Persephone. *She has since published numerous works of fiction, poetry, and criticism including the novels* Surfacing *(1972),* Cat's Eye *(1988), and the futuristic* The Handmaid's Tale *(1985), which was made into a film. Her most recent novel is* Alias Grace *(1996). A fierce proponent of Canadian literature as well as an ardent feminist, Atwood has been instrumental in forging a Canadian cultural identity separate from that of England and the United States. She told an interviewer in* Ms. *magazine, "I began as a profoundly apolitical writer, but then I began to do what all novelists and some poets do: I began to describe the world around me."*

You Fit into Me   [1971]

you fit into me
like a hook into an eye

a fish hook
an open eye

▶ QUESTIONS FOR READING AND WRITING

1. The first stanza introduces the second. The second is an abrupt shift. How
   do they differ?
2. How would you describe this relationship? Have you ever had one like it?

Siren Song   [1974]

This is the one song everyone
would like to learn: the song
that is irresistible:

the song that forces men
to leap overboard in squadrons   5
even though they see the beached skulls

the song nobody knows
because anyone who has heard it
is dead, and the others can't remember.

Shall I tell you the secret   10
and if I do, will you get me
out of this bird suit?

I don't enjoy it here
squatting on this island
looking picturesque and mythical   15

with these two feathery maniacs,
I don't enjoy singing
this trio, fatal and valuable.

I will tell the secret to you,
to you, only to you.   20
Come closer. This song

is a cry for help: Help me!
Only you, only you can,
you are unique

at last. Alas   25
it is a boring song
but it works every time.

➤ QUESTIONS FOR READING AND WRITING

1. Who is the speaker in this poem? What is her "siren song"?
2. Do you agree that the song she describes is "irresistible"? Explain.

W. H. AUDEN (1907–1973)

W[ystan] H[ugh] Auden was born in York, England, and educated at Oxford University. Like many intellectuals of his generation, his left-wing politics led him to serve on the loyalist side of the Spanish Civil War, but Auden quickly became disillusioned after witnessing the destruction and looting of Roman Catholic churches and returned to England. He immigrated to America in 1939, becoming a citizen in 1946. In 1947, he coined the term "the Age of Anxiety" in a long poem of the same name, which has since served as a shorthand term for the intellectual mood of the mid-twentieth century. His early work is characterized by his sharp wit and facility with elaborate verse forms. His later work, influenced by his reawakening interest in Christianity, became increasingly religious in tone.

THE UNKNOWN CITIZEN

[1940]

To

SOCIAL SECURITY ACCOUNT NUMBER 067-01-9818

THIS MARBLE MONUMENT IS ERECTED BY THE STATE

He was found by the Bureau of Statistics to be
One against whom there was no official complaint,
And all the reports on his conduct agree
That, in the modern sense of an old-fashioned word, he was a saint,
For in everything he did he served the Greater Community.   5
Except for the war, till the day he retired
He worked in one factory and never got fired,
But satisfied his employers, Fudge Motors, Inc.,
Yet was neither a scab nor odd in his views,
For his Union reports that he paid his dues   10
(Our report on his Union says it was sound),
And our Social Psychology workers found
He was popular with his mates and liked a drink.
The Press are convinced that he bought a paper every day,
And that his reactions to advertisements were normal in every way.   15
Policies taken out in his name prove that he was fully insured,

And a certificate shows that he was once in hospital but left it cured.
Both *Producer's Research* and *High Grade Living* declare
He was fully sensible to the advantages of the Installment Plan,
And had everything necessary to the Modern Man—   20
A victrola, a radio, a car, and a frigidaire.
Our investigators into Public Opinion are content
That he held the proper opinions for the time of year;
When there was peace, he was for peace; when there was war, he went.
He was married and added five children to the population,   25
Which, our eugenist says, was the right number for a parent of his generation,
And our teachers report that he never interfered with their education.
Was he free? Was he happy? The question is absurd:
Had anything been wrong, we should certainly have heard.

► QUESTIONS FOR READING AND WRITING

1. What is the tone of this poem? What lines in the poem indicate this?
2. This poem was written in 1940, so a few of the unknown citizen's posses-
   sions are not state-of-the-art. Can you update them to present-day equiva-
   lents?
3. Based on what is said about him, who is "the Unknown Citizen"? Was he
   "free"? Was he "happy"? Are the questions absurd?

ELIZABETH BISHOP (1911–1979)

Elizabeth Bishop was born in Worcester,
Massachusetts. Her father died when she was
still an infant, and her mother suffered a serious
mental breakdown and was institutionalized.
Bishop was raised first by her mother's family in
Nova Scotia and then, when she was 6, by her
father's parents, who lived in Worcester. Sickly
and shy, she spent most of her childhood
immersed in books, before attending boarding
school during her teens. While at Vassar College,
her poetry attracted the attention of a librarian,
who introduced Bishop to the poet Marianne
Moore. Moore became Bishop's mentor, and her
influence can be seen in Bishop's early work. Following graduation, Bishop lived in Key
West for 9 years, and then moved to Brazil, where she lived for almost 20. Returning to
the United States in 1966, she held positions at the University of Washington and the
Massachusetts Institute of Technology before settling at Harvard University, where she
was teaching when she died. Her collections of poetry include North and South *(1946),*
A Cold Spring *(winner of the Pulitzer Prize in 1956),* Complete Poems *(winner of the*
National Book Award in 1970), and Geography III *(1977). She was also a respected*

travel writer, publishing numerous volumes including Questions of Travel *(1965) and*
Brazil *(1967). Often considered a "poet's poet," Bishop's poems are characterized by a*
spare style and a distinctive, ironic voice.

In the Waiting Room   [1976]

In Worcester, Massachusetts,
I went with Aunt Consuelo
to keep her dentist's appointment
and sat and waited for her
in the dentist's waiting room.   5
It was winter. It got dark
early. The waiting room
was full of grown-up people,
arctics and overcoats,
lamps and magazines.   10
My aunt was inside
what seemed like a long time
and while I waited I read
the *National Geographic*
(I could read) and carefully   15
studied the photographs:
the inside of a volcano,
black, and full of ashes;
then it was spilling over
in rivulets of fire.   20
Osa and Martin Johnson
dressed in riding breeches,
laced boots, and pith helmets.
A dead man slung on a pole
—"Long Pig," the caption said.   25
Babies with pointed heads
wound round and round with string;
black, naked women with necks
wound round and round with wire
like the necks of light bulbs.   30
Their breasts were horrifying.
I read it right straight through.
I was too shy to stop.
And then I looked at the cover:
the yellow margins, the date.   35

Suddenly, from inside,
came an *oh!* of pain
—Aunt Consuelo's voice—
not very loud or long.

I wasn't at all surprised;   40
even then I knew she was
a foolish, timid woman.
I might have been embarrassed,
but wasn't. What took me
completely by surprise   45
was that it was *me:*
my voice, in my mouth.
Without thinking at all
I was my foolish aunt,
I—we—were falling, falling,   50
our eyes glued to the cover
of the *National Geographic,*
February, 1918.

I said to myself: three days
and you'll be seven years old.   55
I was saying it to stop
the sensation of falling off
the round, turning world
into cold, blue-black space.
But I felt: you are an *I,*   60
you are an *Elizabeth,*
you are one of *them.*
Why should you be one, too?
I scarcely dared to look
to see what it was I was.   65
I gave a sidelong glance
—I couldn't look any higher—
at shadowy gray knees,
trousers and skirts and boots
and different pairs of hands   70
lying under the lamps.
I knew that nothing stranger
had ever happened, that nothing
stranger could ever happen.
Why should I be my aunt,   75
or me, or anyone?
What similarities—
boots, hands, the family voice
I felt in my throat, or even
the *National Geographic*   80
and those awful hanging breasts—
held us all together
or made us all just one?
How—I didn't know any
word for it—how "unlikely" . . .   85

How had I come to be here,
like them, and overhear
a cry of pain that could have
got loud and worse but hadn't?

The waiting room was bright   90
and too hot. It was sliding
beneath a big black wave,
another, and another.

Then I was back in it.
The War was on. Outside,   95
in Worcester, Massachusetts,
were night and slush and cold,
and it was still the fifth
of February, 1918.

➤ QUESTIONS FOR READING AND WRITING

1. Who is the speaker? How old is she? Does it matter? Explain.
2. What does the sound of Aunt Consuelo's voice reveal to her?
3. What do you think the speaker means by "But I felt: you are an *I*, / you are
   an *Elizabeth*, / you are one of *them*"?
4. In the last stanza, she says, "Then I was back in it." Where has she been?
   What is she "back in"?

THE FISH   [1946]

I caught a tremendous fish
and held him beside the boat
half out of water, with my hook
fast in a corner of his mouth.
He didn't fight.   5
He hadn't fought at all.
He hung a grunting weight,
battered and venerable
and homely. Here and there
his brown skin hung in strips   10
like ancient wallpaper,
and its pattern of darker brown
was like wallpaper:
shapes like full-blown roses
stained and lost through age.   15
He was speckled with barnacles,
fine rosettes of lime,
and infested
with tiny white sea-lice,

and underneath two or three   20
rags of green weed hung down.
While his gills were breathing in
the terrible oxygen
—the frightening gills,
fresh and crisp with blood,   25
that can cut so badly—
I thought of the coarse white flesh
packed in like feathers,
the big bones and the little bones,
the dramatic reds and blacks   30
of his shiny entrails,
and the pink swim-bladder
like a big peony.
I looked into his eyes
which were far larger than mine   35
but shallower, and yellowed,
the irises backed and packed
with tarnished tinfoil
seen through the lenses
of old scratched isinglass.°   40
They shifted a little, but not
to return my stare.
—It was more like the tipping
of an object toward the light.
I admired his sullen face,   45
the mechanism of his jaw,
and then I saw
that from his lower lip
—if you could call it a lip—
grim, wet, and weaponlike,   50
hung five old pieces of fish-line,
or four and a wire leader
with the swivel still attached,
with all their five big hooks
grown firmly in his mouth.   55
A green line, frayed at the end
where he broke it, two heavier lines,
and a fine black thread
still crimped from the strain and snap
when it broke and he got away.   60
Like medals with their ribbons
frayed and wavering,
a five-haired beard of wisdom

---

⁴⁰**isinglass** semitransparent material made from fish bladders

trailing from his aching jaw.
I stared and stared
and victory filled up
the little rented boat,
from the pool of bilge
where oil had spread a rainbow
around the rusted engine
to the bailer° rusted orange,
the sun-cracked thwarts,
the oarlocks on their strings,
the gunnels°—until everything
was rainbow, rainbow, rainbow!
And I let the fish go.

65

70

75

⁷¹**bailer** bucket   ⁷⁴**gunnels** gunwales

> **QUESTIONS FOR READING AND WRITING**

1   How much do the details in the poem tell you about the history of this fish?
2. Why do you think the speaker lets the fish go?

ONE ART   [1976]

The art of losing isn't hard to master;
so many things seem filled with the intent
to be lost that their loss is no disaster.

Lose something every day. Accept the fluster
of lost door keys, the hour badly spent.
The art of losing isn't hard to master.

5

Then practice losing farther, losing faster:
places, and names, and where it was you meant
to travel. None of these will bring disaster.

I lost my mother's watch. And look! my last, or
next-to-last, of three loved houses went.
The art of losing isn't hard to master.

10

I lost two cities, lovely ones. And, vaster,
some realms I owned, two rivers, a continent.
I miss them, but it wasn't a disaster.

15

—Even losing you (the joking voice, a gesture
I love) I shan't have lied. It's evident
the art of losing's not too hard to master
though it may look like (*Write* it!) like disaster.

➤ *QUESTIONS FOR READING AND WRITING*

1. What do you think the speaker means when she says, "The art of losing isn't hard to master"?
2. Describe the rhyme scheme and structure of this poem. How do they influence your response to its content?
3. Compare this poem with Elizabeth Gaffney's "Losses That Turn Up in Dreams" on page 173 or Gwendolyn Brooks's "The Mother" on page 139.

WILLIAM BLAKE (1757–1827)

The son of a London haberdasher, William Blake received very little formal education. When he was 10 he entered a drawing school, and later studied for a few months at the Royal Academy of Art. At the age of 14 he was apprenticed to an engraver, and, after seven years, he was able to earn his living illustrating books. From his early twenties to his sixties, when he chose to devote himself exclusively to pictorial art, Blake produced books of his own poetry, which were painstakingly illustrated and handcolored, often with the help of his wife. His early books of poetry, Songs of Innocence *(1789) and* Songs of Experience *(1794), from which the following poems are taken, express Blake's rage at the social injustices of England. His later work, the so-called* Prophetic Works, *are much more difficult. In these highly symbolic and often cryptic poems, Blake created his own complicated mythological system based on his deeply held religious and spiritual beliefs. (His wife said of him, "I have very little of Mr. Blake's company; he is always in Paradise.") His now-famous verses were not very well-known during his lifetime, and it is only in the past century that he has earned a wider readership.*

THE CHIMNEY SWEEPER   [1789]

When my mother died I was very young,
And my father sold me while yet my tongue
Could scarcely cry "'weep! 'weep! 'weep!"
So your chimneys I sweep, and in soot I sleep.

There's little Tom Dacre, who cried when his head,   5
That curled like a lamb's back, was shaved: so I said
"Hush, Tom! never mind it, for when your head's bare
You know that the soot cannot spoil your white hair."

And so he was quiet, and that very night,
As Tom was a-sleeping, he had such a sight!   10
That thousands of sweepers, Dick, Joe, Ned, and Jack,
Were all of them locked up in coffins of black.

And by came an Angel who had a bright key,
And he opened the coffins and set them all free;
Then down a green plain leaping, laughing, they run,   15
And wash in a river, and shine in the sun.

Then naked and white, all their bags left behind,
They rise upon clouds and sport in the wind;
And the Angel told Tom, if he'd be a good boy,
He'd have God for his father, and never want joy.   20

And so Tom awoke; and we rose in the dark,
And got with our bags and our brushes to work.
Though the morning was cold, Tom was happy and warm;
So if all do their duty they need not fear harm.

➤ QUESTIONS FOR READING AND WRITING

1. Describe the tone and rhythm of this poem. How does it shape your
    response to the story of the chimney sweeper?
2. Interpret Tom's dream. Does religion play a useful role in his life? Explain.
3. Reread the last line of the poem. Do you think this is really the message of
    the poem? Why or why not?
4. Can you imagine a similar poem being written about poverty-stricken
    people who live in the world today? Explain.

LONDON   [1794]

I wander through each chartered street,
Near where the chartered Thames does flow,
And mark in every face I meet
Marks of weakness, marks of woe.

In every cry of every man,   5
In every infant's cry of fear,
In every voice, in every ban,
The mind-forged manacles I hear.

How the chimney-sweeper's cry
Every black'ning church appalls   10
And the hapless soldier's sigh
Runs in blood down palace walls.

But most through midnight streets I hear
How the youthful harlot's curse
Blasts the new born infant's tear   15
And blights with plagues the marriage hearse.

► *QUESTIONS FOR READING AND WRITING*

1. What are "mind-forged manacles"? Can you think of any "mind-forged manacles" that exist today?
2. What is the "youthful harlot's curse" and what does it have to do with blasting "the new born infant's tear" or plaguing "the marriage hearse"?
3. Compare this vision of the city with that of William Wordsworth's as expressed in "Composed upon Westminster Bridge" (p. 270).

THE LAMB [1789]

Little Lamb, who made thee?
Dost thou know who made thee?
Gave thee life & bid thee feed,
By the stream & o 'er the mead;
Gave thee clothing of delight, 5
Softest clothing wooly bright;
Gave thee such a tender voice,
Making all the vales rejoice!
Little lamb, who made thee?
Dost thou know who made thee? 10

Little Lamb, I'll tell thee,
Little Lamb, I'll tell thee:
He is calléd by thy name,
For he calls himself a Lamb:
He is meek & he is mild, 15
He became a little child:
I a child & thou a lamb,
We are calléd by his name.
Little Lamb, God bless thee!
Little Lamb, God bless thee! 20

THE TYGER [1794]

Tyger! Tyger! burning bright
In the forests of the night,
What immortal hand or eye
Could frame thy fearful symmetry?

In what distant deeps or skies 5
Burnt the fire of thine eyes?
On what wings dare he aspire?
What the hand dare seize the fire?

And what shoulder, and what art,
Could twist the sinews of thy heart?
And when thy heart began to beat,
What dread hand? and what dread feet?

10

What the hammer? what the chain?
In what furnace was thy brain?
What the anvil? what dread grasp
Dare its deadly terrors clasp?

15

When the stars threw down their spears,
And watered heaven with their tears,
Did he smile his work to see?
Did he who made the Lamb make thee?

20

Tyger! Tyger! burning bright
In the forests of the night,
What immortal hand or eye,
Dare frame thy fearful symmetry?

➤ QUESTIONS FOR READING AND WRITING

1. Compare "The Lamb" and "The Tyger."
2. How do the structure and rhymes of each poem influence your response?
3. Why do you think the speaker in "The Tyger" asks, "Did he who made the Lamb make thee?"

ROBERT BRIDGES (1844–1930)

Robert Bridges was born the son of a prosperous landowner and took his degree at Corpus Christi College, Oxford, where he made friends with Gerald Manley Hopkins. He was a medical student at St. Bartholomew's Hospital, London, and practiced medicine until 1881 when illness forced his retirement. For the rest of his life he dedicated himself to his writing. In 1913 he was named Poet Laureat of England.

LONDON SNOW

[1880]

When men were all asleep the snow came flying,
In large white flakes falling on the city brown,

Stealthily and perpetually settling and loosely lying,
    Hushing the latest traffic of the drowsy town;
Deadening, muffling, stifling its murmers failing;   5
Lazily and incessantly floating down and down;
    Silently sifting and veiling road, roof and railing;
Hiding difference, making unevenness even,
Into angles and crevices softly drifting and sailing.
    All night it fell, and when full inches seven   10
It lay in the depth of its uncompacted lightness,
The clouds blew off from a high and frosty heaven;
    And all woke earlier for the unaccustomed brightness
Of the winter dawning, the strange unheavenly glare:
The eye marvelled—marvelled at the dazzling whiteness;   15
    The ear hearkened to the stillness of the solemn air;
No sound of wheel rumbling nor of foot falling,
And the busy morning cries came thin and spare.
    Then boys I heard, as they went to school, calling;
They gathered up the crystal manna to freeze   20
Their tongues with tasting, their hands with snowballing;
    Or rioted in a drift, plunging up to the knees;
Or peering up from under the white-mossed wonder,
"O look at the trees!" they cried. "O look at the trees!"
    With lessened load, a few carts creak and blunder,   25
Following along the white deserted way,
A country company long dispersed asunder:
    When, now, already the sun, in pale display
Standing by Paul's high dome, spread forth below
His sparkling beams, and awoke the stir of the day.   30
    For now doors open, and war is waged with the snow;
And trains of sombre men, past tale of number,
Tread long brown paths, as toward their toil they go:
    But even for them awhile no cares encumber
Their minds diverted; the daily word is unspoken,   35
The daily thoughts of labour and sorrow slumber
At the sight of the beauty that greets them, for the charm they
    have broken.

➤ QUESTIONS FOR READING AND WRITING

1. To what extent does your own experience affect your response to this poem?
2. The speaker says, "For now doors open, and war is waged with the snow." Pick out phrases in the poem that describe "the charm they have broken."

GWENDOLYN BROOKS (1917–2000)

Born in Topeka, Kansas, Gwendolyn Brooks was raised on the South Side of Chicago. She graduated from Wilson Junior College in 1936, and married in 1939. Though Brooks began writing poetry as a child she did not find her vocation until she entered a poetry workshop at a local community arts center in the early 1940s. Influenced by Langston Hughes and other poets of the Harlem Renaissance, Brooks attempted to wed the familiar idiom and rhythms of the colloquial speech of Chicago's South Side to the traditional poetic forms she encountered in the workshop. Her first collection of poetry, A Street in Bronzeville, *appeared in 1945. In 1949, with the publication of* Annie Allen, *she became the first African-American woman awarded the Pulitzer Prize. After attending a conference of African-American writers at Fisk University in 1967, Brooks became convinced that "black poets should write as blacks, about blacks, and address themselves to blacks." As a result, she became a devoted teacher of writing, particularly in the African-American community, and abandoned her New York publisher in favor of small African-American presses. In addition to numerous volumes of poetry, she published children's books, a novel,* Maud Martha *(1953), and an autobiography,* Report from Part I *(1972), and received over 50 honorary degrees.*

WE REAL COOL   [1960]

The Pool Players.
Seven at the Golden Shovel.

We real cool. We
Left school. We

Lurk late. We
Strike straight. We   5

Sing sin. We
Thin gin. We

Jazz June. We
Die soon.   10

➤ QUESTIONS FOR READING AND WRITING

1. Who is the speaker in this poem?
2. What is the relationship between rhyme and rhythm and meaning in this poem?
3. Were you surprised by the last line? Explain.

THE MOTHER [1945]

Abortions will not let you forget.
You remember the children you got that you did not get,
The damp small pulps with a little or with no hair,
The singers and workers that never handled the air.
You will never neglect or beat   5
Them, or silence or buy with a sweet.
You will never wind up the sucking-thumb
Or scuttle off ghosts that come.
You will never leave them, controlling your luscious sigh,
Return for a snack of them, with gobbling mother-eye.   10

I have heard in the voices of the wind the voices of my dim killed
    children.
I have contracted. I have eased
My dim dears at the breasts they could never suck.
I have said, Sweets, if I sinned, if I seized
Your luck   15
And your lives from your unfinished reach,
If I stole your births and your names,
Your straight baby tears and your games,
Your stilted or lovely loves, your tumults, your marriages, aches,
    and your deaths,
If I poisoned the beginnings of your breaths,   20
Believe that even in my deliberateness I was not deliberate.
Though why should I whine,
Whine that the crime was other than mine?—
Since anyhow you are dead.
Or rather, or instead,   25
You were never made.
But that too, I am afraid,
Is faulty: oh, what shall I say, how is the truth to be said?
You were born, you had body, you died.
It is just that you never giggled or planned or cried.   30

Believe me, I loved you all.
Believe me, I knew you, though faintly, and I loved, I loved you
All.

➤ QUESTIONS FOR READING AND WRITING

1. Who is the speaker in this poem and what is she mourning? What does she miss most?
2. She says, "Believe me, I loved you all." Do you think she does? Explain.

ELIZABETH BARRETT BROWNING

(1806–1861)

Elizabeth Barrett Browning was born in Durham, England, the oldest of 11 children, and at 15 suffered a spinal injury that left her partially paralyzed. In 1845 she met Robert Browning and the two fell in love. They were forced to elope, however, because of her extremely possessive father. A very popular poet during her lifetime, she published many volumes of poetry, including her most famous collection, Sonnets from the Portuguese, *love poems written to her husband. "How Do I Love Thee?" is one of the sonnets in this collection*

HOW DO I LOVE THEE? [1850]

How do I love thee? Let me count the ways.
I love thee to the depth and breadth and height
My soul can reach, when feeling out of sight
For the ends of being and ideal grace.
I love thee to the level of every day's   5
Most quiet need, by sun and candle-light.
I love thee freely, as men strive for right.
I love thee purely, as they turn from praise.
I love thee with the passion put to use
In my old griefs, and with my childhood's faith.   10
I love thee with a love I seemed to lose
With my lost saints. I love thee with the breath,
Smiles, tears, of all my life; and, if God choose,
I shall but love thee better after death.

➤ QUESTIONS FOR READING AND WRITING

1. The sentiments expressed in this poem are very idealistic. Do you think love can be this powerful and absolute? Explain.
2. Pick out some of the similes and metaphors in this poem and describe what makes them effective.
3. Compare this sonnet with "Let Me Not to the Marriage of True Minds" (p. 250), "Love Is Not All" (p. 73) or "Sonnet Ending with a Film Subtitle" (p. 179).

ROBERT BROWNING (1812–1889)

The son of a banker, Robert Browning was born in a suburb of London, and first learned the joy of reading in his father's vast library. He published his first collection of poems, Pauline, in 1833, and over the next 30 years followed it with numerous other volumes, which, though they contained some of his greatest works, were financially unsuccessful. In 1846, in one of the most famous matches in literary history, he married the celebrated poet Elizabeth Barrett, who wrote the sonnet that begins, "How do I love thee? Let me count the ways" to him. Because of her ill health and to escape her overbearing father, the couple moved to Italy. After her death in 1861, he returned to England and wrote The Ring and the Book *(1868–1869), a long narrative poem about a famous seventeenth-century murder case. The poem was Browning's first major success and brought him the wide recognition and respect that had thus far eluded him. Many of his best regarded poems, including "Porphyria's Lover," take the form of dramatic monologues, in which the poet creates a character who reveals himself or herself while delivering an extended speech, often to a silent listener.*

PORPHYRIA'S LOVER

[1834]

The rain set early in tonight,
    The sullen wind was soon awake,
It tore the elm-tops down for spite,
    And did its worst to vex the lake:
I listened with heart fit to break.   5
    When glided in Porphyria; straight
She shut the cold out and the storm,
    And kneeled and made the cheerless grate
Blaze up, and all the cottage warm;
    Which done, she rose, and from her form   10
Withdrew the dripping cloak and shawl,
    And laid her soiled gloves by, untied
Her hat and let the damp hair fall,
    And, last, she sat down by my side
And called me. When no voice replied,   15
    She put my arm about her waist,
And made her smooth white shoulder bare,

And all her yellow hair displaced,
And, stooping, made my cheek lie there,
   And spread, o'er all, her yellow hair,   20
Murmuring how she loved me—she
   Too weak, for all her heart's endeavor,
To set its struggling passion free
   From pride, and vainer ties dissever,
And give herself to me forever.   25
   But passion sometimes would prevail,
Nor could tonight's gay feast restrain
   A sudden thought of one so pale
For love of her, and all in vain:
   So, she was come through wind and rain.   30
Be sure I looked up at her eyes
   Happy and proud; at last I knew
Porphyria worshiped me: surprise
   Made my heart swell, and still it grew
While I debated what to do.   35
   That moment she was mine, mine, fair,
Perfectly pure and good: I found
   A thing to do, and all her hair
In one long yellow string I wound
   Three times her little throat around,   40
And strangled her. No pain felt she;
   I am quite sure she felt no pain.
As a shut bud that holds a bee,
   I warily opened her lids: again
Laughed the blue eyes without a stain.   45
   And I untightened next the tress
About her neck; her cheek once more
   Blushed bright beneath my burning kiss:
I propped her head up as before,
   Only, this time my shoulder bore   50
Her head, which droops upon it still:
   The smiling rosy little head,
So glad it has its utmost will,
   That all it scorned at once is fled,
And I, its love, am gained instead!   55
   Porphyria's love: she guessed not how
Her darling one wish would be heard.
   And thus we sit together now,
And all night long we have not stirred,
   And yet God has not said a word!   60

▶ QUESTIONS FOR READING AND WRITING

   1. What details set the mood early in the poem?

2. Paraphrase the speaker's argument. According to him, why is it appropriate to strangle Porphyria?
3. Interpret the last line of the poem. Is the speaker showing consciousness of guilt?
4. Compare the love described in this poem with that described in Elizabeth Barrett Browning's "How Do I Love Thee?" (p. 140).

LEWIS CARROLL [CHARLES LUTWIDGE DODSON] (1832–1898)

Lewis Carroll was born in England and attended Oxford University, where he later returned to teach Mathematics. He is best known for the stories he wrote for a friend's daughter, Alice Liddell. His works include Alice's Adventures in Wonderland *(1865) and* Through the Looking Glass *and* What Alice Found There *(1871).*

JABBERWOCKY   [1871]

'Twas brillig, and the slithy toves
    Did gyre and gimble in the wabe:
All mimsy were the borogoves,
    And the mome raths outgrabe.

"Beware the Jabberwock, my son!   5
    The jaws that bite, the claws that catch!
Beware the Jubjub bird, and shun
    The frumious Bandersnatch!"

He took his vorpal sword in hand;
    Long time the manxome foe he sought—   10
So rested he by the Tumtum tree
    And stood a while in thought.

And, as in uffish thought he stood,
    The Jabberwock, with eyes of flame,
Came whiffling through the tulgey wood,   15
    And burbled as it came!

One, two! One, two! An through and through
   The vorpal blade went snicker-snack!
He left it dead, and with its head
   He went galumphing back.

20

"And hast thou slain the Jabberwock?
   Come to my arms, my beamish boy!
O frabjous day! Callooh, Callay!"
   He chortled in his joy.

'Twas brillig, and the slithy toves
   Did gyre and gimble in the wabe:
All mimsy were the borogoves,
   And the mome raths outgrabe

25

➤ QUESTIONS FOR READING AND WRITING

1. What do you think this poem is about?
2. In what way do the sounds of the words convey its meaning? A number of these words may be unfamiliar to you. Some (like "chortled") are in the dictionary. But many others are not. How can you account for their meaning?

JUDITH ORTIZ COFER (b. 1952)

The daughter of a Puerto Rican mother and a United States mainland father, Judith Ortiz Cofer was born in Puerto Rico but immigrated to the mainland in 1956. Educated at Augusta College and Florida Atlantic University, Cofer did further graduate work at Oxford University in 1977 and then worked as an English teacher and bilingual instructor in Florida. Due to her bilingual upbringing, much of Cofer's work is concerned with the power of language and its uses. She has published several volumes of poetry and a novel, The Line of the Sun *(1989).*

MY FATHER IN THE NAVY: A CHILDHOOD MEMORY

[1987]

Stiff and immaculate
in the white cloth of his uniform
and a round cap on his head like a halo,
he was an apparition on leave from a shadow-world
and only flesh and blood when he rose from below
the waterline where he kept watch over the engines
and dials making sure the ship parted the waters
on a straight course.

5

Mother, brother, and I kept vigil
on the nights and dawns of his arrivals,   10
watching the corner beyond the neon sign of a quasar
for the flash of white our father like an angel
heralding a new day.
His homecomings were the verses
we composed over the years making up   15
the siren's song that kept him coming back
from the bellies of iron whales
and into our nights
like the evening prayer.

➤ QUESTIONS FOR READING AND WRITING

1. To what extent is your response to this poem affected by your own experience?
2. What does the speaker in the poem look forward to about her father? What lines in the poem indicate that?
3. What does the speaker mean by "he was an apparition on leave from a shadow-world"?

WANDA COLEMAN (b. 1946)

Wanda Coleman has received fellowships from the National Endowment for the Arts and the Guggenheim Foundation and was awarded the 1999 Lenore Marshall Poetry Prize. Her most recent books of poetry include Bathwater Wine *(1998),* Native in a Strange Land *(1996), and* Hand Dance *(1993). When not writing, she hosts an interview program on Pacific Radio. She told* Contemporary Authors, *"Words seem inadequate in expressing the anger and outrage I feel at the persistent racism that permeates every aspect of black American life. Since words are what I am best at, I concern myself with this as an urban actuality as best I can."*

SWEET MAMA WANDA TELLS FORTUNES FOR A PRICE   [1979]

dark stairs
me walking up them
the room
is cold
i am here to fuck   5
then go back
to the streets

he sighs
touches
likes my lips
my cocoa thighs   10
we lay down
the bed yields
he comes off calling mama

outside   15
i count my cash
it's been a good night
the street is cold
i head east

➤ QUESTIONS FOR READING AND WRITING

1. Who is the speaker in this poem? What kind of "fortunes" does she tell?
2. What is the tone of the poem? What indicates that?
3. What does the speaker mean by "the street is cold"?

BILLY COLLINS (b. 1941)

*Billy Collins is the author of seven books of
poetry, and his work has appeared in a variety
of publications, including* Poetry, American
Poetry Review, American Scholar, Harper's,
Paris Review, *and the* New Yorker. *He has
received fellowships from the National
Endowment for the Arts and the Guggenheim
Foundation, and was chosen to serve as
"Literary Lion" by the New York Public
Library. In 2001, he was named U.S. Poet
Laureate and published his most recent collec-
tion* Sailing Alone Around the Room. *He
teaches at Lehman College, of the City
University of New York, and lives in Somers, New York.*

VICTORIA'S SECRET   [1998]

The one in the upper left-hand corner
is giving me a look
that says I know you are here
and I have nothing better to do
for the remainder of human time   5
than return your persistent but engaging stare.

She is wearing a deeply scalloped
flame-stitch halter top
with padded push-up styling
and easy side-zip tap pants.   10

The one on the facing page, however,
who looks at me over her bare shoulder,
cannot hide the shadow of annoyance in her brow.
You have interrupted me,
she seems to be saying,   15
with your coughing and your loud music.
Now please leave me alone;
let me finish whatever it was I was doing
in my organza-trimmed
whisperweight camisole with   20
keyhole closure and a point d'esprit mesh back.

I wet my thumb and flip the page.
Here, the one who happens to be reclining
in a satin and lace merry window
with an inset lace-up front,   25
decorated underwire cups and bodice
with lace ruffles along the bottom
and hook-and-eye closure in the back,
is wearing a slightly contorted expression,
her head thrust back, mouth partially open,   30
a confusing mixture of pain and surprise
as if she had stepped on a tack
just as I was breaking down
her bedroom door with my shoulder.

Nor does the one directly beneath her   35
look particularly happy to see me.
She is arching one eyebrow slightly
as if to say, so what if I am wearing nothing
but this stretch panne velvet bodysuit
with a low sweetheart neckline   40
featuring molded cups and adjustable straps.
Do you have a problem with that?!

The one on the far right is easier to take,
her eyes half-closed
as if she were listening to a medley   45
of lullabies playing faintly on a music box.
Soon she will drop off to sleep,
her head nestled in the soft crook of her arm,
and later she will wake up in her
Spandex slip dress with the high side slit,   50
deep scoop neckline, elastic shirring,
and concealed back zip and vent.

But opposite her,
stretched out catlike on a couch
in the warm glow of a paneled library,   55
is one who wears a distinctly challenging expression,
her face tipped up, exposing
her long neck, her perfectly flared nostrils.
Go ahead, her expression tells me,
take off my satin charmeuse gown   60
with a sheer, jacquard bodice
decorated with a touch of shimmering Lurex.
Go ahead, fling it into the fireplace.
What do I care, her eyes say, we're all going to hell anyway.

I have other mail to open,   65
but I cannot help noticing her neighbor
whose eyes are downcast,
her head ever so demurely bowed to the side
as if she were the model who sat for Coreggio
when he painted "The Madonna of St. Jerome,"   70
only, it became so ungodly hot in Parma
that afternoon, she had to remove
the traditional blue robe
and pose there in his studio
in a beautifully shaped satin teddy   75
with an embossed V-front,
princess seaming to mold the bodice,
and puckered knit detail.

And occupying the whole facing page
is one who displays that expression   80
we have come to associate with photographic beauty.
Yes, she is pouting about something,
all lower lip and cheekbone.
Perhaps her ice cream has tumbled
out of its cone onto the parquet floor.   85
Perhaps she has been waiting all day
for a new sofa to be delivered,
waiting all day in a stretch lace hipster
with lattice edging, satin frog closures,
velvet scrollwork, cuffed ankles,   90
flare silhouette, and knotted shoulder straps
available in black, champagne, almond,
cinnabar, plum, bronze, mocha,
peach, ivory, caramel, blush, butter, rose, and periwinkle.
It is, of course, impossible to say,   95
impossible to know what she is thinking,
why her mouth is the shape of petulance.

But this is already too much.
Who has the time to linger on these delicate
lures, these once unmentionable things?   100
Life is rushing by like a mad, swollen river.
One minute roses are opening in the garden
and the next, snow is flying past my window.
Plus the phone is ringing.
The dog is whining at the door.   105
Rain is beating on the roof.
And as always there is a list of things I have to do
before the night descends, black and silky,
and the dark hours begin to hurtle by,
before the little doors of the body swing shut   110
and I ride to sleep, my closed eyes
still burning from all the glossy lights of day.

➤ QUESTIONS FOR READING AND WRITING

1. The title of the poem, "Victoria's Secret," is a reference to a well-known store catalog that features women modeling lingerie. What do you think makes the speaker's commentary so humorous as he peruses the pictures?
2. His descriptions of what the models are wearing are very detailed. Why?
3. To what extent is this poem a commentary on American culture? What is Victoria's secret?
4. In what way does the tone of the last stanza differ from the rest? What point do you think the speaker is trying to make?

STEPHEN CRANE (1871–1900)

Stephen Crane was the youngest of 14 children born to a Methodist minister in Newark, New Jersey. After briefly attending LaFayette College and Syracuse University, Crane moved to New York City to work as a freelance journalist. He lived a bohemian (and often impoverished) existence and came to know life firsthand. These experiences inspired his first novel, Maggie, a Girl on the Streets, *which he published at his own expense under a pseudonym. While not widely read due to its realistic language that was considered shocking at the time, the novel impressed members of New York's literary elite, setting the stage for the publication of his second novel,* The Red Badge of Courage *(1895). In 1895, Crane published a book of short poems,* The Black Riders, *and* Other Line, *and another collection of poetry,* War Is Kind, *in 1899, which would later prove influential but went largely unnoticed until after his death. Crane died of tuberculosis when he was only 28.*

A MAN SAID TO THE UNIVERSE [1899]

A man said to the universe:
"Sir, I exist!"
"However," replied the universe,
"The fact has not created in me
A sense of obligation." 5

▶ QUESTIONS FOR READING AND WRITING

1. What do you think the man expects from the universe? Why does he say, "I exist"? Are you surprised by the universe's response? Explain.
2. Compare this poem to "Dover Beach" on page 123.

E. E. CUMMINGS (1894–1962)

E[dwin] E[stlin] Cummings was born in Cambridge, Massachusetts. He began writing poetry as a child and claimed that he wrote at least one poem a day between the ages of 8 and 22. He attended Harvard University, earning a bachelor's degree in 1915 and a master's degree in 1916. During World War I, he served as an ambulance driver and was confined for a time in a French internment camp for what proved to be a mistaken suspicion of treason. In 1922, he wrote of these experiences in his novel The Enormous Room, *which proved to be a great critical success. In the 1920s, he published the collections of poetry—including* & *(1925), XLI* Poems *(1925), and* is 5 *(1926)—that would establish him as America's foremost avant-garde poet. His* Complete Poems: 1910 to 1962 *was published in 1980. Though his poems employ slang, dialect, and all kinds of typographical games, they are often much more accessible than they immediately appear.*

anyone lived in a pretty how town [1940]

anyone lived in a pretty how town
(with up so floating many bells down)
spring summer autumn winter
he sang his didn't he danced his did.

Women and men (both little and small) 5
cared for anyone not at all
they sowed their isn't they reaped their same
sun moon stars rain

children guessed (but only a few
and down they forgot as up they grew
autumn winter spring summer)
that noone loved him more by more

10

when by now and tree by leaf
she laughed his joy she cried his grief,
bird by snow and stir by still
anyone's any was all to her

15

someones married their everyones
laughed their cryings and did their dance
(sleep wake hope and then) they
said their nevers they slept their dream

20

stars rain sun moon
(and only the snow can begin to explain
how children are apt to forget to remember
with up so floating many bells down)

one day anyone died i guess
(and noone stooped to kiss his face)
busy folk buried them side by side
little by little and was by was

25

all by all and deep by deep
and more by more they dream their sleep
noone and anyone earth by april
wish by spirit and if by yes.

30

Women and men (both dong and ding)
summer autumn winter spring
reaped their sowing and went their came
sun moon stars rain

35

➤ QUESTIONS FOR READING AND WRITING

1. How was your reading affected by the unusual style of the writing? Pick out some lines and describe what you think they mean.
2. Who is "anyone"?
3. What do you think the poem means?

SOMEWHERE I HAVE NEVER TRAVELLED, GLADLY BEYOND   [1931]

somewhere i have never travelled, gladly beyond
any experience, your eyes have their silence:
in your most frail gesture are things which enclose me,
or which i cannot touch because they are too near

your slightest look easily will unclose me   5
though i have closed myself as fingers,
you open always petal by petal myself as Spring opens
(touching skillfully,mysteriously)her first rose

or if your wish be to close me,i and
my life will shut very beautifully,suddenly,   10
as when the heart of this flower imagines
the snow carefully everywhere descending;

nothing which we are to perceive in this world equals
the power of your intense fragility: whose texture
compels me with the colour of its countries,   15
rendering death and forever with each breathing

(i do not know what it is about you that closes
and opens; only something in me understands
the voice of your eyes is deeper than all roses)
nobody, not even the rain, has such small hands   20

➤ QUESTIONS FOR READING AND WRITING

1. Where is "somewhere"? Who is the "you" in the poem?
2. Compare this poem to the excerpt from Walt Whitman's *Song of Myself* on page 266.

EMILY DICKINSON (1830–1886)

Emily Dickinson was born in Amherst, Massachusetts, where her father, a one-time congressman, was the lawyer and treasurer of Amherst College. Dickinson spent an unhappy year at the New England Female Seminary (which would become Mount Holyoke College). Returning home, she gradually removed herself from outside responsibilities, eventually leading an almost solitary existence. She published only a tiny number of the nearly 2000 exquisitely crafted and startlingly original poems she composed during her lifetime. Following her death, her family discovered her poems in a trunk in the attic. After making numerous changes, they published nine volumes of her work. Not until Thomas H. Johnson published his three-volume edition, Poems, in 1955, did Dickinson's verses become available as she originally composed them. Her stature has continued to grow and, today, she is considered one of the great geniuses of nineteenth-century American poetry.

Tell All the Truth but Tell It Slant   [CA. 1868]

Tell all the Truth but tell it slant—
Success in Circuit lies
Too bright for our infirm Delight
The Truth's superb surprise

As Lightning to the Children eased   5
With explanation kind
The Truth must dazzle gradually
Or every man be blind—

▶ QUESTIONS FOR READING AND WRITING

1. What advice is the speaker in this poem giving?
2. How does this poem compare with the popular saying, "Honesty is the best policy"? Do you think it's right to "tell it slant"?
3. Consider the words and images in this brief poem. Do you think they convey the message of the poem effectively?

After Great Pain, a Formal Feeling Comes   [CA. 1862]

After great pain, a formal feeling comes—
The Nerves sit ceremonious, like Tombs—
The stiff Heart questions was it He, that bore,
And Yesterday, or Centuries before?

The Feet, mechanical, go round—   5
Of Ground, or Air, or Ought—
A Wooden way
Regardless grown,
A Quartz contentment, like a stone—

This is the Hour of Lead—   10
Remembered, if outlived,
As Freezing persons, recollect the Snow—
First—Chill—then Stupor—then the letting go—

▶ QUESTIONS FOR READING AND WRITING

1. What kind of "great pain" does the speaker make reference to?
2. To what extent is your response affected by your own experience? Do the images work for you? Explain.

Much Madness Is Divinest Sense   [CA. 1862]

Much Madness is divinest Sense—
To a discerning Eye—
Much Sense—the starkest Madness—
'Tis the Majority

In this, as All, prevail—
Assent—and you are sane—
Demur—you're straightway dangerous—
And handled with a Chain—

5

➤ QUESTIONS FOR READING AND WRITING

1. What do you think the speaker means by "Much Madness"? By "Much Sense"?
2. Who is the "Majority" that prevail? Do you think they should? Explain.

THERE'S A CERTAIN SLANT OF LIGHT   [CA. 1861]

There's a certain Slant of light,
Winter Afternoons—
That oppresses, like the Heft
Of Cathedral Tunes—

Heavenly Hurt, it gives us—   5
We can find no scar,
But internal difference,
Where the Meanings, are—

None may teach it—Any—
'Tis the Seal Despair—   10
An imperial affliction
Sent us of the Air—

When it comes, the Landscape listens—
Shadows—hold their breath—
When it goes, 'tis like the Distance   15
On the look of Death—

➤ QUESTIONS FOR READING AND WRITING

1. What is the setting for this poem? Why does the speaker call it a "Slant of light" rather than a "light"?
2. What does the speaker mean by "None may teach it"?

SHE SWEEPS WITH MANY-COLORED BROOMS   [CA. 1861]

She sweeps with many-colored Brooms—
And leaves the Shreds behind—
Oh Housewife in the Evening West—
Come back, and dust the Pond!

You dropped a Purple Ravelling in—   5
You dropped an Amber thread—
And now you've littered all the East
With Duds of Emerald!

And still, she plies her spotted Brooms,
And still the Aprons fly,   10
Till Brooms fade softly into stars—
And then I come away—

➤ QUESTIONS FOR READING AND WRITING

1. Who is the "She" of the poem? What are her "many-colored Brooms" and what do they sweep?
2. In what way do the "Brooms fade softly into stars"?

SUCCESS IS COUNTED SWEETEST   [1878 (CA. 1859)]

Success is counted sweetest
By those who ne'er succeed.
To comprehend a nectar
Requires sorest need.

Not one of all the purple Host   5
Who took the Flag today
Can tell the definition
So clear of Victory

As he defeated—dying—
On whose forbidden ear   10
The distant strains of triumph
Burst agonized and clear!

➤ QUESTIONS FOR READING AND WRITING

1. Do you agree that "Success is counted sweetest / By those who ne'er succeed"? Explain.
2. To what extent does your own experience influence your response?

I HEARD A FLY BUZZ—WHEN I DIED—   [1896]

I heard a Fly buzz—when I died—
The Stillness in the Room
Was like the Stillness in the Air—
Between the Heaves of Storm—

The Eyes around—had wrung them dry—   5
And Breaths were gathering firm
For that last Onset—when the King
Be witnessed—in the Room——

I willed my Keepsakes—Signed away
What portion of me be   10
Assignable—and then it was
There interposed a Fly—

With Blue—uncertain stumbling Buzz—
Between the light—and me—
And then the Windows failed—and then   15
I could not see to see—

► QUESTIONS FOR READING AND WRITING

1. Who is the speaker in this poem?
2. Why do you think the poet choose a "Fly" and not something more exotic?

JOHN DONNE (1572–1631)

*John Donne was born into a Roman Catholic
family and attended Oxford and Cambridge
Universities. As a young man, in response to the
rabid anti-Catholic sentiments of Elizabethan
England, he abandoned his faith and determined to make his way in the court of Queen
Elizabeth I using his charm, learning, and poetic
abilities. In 1601, he destroyed his chances for
serious advancement after secretly marrying
Ann More, the niece of Sir Thomas Egerton, his
employer. Donne then struggled to make ends
meet, publishing treatises and poetry only occasionally. In 1615, after years of resistance, he
converted to Anglicanism and became a priest. Donne became renowned for his preach-
ing, and was soon considered one of the greatest preachers of the age. In 1621, he was
appointed Dean of St. Paul's Cathedral, a post he held until his death. His poetry, most
of which was published posthumously, is usually divided into two periods: his love poetry
is said to date from the beginning of his career, while his religious poems are said to date
from his later years. The greatest of the so-called metaphysical school of poets, Donne's
poetry is remarkable for its elaborate conceits (extended metaphors), unconventional
imagery, and highly compressed meanings.*

THE FLEA   [1633]

Mark but this flea, and mark in this
How little that which thou deny'st me is;
It sucked me first, and now sucks thee,
And in this flea our two bloods mingled be;
Thou know'st that this cannot be said   5
A sin, nor shame, nor loss of maidenhead;
    Yet this enjoys before it woo,
    And pampered swells with one blood made of two,
    And this, alas, is more than we would do.

Oh stay, three lives in one flea spare,   10
Where we almost, yea, more than married are.
This flea is you and I, and this
Our marriage bed and marriage temple is;
Though parents grudge, and you, we are met
And cloistered in these living walls of jet.   15
   Though use make you apt to kill me,
   Let not to that, self-murder added be,
   And sacrilege, three sins in killing three.

Cruel and sudden, hast thou since
Purpled thy nail in blood of innocence?   20
Wherein could this flea guilty be,
Except in that drop it sucked from thee?
Yet thou triumph'st and say'st that thou
Find'st not thyself, nor me, the weaker now;
   'Tis true. Then learn how false fears be;   25
   Just so much honor, when thou yield'st to me,
   Will waste, as this flea's death took life from thee.

► QUESTIONS FOR READING AND WRITING

1. What does the speaker in the poem want? Are you convinced he should get it?
2. Why does he believe that the flea unites him with his love? What does he mean by "Let not to that, self-murder added be, / And sacrilege, three sins in killing three"?
3. Each stanza begins with three rhyming pairs of lines or couplets and ends with three rhyming lines. How is your reading affected by this? Do you think this form conveys the meaning of the poem effectively?

DEATH, BE NOT PROUD   [1633]

Death, be not proud, though some have callèd thee
Mighty and dreadful, for thou art not so;
For those whom thou think'st thou dost overthrow
Die not, poor Death, nor yet canst thou kill me.
From rest and sleep, which but thy pictures be,   5
Much pleasure, then from thee much more must flow,
And soonest our best men with thee do go,
Rest of their bones, and soul's delivery.
Thou art slave to fate, chance, kings, and desperate men,
And dost with poison, war, and sickness dwell,   10
And poppy or charms can make us sleep as well,
And better than thy stroke; why swell'st thou then?
One short sleep past, we wake eternally
And death shall be no more; Death, thou shalt die.

➤ *QUESTIONS FOR READING AND WRITING*

1. Why do you think the speaker suggests that Death is proud? Do you agree?
   Explain.
2. The speaker concludes, "Death, thou shalt die." What is the speaker's reasoning to support this? Do you agree? Explain.
3. Compare this poem to John Keats's "When I Have Fears That I May Cease
   to Be" on page 191 or Philip Larkin's "Aubade" on page 199.

A VALEDICTION: FORBIDDING MOURNING   [1633]

As virtuous men pass mildly away,
And whisper to their souls to go,
Whilst some of their sad friends do say,
"The breath goes now," and some say "No,"

So let us melt, and make no noise,   5
No tear-floods, nor sigh-tempests move;
'Twere profanation of our joys
To tell the laity our love.

Moving of th' earth brings harms and fears;
Men reckon what it did and meant;   10
But trepidation of the spheres,
Though greater far, is innocent.

Dull sublunary lovers' love
(Whose soul is sense) cannot admit
Absence, because it doth remove   15
Those things which elemented it.

But we by a love so much refined
That ourselves know not what it is,
Inter-assurèd of the mind,
Care less, eyes, lips, and hands to miss.   20

Our two souls, therefore, which are one,
Though I must go, endure not yet
A breach, but an expansion,
Like gold to airy thinness beat.

If they be two, they are two so   25
As stiff twin compasses are two:
Thy soul, the fixed foot, makes no show
To move, but doth, if th' other do.

And though it in the center sit,
Yet when the other far doth roam,   30
It leans and harkens after it,
And grows erect as that comes home.

Such wilt thou be to me, who must,
Like th' other foot, obliquely run;
Thy firmness makes my circle just,   35
And makes me end where I begun.

➤ *QUESTIONS FOR READING AND WRITING*

1. The speaker says, "But we by a love so much refined / That ourselves know not what it is." What do you think he means?
2. Do you agree with the speaker's conclusion in this poem?

MARK DOTY (b.1953)

Mark Doty is the author of several collections of poems including Atlantis; Turtle, Swan; Bethlehem in Broad Daylight; *and* My Alexandria, *which won the National Book Critics Circle Award, the Los Angeles Times Book Award, the T. S. Eliot Award, and the National Poetry Series, and was a finalist for the National Book Award. Doty has also been the recipient of grants from the National Endowment for the Arts and the Guggenheim Foundation. He lives in Provincetown, Massachusetts.*

BRILLIANCE   [1993]

Maggie's taking care of a man
who's dying; he's attended to everything,
said goodbye to his parents,

paid off his credit card.
She says *Why don't you just*   5
run it up to the limit?

but he wants everything
squared away, no balance owed,
though he misses the pets

he's already found a home for   10
—he can't be around dogs or cats,
too much risk. He says,

I can't have anything.
She says, *A bowl of goldfish?*
He says he doesn't want to start   15

with anything and then describes
the kind he'd maybe like,
how their tails would fan

to a gold flaring. They talk
about hot jewel tones,   20
gold lacquer, say maybe

they'll go pick some out
though he can't go much of anywhere and then
abruptly he says *I can't love*

anything I can't finish.   25
He says it like he's had enough
of the whole scintillant world,

though what he means is
he'll never be satisfied and therefore
has established this discipline,   30

a kind of severe rehearsal.
That's where they leave it,
him looking out the window,

her knitting as she does because
she needs to do something.   35
Later he leaves a message:

Yes to the bowl of goldfish.
Meaning: let me go, if I have to,
in brilliance. In a story I read,

a Zen master who'd perfected   40
his detachment from the things of the world
remembered, at the moment of dying,

a deer he used to feed in the park,
and wondered who might care for it,
and at that instant was reborn   45

in the stunned flesh of a fawn.
So, Maggie's friend—
is he going out

into the last loved object
of his attention?   50
Fanning the veined translucence

of an opulent tail,
undulant in some uncapturable curve,
is he bronze chrysanthemums,

copper leaf, hurried darting,   55
doubloons, icon-colored fins
troubling the water?

➤ *QUESTIONS FOR READING AND WRITING*

1. Why do you think the dying man wants a bowl of goldfish?
2. To what extent is "Brilliance" an appropriate title for this poem?

PAUL LAURENCE DUNBAR

(1872–1906)

Paul Laurence Dunbar was born and raised in Dayton, Ohio. Both of his parents had been slaves. Dunbar excelled in high school, where he was the only African American in his class, and served both as the class president and class poet. While in high school, he worked as an editor at the Dayton Tattler, *a short-lived newspaper for blacks. His widowed mother's financial situation ruled out college, and, unable to find a position as a writer because of his race, he found work at a number of jobs (including one as an elevator operator), which allowed him the leisure to continue writing and publishing poems. By 1892 he had earned enough recognition that he could pursue a literary career. He wrote prolifically but was plagued by ill health. In 1906, at the age of 33, he died of tuberculosis. Though he is best known, for his poems, which were the first to incorporate African-American speech, Dunbar published numerous novels, short stories, and essays.*

WE WEAR THE MASK   [1895]

We wear the mask that grins and lies,
It hides our cheeks and shades our eyes—
This debt we pay to human guile;
With torn and bleeding hearts we smile,
And mouth with myriad subtleties.   5

Why should the world be overwise,
In counting all our tears and sighs?
Nay, let them only see us, while
    We wear the mask.

We smile, but, O great Christ, our cries   10
To thee from tortured souls arise.
We sing, but oh the clay is vile
Beneath our feet, and long the mile;
But let the world dream otherwise,
    We wear the mask!   15

➤ *QUESTIONS FOR READING AND WRITING*

1. Who is the "we" the speaker refers to?
2. What does the "mask" look like? What are the different forms it takes?
3. To what extent does the year in which the poem was published amplify its content?

T. S. ELIOT (1888–1965)

*Born to a wealthy family in St. Louis, Missouri,
T[homas] S[tearns] Eliot attended Harvard
University, where he studied literature as an
undergraduate, and, as a graduate student,
Sanskrit and philosophy. After further studies
at the Sorbonne and Oxford University, he settled in England in 1915, taking a job first at an
insurance company and later in publishing,
becoming a British citizen in 1926. Eliot, with
his first volume of poetry,* Prufrock and Other
Observations *(1917), and the 1922 publication of* The Waste Land, *transformed the landscape of modern poetry, shattering literary
conventions in order to give voice to what he felt was the spiritual emptiness of the
modern world. An influential critic, he also wrote verse plays, including* Murder in the
Cathedral *(1935) and* The Cocktail Party *(1949). He was awarded the Nobel Prize in
1948 and was one of the most influential poets of the twentieth century.*

THE LOVE SONG OF J. ALFRED PRUFROCK   [1917]

*S'io credessi che mia risposta fosse
a persona che mai tornasse al mondo,
questa fiamma staria senza più scosse.
Ma per ciò che giammai di questo fondo
non tornò vivo alcun, s'i'odo il vero,
senza tema d'infamia ti rispondo.*°   5

Let us go then, you and I,
When the evening is spread out against the sky
Like a patient etherised upon a table;
Let us go, through certain half-deserted streets,   10
The muttering retreats
Of restless nights in one-night cheap hotels

°The statement introducing the confession of the poet Guido da Montefeltro in Dante's *Inferno* (1321).
canto xxxii, 61–66. "If I thought I was speaking to someone who would go back to the world, this flame
would shake no more. But since nobody has ever gone back alive from this place, if what I hear is true.
I answer you without fear of infamy."

And sawdust restaurants with oyster-shells:
Streets that follow like a tedious argument
Of insidious intent   15
To lead you to an overwhelming question . . .
Oh, do not ask, "What is it?"
Let us go and make our visit.

In the room the women come and go
Talking of Michelangelo.°   20

The yellow fog that rubs its back upon the window-panes,
The yellow smoke that rubs its muzzle on the window-panes,
Licked its tongue into the corners of the evening,
Lingered upon the pools that stand in drains,
Let fall upon its back the soot that falls from chimneys,   25
Slipped by the terrace, made a sudden leap,
And seeing that it was a soft October night,
Curled once about the house, and fell asleep.

And indeed there will be time
For the yellow smoke that slides along the street   30
Rubbing its back upon the window-panes;
There will be time, there will be time
To prepare a face to meet the faces that you meet;
There will be time to murder and create,

And time for all the works and days° of hands   35
That lift and drop a question on your plate;
Time for you and time for me,
And time yet for a hundred indecisions,
And for a hundred visions and revisions,
Before the taking of a toast and tea.   40

In the room the women come and go
Talking of Michelangelo.

And indeed there will be time
To wonder, "Do I dare?" and, "Do I dare?"
Time to turn back and descend the stair,   45
With a bald spot in the middle of my hair—
(They will say: "How his hair is growing thin!")
My morning coat, my collar mounting firmly to the chin,
My necktie rich and modest, but asserted by a simple pin—
(They will say: "But how his arms and legs are thin!")   50

<hr>

°**Michelangelo** (1474–1564) the most famous artist of the Italian Renaissance   ³⁵**works and days** possibly an allusion to *Works and Days*, a poem giving practical advice on farming by the Greek poet Hestod (eighth century B.C.)

Do I dare
Disturb the universe?
In a minute there is time
For decisions and revisions which a minute will reverse.

For I have known them all already, known them all—   55
Have known the evenings, mornings, afternoons,
I have measured out my life with coffee spoons;
I know the voices dying with a dying fall
Beneath the music from a farther room.
　　So how should I presume?   60

And I have known the eyes already, known them all—
The eyes that fix you in a formulated phrase,
And when I am formulated, sprawling on a pin,
When I am pinned and wriggling on the wall,
Then how should I begin   65
To spit out all the butt-ends of my days and ways?
　　And how should I presume?

And I have known the arms already, known them all—
Arms that are braceleted and white and bare
(But in the lamplight, downed with light brown hair!°)   70
Is it perfume from a dress
That makes me so digress?

Arms that lie along a table, or wrap about a shawl.
　　And should I then presume?
　　And how should I begin?   75

　　　　　　　　　　· · · · ·

Shall I say, I have gone at dusk through narrow streets
And watched the smoke that rises from the pipes
Of lonely men in shirt-sleeves, leaning out of windows? . . .

I should have been a pair of ragged claws
Scuttling across the floors of silent seas.   80

　　　　　　　　　　· · · · ·

And the afternoon, the evening, sleeps so peacefully!
Smoothed by long fingers,
Asleep . . . tired . . . or it malingers,
Stretched on the floor, here beside you and me.
Should I, after tea and cakes and ices,   85
Have the strength to force the moment to its crisis?

°see Shakespeare's *Twelfth Night* (1623), Act I Scene I 1–4

But though I have wept and fasted, wept and prayed,
Though I have seen my head (grown slightly bald) brought in upon a platter,°
I am no prophet—and here's no great matter;
I have seen the moment of my greatness flicker,   90
And I have seen the eternal Footman hold my coat, and snicker,
And in short, I was afraid.

And would it have been worth it, after all,
After the cups, the marmalade, the tea,
Among the porcelain, among some talk of you and me,   95
Would it have been worth while,
To have bitten off the matter with a smile,
To have squeezed the universe into a ball°
To roll it toward some overwhelming question,
To say: "I am Lazarus,° come from the dead   100
Come back to tell you all, I shall tell you all"—
If one, settling a pillow by her head,
     Should say: "That is not what I meant at all.
     That is not it, at all."

And would it have been worth it, after all,   105
Would it have been worth while,
After the sunsets and the dooryards and the sprinkled streets,
After the novels, after the teacups, after the skirts that trail along the floor—
And this, and so much more?—

It is impossible to say just what I mean!   110
But as if a magic lantern threw the nerves in patterns on a screen:
Would it have been worth while
If one, settling a pillow or throwing off a shawl,
And turning toward the window, should say:
     "That is not it at all,   115
     That is not what I meant, at all."

                              . . . . .

No! I am not Prince Hamlet, nor was meant to be;
Am an attendant lord, one that will do
To swell a progress, start a scene or two,
Advise the prince; no doubt, an easy tool,   120
Deferential, glad to be of use,
Politic, cautious, and meticulous;
Full of high sentence, but a bit obtuse;
At times, indeed, almost ridiculous—
Almost, at times, the Fool.   125

---

[88] An allusion to John the Baptist, the New Testament prophet, whose head was presented to Queen
Herodias on a charger Matthew 14:3–11.   [98]see Andrew Marvell's "To His Coy Mistress" (1641),
lines 41–42, p. 211.   [100]**Lazarus** the man raised by Jesus from the dead. John 11:1–44.

I grow old . . . I grow old . . .
I shall wear the bottoms of my trousers rolled.

Shall I part my hair behind? Do I dare to eat a peach?
I shall wear white flannel trousers, and walk upon the beach.
I have heard the mermaids singing, each to each.   130

I do not think that they will sing to me.

I have seen them riding seaward on the waves
Combing the white hair of the waves blown back
When the wind blows the water white and black.

We have lingered in the chambers of the sea   135
By sea-girls wreathed with seaweed red and brown
Till human voices wake us, and we drown.

▶ *QUESTIONS FOR READING AND WRITING*

1. What is the tone of the poem? How does the language in the poem convey that tone? Is this a love song, as the title indicates?
2. Who is J. Alfred Prufrock? What is his world like? He says, "I have measured out my life with coffee spoons." What do you think he means? Find other images in the poem that convey his self-image.
3. What does he mean when he says, "Do I dare / Disturb the universe?" What is he afraid of?
4. Do you ever feel like you need "To prepare a face to meet the faces that you meet"? If so, to what extent does that help you understand J. Alfred Prufrock—and this poem?

MARTÍN ESPADA (b. 1957)

Martín Espada was born in Brooklyn, New York, of Puerto Rican ancestry. In 1991, he received the Peterson Poetry Prize for Rebellion in the Circle of a Lover's Hands. *In addition to writing poetry, he works as a lawyer and often defends the civil rights of immigrants. He lives in Boston.*

LATIN NIGHT AT THE PAWNSHOP

Chelsea, Massachusetts
Christmas, 1987   [1987]

The apparition of a salsa band
gleaming in the Liberty Loan
pawnshop window:

Golden trumpet,
silver trombone,   5
congas, maracas, tambourine,
all with price tags dangling
like the city morgue ticket
on a dead man's toe.

➤ QUESTIONS FOR READING AND WRITING

1. In what way does Christmas provide an important context for this poem?
2. How do the images in the pawnshop window reflect people's lives—and deaths?

LAWRENCE FERLINGHETTI (b. 1919)

Lawrence Ferlinghetti was born in Yonkers, New York. His father died before he was born, and his mother was institutionalized following a severe mental breakdown. Shuttled between relatives, he lived in France and a public orphanage before settling with a rich family in Bronxville, New York, where his aunt was working as a governess. After attending the University of North Carolina, where he majored in journalism, Ferlinghetti enlisted in the navy. During World War II, he served as a commander in the Normandy invasion, and afterward took advantage of the G.I. Bill, *earning a master's degree from Columbia University in 1948 and a doctorate from the Sorbonne in Paris in 1951. Returning to the United States, he settled in San Francisco where he cofounded* City Lights *magazine, the City Lights Pocket Book Shop, and the City Lights Press. The store—the first in the country to specialize in paperbacks—and the press became the focal point of the Beat Generation—a group of enormously influential American writers and artists that included Allen Ginsberg, Jack Kerouac, and William Burroughs. A prolific poet, playwright, and editor, Ferlinghetti's most famous work continues to be his collection of poems,* A Coney Island of the Mind *(1958), which, with its embrace of open-form and colloquial speech, is considered one of the key works of the Beat movement. Today,*

Ferlinghetti continues to operate the City Lights bookstore when he is not traveling giving poetry readings. "Constantly Risking Absurdity" is taken from A Coney Island of the Mind.

CONSTANTLY RISKING ABSURDITY   [1958]

Constantly risking absurdity
                              and death
              whenever he performs
                            above the heads
                                        of his audience   5
              the poet like an acrobat
                                climbs on rime
                                    to a high wire of his own making
              and balancing on eyebeams
                                    above a sea of faces   10
                  paces his way
                                to the other side of day
              performing entrechats

                              and sleight-of-foot tricks
              and other high theatrics   15

                          and all without mistaking
                  any thing
                            for what it may not be

    For he's the super realist
                              who must perforce perceive   20
                  taut truth
                            before the taking of each stance or step
          in his supposed advance
                              toward that still higher perch
      where Beauty stands and waits   25
                          with gravity
                                to start her death-defying leap

    And he
            a little charleychaplin man
                        who may or may not catch   30
              her fair eternal form
                          spreadeagled in the empty air
          of existence

➤ QUESTIONS FOR READING AND WRITING

1. The speaker compares a poet to an acrobat. In what way is the structure of the poem like acrobatics? Does the comparison work for you?
2. To what extent is the poet a "super realist" who tries to catch "Beauty"?

ROBERT FRANCIS (1901–1987)

Robert Francis was born in Upland, Pennsylvania, and graduated from Harvard University in 1923. A professional writer his entire life, he toured throughout the United States teaching writing workshops and delivering lectures. His collections of poetry include: Stand With Me *(1936),* The Sound I Listened For *(1944), and* Robert Francis: Collected Poems 1936–1976 *(1976). His autobiography* The Trouble with Francis *was published in 1971.*

PITCHER   [1960]

His art is eccentricity, his aim
How not to hit the mark he seems to aim at,

His passion how to avoid the obvious,
His technique how to vary the avoidance.

The others throw to be comprehended. He   5
Throws to be a moment misunderstood.

Yet not too much. Not errant, arrant, wild,
But every seeming aberration willed.

Not to, yet still, still to communicate
Making the batter understand too late.   10

▶ QUESTIONS FOR READING AND WRITING

1. In what way is the pitcher's "aim / How not to hit the mark he seems to aim at"?
2. Why would he want to make "the batter understand too late"?

ROBERT FROST (1874–1963)

Robert Frost was born in San Francisco, California, to a headmaster and schoolteacher who met at a tiny private school in Pennsylvania. When his father died of tuberculosis in 1885, his mother returned the family to New England. Frost attended a local high school where, together with the woman he would eventually marry, Elinor White, he served as class valedictorian. It was in high school, where he was known as the class poet, that Frost seriously began writing poetry. In the many years that followed, Frost continued to write while he attended college (short stints at Dartmouth and Harvard) and held a series of odd jobs, including work as a cobbler, journalist, teacher, and at a cotton mill. From 1900 to 1905, he lived on a farm in Derry, New Hampshire, purchased for him by his grandfather, but financial hardships—he and Elinor had five children by this point— forced him to return to teaching. In 1912, frustrated by his inability to publish in the United States, Frost moved his family to England, where he published his first two books of poetry, A Boy's Will *(1913) and* North of Boston *(1914). By the time he returned to the United States in 1915, he was well on his way to*

becoming the most famous American poet of the century. In 1961, an infirm Frost read his poem "The Gift Outright" at the inauguration of President John F. Kennedy. His poetry, which takes much of its inspiration from the countryside of New England, is often deceptively simple, as it artfully and effortlessly weaves together traditional metrical forms with colloquial American speech.

MENDING WALL

[1914]

Something there is that doesn't love a wall,
That sends the frozen-ground-swell under it,
And spills the upper boulders in the sun;
And makes gaps even two can pass abreast.
The work of hunters is another thing: 5
I have come after them and made repair
Where they have left not one stone on a stone,
But they would have the rabbit out of hiding,
To please the yelping dogs. The gaps I mean,
No one has seen them made or heard them made,   10
But at spring mending-time we find them there.
I let my neighbor know beyond the hill;
And on a day we meet to walk the line
And set the wall between us once again.
We keep the wall between us as we go.   15
To each the boulders that have fallen to each.
And some are loaves and some so nearly balls
We have to use a spell to make them balance:
"Stay where you are until our backs are turned!"
We wear our fingers rough with handling them.   20
Oh, just another kind of outdoor game,
One on a side. It comes to little more:

There where it is we do not need the wall:
He is all pine and I am apple orchard.
My apple trees will never get across   25
And eat the cones under his pines, I tell him.
He only says, "Good fences make good neighbors."
Spring is the mischief in me, and I wonder
If I could put a notion in his head:
"*Why* do they make good neighbors? Isn't it   30
Where there are cows? But here there are no cows.
Before I built a wall I'd ask to know
What I was walling in or walling out,
And to whom I was like to give offense.
Something there is that doesn't love a wall,   35
That wants it down." I could say "Elves" to him,
But it's not elves exactly, and I'd rather
He said it for himself. I see him there
Bringing a stone grasped firmly by the top
In each hand, like an old-stone savage armed.   40
He moves in darkness as it seems to me,
Not of woods only and the shade of trees.
He will not go behind his father's saying,
And he likes having thought of it so well
He says again, "Good fences make good neighbors."   45

➤ QUESTIONS FOR READING AND WRITING

1. Have you ever felt walled in or out? Explain.
2. What is the "Something" in "Something there is that doesn't love a wall"?
3. What does the line "He moves in darkness as it seems to me" mean to you?
4. Does the speaker in the poem agree that "Good fences make good neighbors"? Do you?

FIRE AND ICE   [1923]

Some say the world will end in fire,
Some say in ice.
From what I've tasted of desire
I hold with those who favor fire.
But if I had to perish twice,   5
I think I know enough of hate
To say that for destruction ice
Is also great
And would suffice.

➤ QUESTIONS FOR READING AND WRITING

1. What do you think fire and ice symbolize in this poem?

2. How are you affected by the rhyme scheme? In what way does it serve as a vehicle for the poem's meaning?

"OUT, OUT —"   [1916]

The buzz saw snarled and rattled in the yard
And made dust and dropped stove-length sticks of wood,
Sweet-scented stuff when the breeze drew across it.
And from there those that lifted eyes could count
Five mountain ranges one behind the other   5
Under the sunset far into Vermont.
And the saw snarled and rattled, snarled and rattled,
As it ran light, or had to bear a load.
And nothing happened: day was all but done.
Call it a day, I wish they might have said   10
To please the boy by giving him the half hour
That a boy counts so much when saved from work.
His sister stood beside them in her apron
To tell them "Supper." At the word, the saw,
As if to prove saws knew what supper meant,   15
Leaped out at the boy's hand, or seemed to leap—
He must have given the hand. However it was,
Neither refused the meeting. But the hand!
The boy's first outcry was a rueful laugh,
As he swung toward them holding up the hand   20
Half in appeal, but half as if to keep
The life from spilling. Then the boy saw all—
Since he was old enough to know, big boy
Doing a man's work, though a child at heart—
He saw all spoiled. "Don't let him cut my hand off—   25
The doctor, when he comes. Don't let him, sister!"
So. But the hand was gone already.
The doctor put him in the dark of ether.
He lay and puffed his lips out with his breath.
And then—the watcher at his pulse took fright.   30
No one believed. They listened at his heart.
Little—less—nothing!—and that ended it.
No more to build on there. And they, since they
Were not the one dead, turned to their affairs.

➤ QUESTIONS FOR READING AND WRITING

1. To what extent does your own experience affect your response to this poem?
2. In what way does the setting of the poem emphasize what happens to the boy?

3. At the end of the poem, the speaker says, "And they, since they / Were not the one dead, turned to their affairs." Do you think "they" are being heartless? Why or why not?

4. The title of this poem is taken from Shakespeare's play *Macbeth*. When he receives the news that his young wife is dead, Macbeth begins a soliloquy that includes the line "Out, out, brief candle!" See if you can find the rest of this soliloquy (Macbeth, act 5, scene 5) and compare it to this poem.

ELIZABETH GAFFNEY (b. 1953)

Elizabeth Gaffney's poems have appeared in Wordsmith, Southern Poetry Review, College English, Descant, Wind, *and other publications. A graduate of Fordham University, she has a doctorate from the State University of New York, at Stony Brook and teaches at SUNY Westchester Community College. She lives in Pelham, New York, with her husband and three children.*

LOSSES THAT TURN UP IN DREAMS

[1992]

The notebook I left on a windowsill
in Keating Hall two years ago
floats back to me full of poems.
The silver pin shaped like a bird's wings,
my mother's gold chain   5
stolen with the burnished purse I loved,
its leather worn to smoothness
from years of use—in dreams
appear again my homing pigeons.

Their familiar feel reassures me   10
that nothing's ever gone for good;
the sunglasses, pens, umbrellas,
the scarf of red and blue challis,
the lost socks, the trivial objects
I weep for are losses so palpable,   15

all equal in the land of dreams,
where the baby I lost one October night
comes home to nest, poor ghost,
and my mother, grandmother, uncles

crowd small rooms, and I am one   20
with the tree that bloomed on my birthday,
a daughter, filling up with milk and love.

➤ QUESTIONS FOR READING AND WRITING

1. What losses is the speaker talking about?
2. In what way are the objects that she mentions "homing pigeons"? Can you
   think of objects in your own life that are "homing pigeons"?
3. What does she mean by "I am one / with the tree that bloomed on my
   birthday"?

ALLEN GINSBERG (1926–1997)

*Allen Ginsberg was born in Newark, New
Jersey, and educated at Columbia University.
He eventually moved to San Francisco, where
he was one of the central figures of the so-called
"beat generation" of the 1950s. In the 1960s, he
was arrested several times for his political
activism and outspoken homosexuality. He
published many volumes of his collected works
including* The Fall of America: Poems of
These States *(1974), which won the National
Book Award.*

A SUPERMARKET IN CALIFORNIA   [1956]

What thoughts I have of you tonight, Walt Whitman, for I walked down the
sidestreets under the trees with a headache self-conscious looking at the full
moon.

In my hungry fatigue, and shopping for images, I went into the neon fruit
supermarket, dreaming of your enumerations!

What peaches and what penumbras! Whole families shopping at night!
Aisles full of husbands! Wives in the avocados, babies in the tomatoes!—and
you, García Lorca, what were you doing down by the watermelons?

I saw you, Walt Whitman, childless, lonely old grubber, poking among the
meats in the refrigerator and eyeing the grocery boys.

I heard you asking questions of each: Who killed the pork chops? What price
bananas? Are you my Angel?   5

I wandered in and out of the brilliant stacks of cans following you, and followed in my imagination by the store detective.

We strode down the open corridors together in our solitary fancy tasting artichokes, possessing every frozen delicacy, and never passing the cashier.

Where are we going, Walt Whitman? The doors close in an hour. Which way does your beard point tonight?

(I touch your book and dream of our odyssey in the supermarket and feel absurd.)

Will we walk all night through solitary streets? The trees add shade to shade, lights out in the houses, we'll both be lonely.   10

Will we stroll dreaming of the lost America of love past blue automobiles in driveways, home to our silent cottage?

Ah, dear father, graybeard, lonely old courage-teacher, what America did you have when Charon quit poling his ferry and you got out on a smoking bank and stood watching the boat disappear on the black waters of Lethe?

▶ *QUESTIONS FOR READING AND WRITING*

1. The speaker makes a reference to Walt Whitman. Compare this poem to the excerpt from *Song of Myself* on page 265.
2. Do you think a supermarket is an appropriate setting for a poem? Explain.

NIKKI GIOVANNI (b. 1943)

One of the most prominent poets to emerge from the black literary movement of the 1960s, Nikki Giovanni was born in Knoxville, Tennessee. Her father was a probation officer, and her mother was a social worker. Growing up, she was particularly close to her maternal grandmother and spent summers with her in Knoxville even after her family moved to Cincinnati, Ohio. It was while she was at Fisk University in Nashville that she grew politically aware, serving in Fisk's chapter of the SNCC (Student Nonviolent Coordinating Committee), which promoted the concept of "black power" in confronting the social and economic problems of the time. Her first books of poetry, Black Feeling and Black Talk *(1968),* Black Judgment *(1968), and* Re: Creation *(1970), were enormously successful and brought her much acclaim. A vibrant personality, she has toured the United States giving lectures and reading her poetry, and has recorded numerous albums of her poetry, including* Truth Is on Its Way, *which was*

the best-selling spoken-word album of 1971. Though her more recent work is more introspective and less political, she remains deeply committed to the transforming power of poetry. She has said, "If everybody became a poet, the world would be so much better." Her latest book of poetry, Love Poems, *was published in 1997.*

NIKKI-ROSA   [1968]

childhood remembrances are always a drag
if you're Black
you already remember things like living in Woodlawn
with no inside toilet
and if you become famous or something   5
they never talk about how happy you were to have your mother
all to yourself and
how good the water felt when you got your bath from one of those
big tubs that folk in chicago barbecue in
and somehow when you talk about home   10
it never gets across how much you
understood their feelings
as the whole family attended meetings about Hollydale
and even though you remember
your biographers never understand   15
your father's pain as he sells his stock
and another dream goes
and though you're poor it isn't poverty that
concerns you
and though they fought a lot   20
it isn't your father's drinking that makes any difference
but only that everybody is together and you
and your sister have happy birthdays and very good christmasses
and I really hope no white person ever has cause to write about me
because they never understand Black love is Black wealth and they'll   25
probably talk about my hard childhood and never understand that
all the while I was quite happy

➤ QUESTIONS FOR READING AND WRITING

1. The poem opens with "childhood remembrances are always a drag." Are childhood remembrances a drag for you? Explain.
2. Do you think there is a difference between "childhood remembrances" and childhood itself? Explain.
3. Why does the speaker say, "I really hope no white person ever has cause to write about me"?

LOUISE GLUCK (b. 1943)

Louise Gluck was born in New York City and studied at Sarah Lawrence College and Columbia University. Her collections of poems include Firstborn *(1969),* The House on Marshland *(1975),* Descending Figure *(1980),* The Triumph of Achilles *(1985), and* Ararat *(1990).*

SNOWDROPS   [1992]

Do you know what I was, how I lived? You know
what despair is; then
winter should have meaning for you.

I did not expect to survive,
earth suppressing me. I didn't expect   5
to waken again, to feel
in damp earth my body
able to respond again, remembering
after so long how to open again
in the cold light   10
of earliest spring—

afraid, yes, but among you again
crying yes risk joy

in the raw wind of the new world.

➤ QUESTIONS FOR READING AND WRITING

1. Who is the speaker? In what way does the title describe the speaker's plight?
2. What does the phrase "yes risk joy" mean to you? How has the speaker changed?

JUDY GRAHN (b. 1940)

Judy Grahn was born in Chicago, Illinois. Her father worked as a cook, and her mother was a photographer's assistant. In her twenties, she worked in a series of odd jobs, including short-order cook, artist's model, and nurse's aide before starting the Women's Press Collective with artist Wendy Cadden in Oakland, California, in 1969. In the 1980s, although she was already a well-established poet, she returned to school at San Francisco State University and earned a bachelor's degree. She currently teaches in the New College of California in San Francisco, where she helped create the Gay and Lesbian Studies department. Her publications include The Work of a Common Woman: The Collected Poetry of Judy Grahn, 1964–1977 *(1978),* The Queen of Wands *(1982), and a collection of nonfiction,* Blood and Bread and Roses *(1986).*

ELLA, IN A SQUARE APRON, ALONG HIGHWAY 80   [1971]

She's a copperheaded waitress,
tired and sharp-worded, she hides
her bad brown tooth behind a wicked
smile, and flicks her ass
out of habit, to fend off the pass   5
that passes for affection.
She keeps her mind the way men
keep a knife—keen to strip the game
down to her size. She has a thin spine,
swallows her eggs cold, and tells lies.   10
She slaps a wet rag at the truck drivers
if they should complain. She understands
the necessity for pain, turns away
the smaller tips, out of pride, and
keeps a flask under the counter. Once,   15
she shot a lover who misused her child.
Before she got out of jail, the courts had pounced
and given the child away. Like some isolated lake,
her flat blue eyes take care of their own stark
bottoms. Her hands are nervous, curled, ready   20
to scrape.
This common woman is as common
as a rattlesnake.

➤ QUESTIONS FOR READING AND WRITING

1. Who is Ella? What words or phrases in the poem help you see her?
2. What does the speaker mean by "The common woman is as common / as a rattlesnake"?

MARILYN HACKER (b. 1942)

Marilyn Hacker is a native of New York City. Her collections of poetry include Presentation Piece *(1974),* Separations *(1976),* Taking Notice *(1980), which includes the poem below, "Sonnet Ending with a Film Subtitle," and* Selected Poems *(1994). She has received a National Book Award (1975), the Lenore Marshall Poetry Prize for* Winter Numbers *(1994), and a Guggenheim Fellowship.*

SONNET ENDING WITH A FILM SUBTITLE   [1976]

for Judith Landry

Life has its nauseating ironies:
The good die young, as often has been shown;
Chaste spouses catch Venereal Disease;
And feminists sit by the telephone.
Last night was rather bleak, tonight is starker.   5
I may stare at the wall till half-past-one.
My friends are all convinced Dorthy Parker
Lives, but is not well, in Marylebone.
I wish that I could imitate my betters
And fortify my rhetoric with guns.   10
Some day we women all will break our fetters
And raise our daughters to be Lesbians.
(I wonder if the bastard kept my letters?)
Here follow untranslatable French puns.

➤ QUESTIONS FOR READING AND WRITING

1. Describe the tone of this sonnet. Do you agree with its message? Explain.
2. Compare this sonnet to Shakespeare's sonnet "Let Me Not to the Marriage of True Minds" on page 250 and Elizabeth Barrett Browning's "How Do I Love Thee" on page 140.

THOMAS HARDY (1840–1928)

Thomas Hardy was born near Dorchester in southwestern England. Apprenticed to an architect at the age of 15, Hardy received very little formal schooling outside of the local schools he attended as a boy, but improved himself by reading in his spare time. Unhappy as an architect, he began writing fiction and poetry and, though his first novel was not a success, the success of his second, Under the Greenwood Tree *(1872), allowed him to devote himself to a literary career. Hardy followed this with a string of 11 remarkable novels set in his native Dorchester (called Wessex in the novels) including* Far from the Madding Crowd *(1874),* The Return of the Native *(1879),* The Mayor of Casterbridge *(1887), and* Tess of the D'Ubervilles *(1891). These often bleak novels share a common theme—that human destiny is controlled not by human will but by forces beyond humankind's control. Disillusioned after the hostile reception to* Jude the Obscure *(1895), considered by many modern critics to be his greatest work, Hardy turned to writing highly original poetry that often explored the same themes as his novels. His* Collected Poems *was published in 1931.*

THE MAN HE KILLED

[1902]

      Had he and I but met
      By some old ancient inn,
We should have sat us down to wet
      Right many a nipperkin!

      But ranged as infantry,   5
      And staring face to face,
I shot at him as he at me,
      And killed him in his place.

      I shot him dead because—
      Because he was my foe.   10
Just so: my foe of course he was;
      That's clear enough; although

      He thought he'd 'list, perhaps,
      Off-hand-like—just as I—
Was out of work—had sold his traps—   15
      No other reason why.

      Yes; quaint and curious war is!
      You shoot a fellow down
You'd treat, if met where any bar is,
      Or help to half-a-crown.   20

> ## QUESTIONS FOR READING AND WRITING

1. Who is the speaker in the poem? What does his speech tell you about him?
2. Do you think he is trying to justify his actions? Explain.
3. What do you think he concludes? To what extent do you agree?
4. Compare this poem to Stephen Crane's "War Is Kind" on page 61.

HAP   [1866]

If but some vengeful god would call to me
From up the sky, and laugh: "Thou suffering thing,
Know that thy sorrow is my ecstasy,
That thy love's loss is my hate's profiting!"

Then would I bear it, clench myself, and die,   5
Steeled by the sense of ire unmerited;
Half-eased in that a Powerfuller than I
Had willed and meted me the tears I shed.

But not so. How arrives it joy lies slain,
And why unblooms the best hope ever sown?   10
—Crass Casualty obstructs the sun and rain,
And dicing Time for gladness casts a moan . . .
These purblind Doomsters had as readily strown
Blisses about my pilgrimage as pain.

> ## QUESTIONS FOR READING AND WRITING

1. Why do you think the speaker wishes for a "vengeful god"? What does he suggest we have instead?
2. Compare this poem to Stephen Crane's "A Man Said to the Universe" on page 150.

JOY HARJO (b. 1951)

Joy Harjo was born in Tulsa, Oklahoma, and is a member of the Creek tribe. Her work is often derived from jazz, story, and prayer. She frequently performs her own poetry and plays saxophone with her band, Poetic Justice. Harjo teaches at the University of New Mexico.

Song for the Deer and Myself to Return On [1990]

This morning when I looked out the roof window
before dawn and a few stars were still caught
in the fragile weft of ebony night
I was overwhelmed. I sang the song Louis taught me:
a song to call the deer in Creek, when hunting,   5
and I am certainly hunting something as magic as deer
in this city far from the hammock of my mother's belly.
It works, of course, and deer came into this room
and wondered at finding themselves
in a house near downtown Denver.   10
Now the deer and I are trying to figure out a song
to get them back, to get all of us back,
because if it works I'm going with them.
And it's too early to call Louis
and nearly too late to go home.   15

➤ QUESTIONS FOR READING AND WRITING

1. Why do you think the speaker sings a song to call the deer?
2. She says "It works, of course, and deer came into this room." Do they?
3. What does the speaker mean by "the deer and I are trying to figure out a
   song to . . . get all of us back"?

SEAMUS HEANEY (b. 1939)

*Sometimes referred to as Ireland's greatest poet
since Yeats, Seamus Heaney was born on a
farm in County Derry in Northern Ireland. He
graduated from Queen's University in Belfast
in 1961. He published his first book of poetry,*
Eleven Poems, *in 1965. He was awarded the
Nobel Prize in 1995. Currently he divides his
time between Dublin and the United States,
where he holds a teaching position at Harvard
University. The rich, and often violent, history
of Ireland and its people is the concern of much
of his poetry. His critically acclaimed verse
translation of* Beowulf *was published in 2000,
and his latest bood of poems,* Electric Light *in 2001.*

Digging [1965]

Between my finger and my thumb
The squat pen rests; snug as a gun.

Under my window, a clean rasping sound
When the spade sinks into gravelly ground:
My father, digging. I look down   5

Till his straining rump among the flowerbeds
Bends low, comes up twenty years away
Stooping in rhythm through potato drills
Where he was digging.

The coarse boot nestled on the lug, the shaft   10
Against the inside knee was levered firmly.
He rooted out tall tops, buried the bright edge deep
To scatter new potatoes that we picked
Loving their cool hardness in our hands.

By God, the old man could handle a spade.   15
Just like his old man.

My grandfather cut more turf in a day
Than any other man on Toner's bog.
Once I carried him milk in a bottle
Corked sloppily with paper. He straightened up   20
To drink it, then fell to right away

Nicking and slicing neatly, heaving sods
Over his shoulder, going down and down
For the good turf. Digging.

The cold smell of potato mould, the squelch and slap   25
Of soggy peat, the curt cuts of an edge
Through living roots awaken in my head.
But I've no spade to follow men like them.

Between my finger and my thumb
The squat pen rests.   30
I'll dig with it.

> ## ► QUESTIONS FOR READING AND WRITING

1. What kind of work did the speaker's father and grandfather do? To
   what extent is your response to this poem influenced by your own background?
2. The speaker begins the poem by saying, "The squat pen rests; snug as a
   gun." But in the last stanza he says of the squat pen, "I'll dig with it." What
   kind of work does he do and what does he mean?

MID-TERM BREAK   [1965]

I sat all morning in the college sick bay
Counting bells knelling classes to a close.
At two o'clock our neighbors drove me home.

In the porch I met my father crying—
He had always taken funerals in his stride—   5
And Big Jim Evans saying it was a hard blow.

The baby cooed and laughed and rocked the pram
When I came in, and I was embarrassed
By old men standing up to shake my hand

And tell me they were "sorry for my trouble."   10
Whispers informed strangers I was the eldest,
Away at school, as my mother held my hand

In hers and coughed out angry tearless sighs.
At ten o'clock the ambulance arrived
With the corpse, stanched and bandaged by the nurses.   15

Next morning I went up into the room. Snowdrops
And candles soothed the bedside; I saw him
For the first time in six weeks. Paler now,

Wearing a poppy bruise on his left temple.
He lay in the four foot box as in his cot.   20
No gaudy scars, the bumper knocked him clear.

A four foot box, a foot for every year.

▶ QUESTIONS FOR READING AND WRITING

1. The boy is told by the old men that they are "'sorry for [his] trouble.'"
   What trouble is that? What's happened here?
2. To what extent is your response to this poem affected by your own experience?
3. The last line of the poem, "A four foot box, a foot for every year," stands by
   itself. What is your reaction to it? In what ways is it appropriate to wrap up
   the poem?

GERARD MANLEY HOPKINS (1844–1889)

*Gerard Manley Hopkins was born in Stratford, Essex. He graduated from Balliol
College, Oxford, in 1867. Born an Anglican he became a Roman Catholic while a student at Oxford, and in 1877 he was ordained a Jesuit priest. After serving in several*

parishes, he taught classics at Stonyhurst College, and eventually held the chair of Greek at the Royal University, Dublin, until his death. His complete works were published 19 years after his death by friend and poet Robert Bridges. His work is characterized by rich, complex sounds and images.

PIED° BEAUTY   [1877]

Glory be to God for dappled things—
For skies of couple-colour as a brinded° cow;
    For rose-moles all in stipple upon trout that swim;
Fresh-firecoal chestnut-falls; finches' wings;
Landscape plotted and pieced—fold, fallow, and plough;   5
    And áll trádes, their gear and tackle and trim.°

All things counter, original, spare,° strange;
Whatever is fickle, freckled (who knows how?)
    With swift, slow; sweet, sour; adazzle, dim;
He fathers-forth whose beauty is past change: 10
                    Praise him.

pied variegated   **²brinded** brindled, streaked   **⁶gear and tackle and trim** equipment   **⁷counter, original, spare** unusual

➤ QUESTIONS FOR READING AND WRITING

1. Read the poem aloud. How do the sounds of the poem affect your response?
2. What do you think the speaker means when he says, "He fathers-forth whose beauty is past change"?

THE WINDHOVER°   [1877]

        To Christ Our Lord

I caught this morning morning's minion, king-
    dom of daylight's dauphin, dapple-dawn-drawn Falcon, in his riding
    Of the rolling level underneath him steady air, and striding

windhover a windhover is a small falcon

High there, how he rung upon the rein of a wimpling wing
In his ecstasy! then off, off forth on swing,   5
    As a skate's heel sweeps smooth on a bow-bend: the hurl and gliding
    Rebuffed the big wind. My heart in hiding
Stirred for a bird, —the achieve of, the mastery of the thing!

Brute beauty and valor and act, oh, air, pride, plume, here
    Buckle! AND the fire that breaks from thee then, a billion   10
Times told lovelier, more dangerous, O my chevalier!

    No wonder of it: shéer plód makes plow down sillion°
Shine, and blue-bleak embers, ah my dear,
    Fall, gall themselves, and gash gold-vermilion.

¹²**sillion** furrow

➤ QUESTIONS FOR READING AND WRITING

1. Describe the sounds of this poem. How do they compare with "Pied Beauty"?
2. What does the speaker mean when he says, "My heart in hiding / Stirred for a bird"?

A. E. HOUSMAN (1859–1936)

An important scholar of Latin as well as a celebrated poet, A[lfred] E[dward] Housman was born in the village of Fockbury in Worcestershire, England. A brilliant student at Oxford University, Housman inexplicably failed his final exams. Determined to redeem himself after his poor showing, he wrote scholarly articles while working at night as a civil servant in the patent office. His brilliant scholarship eventually won him positions at the University of London and Cambridge University. During his life he published only two slim volumes of poetry, A Shropshire Lad *(1898) and* Last Poems *(1922). His poems are tinged with melancholy, often dealing with themes of lost love and youth. His* Complete Poems, *which includes verses that were published posthumously, was published in 1956. Housman's life story was the subject of a play "The Invention of Love" by Tom Stoppard. It was produced on Broadway in 2001.*

WHEN I WAS ONE-AND-TWENTY   [1898]

When I was one-and-twenty
    I heard a wise man say,

"Give crowns and pounds and guineas
    But not your heart away;
Give pearls away and rubies   5
    But keep your fancy free."
But I was one-and-twenty,
    No use to talk to me.

When I was one-and-twenty
    I heard him say again,   10
"The heart out of the bosom
    Was never given in vain;
'Tis paid with sighs a plenty
    And sold for endless rue."
And I am two-and-twenty,   15
    And oh, 'tis true, 'tis true.

➤ *QUESTIONS FOR READING AND WRITING*

1. What do you think of the wise man's advice in the first stanza?
2. Would you have taken his advice? Explain.
3. What's happened to the speaker? Does he regret his decision? Would you?

TO AN ATHLETE DYING YOUNG   [1896]

The time you won your town the race
We chaired you through the market-place;
Man and boy stood cheering by,
And home we brought you shoulder-high.

To-day, the road all runners come,   5
Shoulder-high we bring you home,
And set you at your threshold down,
Townsman of a stiller town.

Smart lad, to slip betimes away
From fields where glory does not stay   10
And early though the laurel grows
It withers quicker than the rose.

Eyes the shady night has shut
Cannot see the record cut,
And silence sounds no worse than cheers   15
After earth has stopped the ears:

Now you will not swell the rout
Of lads that wore their honours out,
Runners whom renown outran
And the name died before the man.   20

So set, before its echoes fade,
The fleet foot on the sill of shade,

And hold to the low lintel up
The still-defended challenge-cup.

And round that early-laurelled head   25
Will flock to gaze the strengthless dead
And find unwithered on its curls
The garland briefer than a girl's.

► *QUESTIONS FOR READING AND WRITING*

1. Who is the "you" addressed by the speaker? Both the first and second stan-
   zas make reference to carrying the subject "shoulder-high." What does the
   term mean in each stanza? In what way is it ironic?
2. Dying young is not a pleasant prospect. But what does the speaker mean
   by "Now you will not swell the rout / Of lads that wore their honours out"?
   Is there a positive side to dying young? Explain.

LANGSTON HUGHES (1902–1967)

*One of the most important figures of the
Harlem Renaissance—a movement of African-
American artists, writers, poets, and musicians
in the 1920s and 1930s centered in the Harlem
neighborhood of New York City—Langston
Hughes was born in Joplin, Missouri, and
graduated from Lincoln University in
Pennsylvania. As a young man, he traveled the
world as a merchant seaman, visiting Africa
and living for a time in Paris and Rome. A
poet, writer of fiction, playwright, lyricist,
editor, critic, and essayist, Hughes published
two volumes of his autobiography,* The Big Sea
(1940) and I Wonder as I Wander *(1956). Hughes's work, which is filled with the
sounds and music of the African-American experience, has influenced generations of
American writers.*

I, Too   [1925]

I, too, sing America.

I am the darker brother.

They send me to eat in the kitchen
When company comes,
But I laugh,   5
And eat well,
And grow strong.

Tomorrow,
I'll be at the table
When company comes.   10
Nobody'll dare
Say to me,
"Eat in the kitchen,"
Then.

Besides,   15
They'll see how beautiful I am
And be ashamed—

I, too, am America.

> QUESTIONS FOR READING AND WRITING

1. Who is the speaker in this poem? What does he mean by "I, too"? Who else is he referring to?
2. Compare this poem to Dunbar's "We Wear the Mask" on page 161 or Hughes's other poems in this book: "Theme for English B" on page 86 and "A Dream Deferred" on page 64.
3. What other works have you read that speak to the same issue?

THE NEGRO SPEAKS OF RIVERS   [1926]

I've known rivers:
I've known rivers ancient as the world and older than the flow of human blood in
    human veins.

My soul has grown deep like the rivers.

I bathed in the Euphrates when dawns were young.
I built my hut near the Congo and it lulled me to sleep.   5
I looked upon the Nile and raised the pyramids above it.
I heard the singing of the Mississippi when Abe Lincoln went down to New
    Orleans, and I've seen its muddy bosom turn all golden in the sunset.

I've known rivers:
Ancient, dusky rivers.

My soul has grown deep like the rivers.   10

➤ *QUESTIONS FOR READING AND WRITING*

1. Who is the speaker in this poem?
2. What does he mean when he says, "My soul has grown deep like the rivers" How deep is his soul? Explain.

TED HUGHES (1930–1998)

Ted Hughes was born in Mytholmroyd in West Yorkshire, England. After attending Cambridge University, he published his critically - acclaimed first volume of poetry, The Hawk in the Rain *(1957). The collection of poems, like much of his subsequent poetry, is set in the Yorkshire countryside and is remarkable for its animal imagery, primitivism, and intensity of feeling. Later works of poetry include* Lupercal *(1960),* Wodwo *(1967),* Selected Poems 1957–1967 *(1972), and most recently,* Rain-Charm for the Duchy and Other Laureate Poems *(1992). Hughes was married to American poet Sylvia Plath and served as editor for her* Collected Poems, *which was published in 1981. In 1984, Hughes was appointed Poet Laureate of England.*

SECRETARY   [1956]

If I should touch her she would shriek and weeping
Crawl off to nurse the terrible wound: all
Day like a starling under the bellies of bulls
She hurries among men, ducking, peeping,
Off in a whirl at the first move of a horn.   5
At dusk she scuttles down the gauntlet of lust
Like a clockwork mouse. Safe home at last
She mends socks with holes, shirts that are torn
For father and brother, and a delicate supper cooks:
Goes to bed early, shuts out with the light   10
Her thirty years, and lies with buttocks tight,
Hiding her lovely eyes until day break.

➤ *QUESTIONS FOR READING AND WRITING*

1. Who is the secretary?
2. Why do you think she hides "her lovely eyes until day break"?

JOHN KEATS (1795–1821)

John Keats was born in London and abandoned a medical career for writing when a number of his poems were published. His work is characterized by a passionate concern with the relationship between beauty and truth and emotion and knowledge. He died of tuberculosis at the age of 26.

WHEN I HAVE FEARS THAT I MAY CEASE TO BE   [1818]

When I have fears that I may cease to be
   Before my pen has gleaned my teeming brain,
Before high-pilèd books, in charact'ry,
   Hold like rich garners the full-ripened grain;
When I behold, upon the night's starred face,   5
   Huge cloudy symbols of a high romance,
And think that I may never live to trace
   Their shadows, with the magic hand of chance;
And when I feel, fair creature of an hour,
   That I shall never look upon thee more,   10
Never have relish in the fairy power
   Of unreflecting love—then on the shore
Of the wide world I stand alone, and think
Till love and fame to nothingness do sink.

➤ QUESTIONS FOR READING AND WRITING

1. Do you ever have fears that you may cease to be? If so, how do those fears affect your response to this poem?
2. Compare this poem to Philip Larkin's "Aubade" on page 199 or John Donne's "Death, Be Not Proud" on page 157.

GALWAY KINNELL (b. 1927)

Born and raised in Providence, Rhode Island, Galway Kinnell first became interested in poetry while attending Wilbraham Academy, a prep school in Massachusetts. He attended college at Princeton University (where his roommate was the poet W. S. Merwin) and later earned a master's degree from the University of Rochester. His first collection of poems, What a Kingdom It Was, *was published in 1960, and his latest,* Imperfect Thirst, *appeared in 1994. A dedicated teacher as well as a poet, Kinnell has taught at numerous universities and held writing workshops throughout the world. He currently divides his time between Vermont and New York City, where he is a professor at New York University. His intensely personal poetry often explores the darkest aspects of human consciousness. In a 1989 interview with* Contemporary Authors, *Kinnell described the ideal reader: "As far as the person who buys and reads your poems is concerned, every living reader is an ideal reader. Anybody who recognizes the poem and puts something of his or her own experience into it is the ideal reader. The less than ideal reader is the one who reads without engagement: very often the critic."*

FROM *THE DEAD SHALL BE RAISED INCORRUPTIBLE*   [1971]

In the Twentieth Century of my trespass on earth,
having exterminated one billion heathens,
heretics, Jews, Moslems, witches, mystical seekers,
black men, Asians, and Christian brothers,
every one of them for his own good,   5

a whole continent of red men for living in unnatural community
and at the same time having relations with the land,
one billion species of animals for being sub-human,
and ready to take on the bloodthirsty creatures from the other planets,
I, Christian man, groan out this testament of my last will.   10
I give my blood fifty parts polystyrene,
twenty-five parts benzene, twenty-five parts good old gasoline,
to the last bomber pilot aloft, that there shall be one acre
in the dull world where the kissing flower may bloom,
which kisses you so long your bones explode under its lips.   15

My tongue goes to the Secretary of the Dead
to tell the corpses, "I'm sorry, fellows,
the killing was just one of those things
difficult to pre-visualize—like a cow,
say, getting hit by lightning."   20

My stomach, which has digested
four hundred treaties giving the Indians
eternal right to their land, I give to the Indians,
I throw in my lungs which have spent four hundred years
sucking in good faith on peace pipes.   25

My soul I leave to the bee
that he may sting it and die, my brain
to the fly, his back the hysterical green color of slime,
that he may suck on it and die, my flesh to the advertising man,
the anti-prostitute, who loathes human flesh for money.   30

I assign my crooked backbone
to the dice maker, to chop up into dice,
for casting lots as to who shall see his own blood
on his shirt front and who his brother's,
for the race isn't to the swift but to the crooked.   35

To the last man surviving on earth
I give my eyelids worn out by fear, to wear
in his long nights of radiation and silence,
so that his eyes can't close, for regret
is like tears seeping through closed eyelids.   40

I give the emptiness my hand: the pinkie picks no more noses,
slag clings to the black stick of the ring finger,
a bit of flame jets from the tip of the fuck-you finger,
the first finger accuses the heart, which has vanished,
on the thumb stump wisps of smoke ask a ride into the emptiness.   45

In the Twentieth Century of my nightmare
on earth, I swear on my chromium testicles
to this testament
and last will
of my iron will, my fear of love, my itch for money, and my madness.   50

➤ QUESTIONS FOR READING AND WRITING

1. Who is the speaker in this poem? What is the poem's tone?
2. The first stanza begins, "In the Twentieth Century of my trespass." The last stanza begins, "In the Twentieth Century of my nightmare." What happens in between?
3. Compare this poem to Wilfred Owen's "Dulce et Decorum Est" on page 227 or Thomas Hardy's "The Man He Killed" on page 180.

SAINT FRANCIS AND THE SOW   [1980]

The bud
stands for all things,
even for those things that don't flower,

for everything flowers, from within, of self-blessing;
though sometimes it is necessary   5
to reteach a thing its loveliness,
to put a hand on its brow
of the flower
and retell it in words and in touch
it is lovely   10
until it flowers again from within, of self-blessing;
as Saint Francis
put his hand on the creased forehead
of the sow, and told her in words and in touch
blessings of earth on the sow, and the sow   15
began remembering all down her thick length,
from the earthen snout all the way
through the fodder and slops to the spiritual curl of the tail,
from the hard spininess spiked out from the spine
down through the great broken heart   20
to the sheer blue milken dreaminess spurting and shuddering
from the fourteen teats into the fourteen mouths sucking and
    blowing beneath them:
the long, perfect loveliness of sow.

▶ QUESTIONS FOR READING AND WRITING

1. What is a sow? Do you think a sow is an appropriate subject for a poem?
   Explain.
2. What does the speaker mean by "until it flowers again from within, of self-
   blessing"?
3. Compare this poem with James Wright's "A Blessing" on page 273 or the
   excerpt from Walt Whitman's *Song of Myself* on page 266.

CAROLYN KIZER (b. 1925)

*Carolyn Kizer was born in Spokane,
Washington, and studied with Theodore
Roethke at the University of Washington. She
won the Pulitzer Prize for Poetry for her collec-
tion* Yin *(1985). "Night Sounds" is taken from*
Mermaids in the Basement.

NIGHT SOUNDS   [1984]

imitated from the Chinese

The moonlight on my bed keeps me awake;
Living alone now, aware of the voices of evening,
A child weeping at nightmares, the faint love-cries of a woman,
Everything tinged by terror or nostalgia.

No heavy, impassive back to nudge with one foot   5
While coaxing, "Wake up and hold me,"
When the moon's creamy beauty is transformed
Into a map of impersonal desolation.

But, restless in this mock dawn of moonlight
That so chills the spirit, I alter our history;   10
You were never able to lie quite peacefully at my side,
Not the night through. Always withholding something.

Awake before morning, restless and uneasy,
Trying not to disturb me, you would leave my bed
While I lay there rigidly, feigning sleep.   15
Still—the night was nearly over, the light not as cold
As a full cup of moonlight.

And there were the lovely times when, to the skies' cold *No*
You cried to me, *Yes!* Impaled me with affirmation.
Now when I call out in fear, not in love, there is no answer.   20
Nothing speaks in the dark but the distant voices,
A child with the moon in his face, a dog's hollow cadence.

➤ *QUESTIONS FOR READING AND WRITING*

1. What are "night sounds"? Are sounds at night different than during the day? Explain.
2. She says, "You were never able to lie quite peacefully at my side, / Not the night through. Always withholding something." Who is the "you" of the poem? What do you think she means?

YUSEF KOMUNYAKAA (b. 1947)

Yusef Komunyakaa was born in Bogalusa, Louisiana, and served in the Vietnam War. His volumes of poetry include Copacetic *(1984),* I Apologize for the Eyes in My Head *(1986), and* Neon Vernacular, *which won the Pulitzer Prize in 1994. "Facing It," a poem about the Vietnam Memorial in Washington, D.C., is taken from* Dien Cai Dau *(1988). He teaches at Indiana University.*

FACING IT   [1988]

My black face fades,
hiding inside the black granite.
I said I wouldn't,
dammit: No tears.
I'm stone. I'm flesh.   5
My clouded reflection eyes me
like a bird of prey, the profile of night
slanted against morning. I turn
this way—the stone lets me go.
I turn that way—I'm inside   10
the Vietnam Veterans Memorial
again, depending on the light
to make a difference.
I go down the 58,022 names,
half-expecting to find   15
my own in letters like smoke.
I touch the name Andrew Johnson;
I see the booby trap's white flash.
Names shimmer on a woman's blouse
but when she walks away   20
the names stay on the wall.
Brushstrokes flash, a red bird's
wings cutting across my stare.
The sky. A plane in the sky.
A white vet's image floats   25
closer to me, then his pale eyes
look through mine. I'm a window.
He's lost his right arm
inside the stone. In the black mirror

a woman's trying to erase names: 30
No, she's brushing a boy's hair.

► *QUESTIONS FOR READING AND WRITING*

1. Who is the speaker in this poem? What is the speaker's point of view?
2. Do you think "Facing It" is an appropriate title for this poem? Explain.
3. How many different things does he see reflected in the wall? In what way is it fitting that he mistakes the woman's brushing the boy's hair as trying to erase names?

MAXINE KUMIN (B. 1925)

Maxine Kumin was born in Philadelphia, Pennsylvania, and currently lives on a farm in New Hampshire. She attended Radcliffe College, earning a bachelor's degree in 1946 and a master's degree in 1948. Though Kumin was always interested in writing poetry, she did not begin to write seriously until, frustrated in her role as a suburban housewife, she began taking workshops at the Boston Center for Adult Education. At one of these workshops she met Anne Sexton, then also a housewife, and the two women became close friends. Over the following years, the women, who collaborated on three children's books, were important influences on each other, often providing suggestions, critiques, and support. Kumin's poetry, less confessional and more optimistic than Sexton's, often finds its subject matter in the details of everyday life in rural New England. Her works include four novels, numerous works for children, two collections of short stories, two collections of critical essays, and numerous volumes of poetry, including Up Country: Poems of New England, *which was awarded the Pulitzer Prize in 1973. Her most recent work,* Connecting the Dots: Poems, *appeared in 1996.*

AFTER LOVE   [1972]

Afterwards, the compromise.
Bodies resume their boundaries.

These legs, for instance, mine.
Your arms take you back in.

Spoons of our fingers, lips   5
admit their ownership.

The bedding yawns, a door
blows aimlessly ajar

and overhead, a plane
singsongs coming down.   10

Nothing is changed, except
there was a moment when

the wolf, the mongering wolf
who stands outside the self

lay lightly down, and slept.   15

► *QUESTIONS FOR READING AND WRITING*

1. What does the speaker mean by "Afterwards, the compromise"?
2. Who is "the mongering wolf / who stands outside the self"?

PHILIP LARKIN (1922–1985)

*Philip Larkin was born to a working-class
family in Coventry, an industrial city in northern England. He attended Oxford University
on a scholarship, and afterward served for
many years as the librarian at the University of
Hull. Though he wrote novels and was an
astute critic of both music—jazz, in particular—and literature, Larkin is remembered
today as one of England's most influential post-
war poets. In his poems, which are often called
antiromantic, Larkin takes a witty, sophisti-
cated, and tough-minded approach to traditional poetic subjects.*

THIS BE THE VERSE   [1971]

They fuck you up, your mum and dad.
    They may not mean to, but they do.
They fill you with the faults they had
    And add some extra, just for you.

But they were fucked up in their turn   5
    By fools in old-style hats and coats,
Who half the time were soppy-stern
    And half at one another's throats.

Man hands on misery to man.
    It deepens like a coastal shelf.   10
Get out as early as you can.
    And don't have any kids yourself.

➤ *QUESTIONS FOR READING AND WRITING*

1. What is the tone of this poem? Were you surprised by it, and the message? Why?
2. Is the advice at the end realistic? Do you agree with it? Explain.

AUBADE   [1977]

I work all day, and get half-drunk at night.
Waking at four to soundless dark, I stare.
In time the curtain-edges will grow light.
Till then I see what's really always there:
Unresting death, a whole day nearer now,   5
Making all thought impossible but how
And where and when I shall myself die.
Arid interrogation: yet the dread
Of dying, and being dead,
Flashes afresh to hold and horrify.   10

The mind blanks at the glare. Not in remorse
—The good not done, the love not given, time
Torn off unused—nor wretchedly because
An only life can take so long to climb
Clear of its wrong beginnings, and may never;   15
But at the total emptiness for ever,
The sure extinction that we travel to
And shall be lost in always. Not to be here,
Not to be anywhere,
And soon; nothing more terrible, nothing more true.   20

This is a special way of being afraid
No trick dispels. Religion used to try,
That vast moth-eaten musical brocade
Created to pretend we never die,
And specious stuff that says *No rational being*   25
Can fear a thing it will not feel, not seeing
That this is what we fear—no sight, no sound,
No touch or taste or smell, nothing to think with,
Nothing to love or link with,
The anaesthetic from which none come round.   30

And so it stays just on the edge of vision,
A small unfocused blur, a standing chill
That slows each impulse down to indecision.
Most things may never happen: this one will,
And realisation of it rages out   35
In furnace-fear when we are caught without
People or drink. Courage is no good:
It means not scaring others. Being brave

Lets no one off the grave.
Death is no different whined at than withstood.   40

Slowly light strengthens, and the room takes shape.
It stands plain as a wardrobe, what we know,
Have always known, know that we can't escape,
Yet can't accept. One side will have to go.
Meanwhile telephones crouch, getting ready to ring   45
In locked-up offices, and all the uncaring
Intricate rented world begins to rouse.
The sky is white as clay, with no sun.
Work has to be done.
Postmen like doctors go from house to house.   50

➤ QUESTIONS FOR READING AND WRITING

1. What is the speaker pondering? Do you think the night intensifies this?
   Explain.
2. Compare this poem to John Donne's "Death, Be Not Proud" on page 157,
   John Keats's "When I Have Fears That I May Cease to Be" on page 191, or
   Alfred, Lord Tennyson's "Ulysses" on page 259.

MICHAEL LASSELL (b. 1947)

*Michael Lassell is the author of six books of
poetry, fiction, and nonfiction including* A
Flame for the Touch That Matters *(1998) and*
Decade Dance *(1990), which won a Lambda
Literary Award. He is also the editor of five
books including (with Elena Georgiou)* The
World in U.S.: Lesbian and Gay Poetry of the
Next Wave *(St. Martin's Press, 2000) and*
Elton John and Tim Rice's Aida: The Making
of a Broadway Show *(Disney Editions, 2000).
He holds degrees from Colgate University,
California Institute of the Arts, and Yale
University, and lives in New York City, where
he is the features editor of* Metropolitan Home
magazine.

HOW TO WATCH YOUR BROTHER DIE   [1990]

for Carl Morse

When the call comes, be calm.
Say to your wife, "My brother is dying. I have to fly

to California."
Try not to be shocked that he already looks like
a cadaver.   5
Say to the young man sitting by your brother's side,
"I'm his brother."
Try not to be shocked when the young man says,
"I'm his lover. Thanks for coming."

Listen to the doctor with a steel face on.   10
Sign the necessary forms.
Tell the doctor you will take care of everything.
Wonder why doctors are so remote.

Watch the lover's eyes as they stare into
your brother's eyes as they stare into   15
space.
Wonder what they see there.
Remember the time he was jealous and
opened your eyebrow with a sharp stick.
Forgive him out loud   20
even if he can't
understand you.
Realize the scar will be
all that's left of him.

Over coffee in the hospital cafeteria   25
say to the lover, "You're an extremely good-looking
young man."
Hear him say,
"I never thought I was good enough looking to
deserve your brother."   30

Watch the tears well up in his eyes. Say,
"I'm sorry, I don't know what it means to be
the lover of another man."
Hear him say,
"It's just like a wife, only the commitment is   35
deeper because the odds against you are so much
greater."
Say nothing, but
take his hand like a brother's.

Drive to Mexico for unproved drugs that might   40
help him live longer.
Explain what they are to the border guard.
Fill with rage when he informs you,
"You can't bring those across."

Begin to grow loud. 45
Feel the lover's hand on your arm
restraining you. See in the guard's eye
how much a man can hate another man.
Say to the lover, "How can you stand it?"
Hear him say, "You get used to it." 50
Think of one of your children getting used to
another man's hatred.

Call your wife on the telephone. Tell her,
"He hasn't much time.
I'll be home soon." Before you hang up, say, 55
"How could anyone's commitment be deeper than
a husband and wife?" Hear her say,
"Please. I don't want to know all the details."

When he slips into an irrevocable coma,
hold his lover in your arms while he sobs, 60
no longer strong. Wonder how much longer
you will be able to be strong.
Feel how it feels to hold a man in your arms
whose arms are used to holding men.
Offer God anything to bring your brother back. 65
Know you have nothing God could possibly want.
Curse God, but do not
abandon Him.

Stare at the face of the funeral director
when he tells you he will not 70
embalm the body for fear of
contamination. Let him see in your eyes
how much a man can hate another man.

Stand beside a casket covered in flowers,
white flowers. Say, 75
"Thank you for coming," to each of several
hundred men
who file past in tears, some of them
holding hands. Know that your brother's life
was not what you imagined. Overhear two 80
mourners say, "I wonder who'll be next?" and
"I don't care anymore,
as long as it isn't you."

Arrange to take an early flight home,
his lover will drive you to the airport. 85
When your flight is announced say,
awkwardly, "If I can do anything, please

let me know." Do not flinch when he says,
"Forgive yourself for not wanting to know him
after he told you. He did."   90
Stop and let it soak in. Say,
"He forgave me, or he knew himself?"
"Both," the lover will say, not knowing what else
to do. Hold him like a brother while he
kisses you on the cheek. Think that   95
you haven't been kissed by a man since
your father died. Think,
"This is no moment not to be strong."

Fly first class and drink Scotch. Stroke
your split eyebrow with a finger and   100
think of your brother alive. Smile
at the memory and think
how your children will feel in your arms,
warm and friendly and without challenge.

▶ QUESTIONS FOR READING AND WRITING

1. What do you think of the title of the poem? Is this how to watch your brother die? Explain.
2. Who is the "you" to whom the speaker addresses himself?
3. What does the speaker mean by "See in the guard's eye how much a man can hate another man." What other images of love or hate can you find in the poem?
4. The poem concludes with, "think how your children will feel in your arms, / warm and friendly and without challenge." Is this a fitting conclusion? Explain.

LI-YOUNG LEE (b. 1957)

Li-Young Lee was born in Jakarta, Indonesia. He came to the United States in 1964 at the age of 7, when his father, a physician and minister, was forced to flee Indonesia due to political persecution. He attended the University of Pittsburgh, the University of Arizona, and the State University of New York at Brockport. His volumes of poetry include Rose *(1986) and* The City in Which I Love You *(1990). In 1994, he published a book of his memoirs,* The Winged Seed. *He currently lives in Chicago.*

THE GIFT
[1986]

To pull the metal splinter from my palm
my father recited a story in a low voice.
I watched his lovely face and not the blade.
Before the story ended he'd removed
the iron sliver I thought I'd die from.   5

I can't remember the tale
but hear his voice still, a well
of dark water, a prayer.
And I recall his hands,
two measures of tenderness   10
he laid against my face,
the flames of discipline
he raised above my head.

Had you entered that afternoon
you would have thought you saw a man   15
planting something in a boy's palm,
a silver tear, a tiny flame.
Had you followed that boy
you would have arrived here,
where I bend over my wife's right hand.   20

Look how I shave her thumbnail down
so carefully she feels no pain.
Watch as I lift the splinter out.
I was seven when my father
took my hand like this,   25
and I did not hold that shard
between my fingers and think,
Metal that will bury me,
christen it Little Assassin,
Ore Going Deep for My Heart,   30
And I did not lift up my wound and cry,
Death visited here!
I did what a child does
when he's given something to keep,
I kissed my father.   35

➤ QUESTIONS FOR READING AND WRITING

1. What is "the gift"?
2. How do you think the italicized phrases *"Metal that will bury me"* and
    "Death visited here!" fit in this poem? Are there any other phrases that
    stand out for you?

3. Can you remember a time when someone gave you a "gift" like this? Explain.

AMY LOWELL (1874–1925)

Amy Lowell was born into a distinguished New England family, where she spent much time browsing through her father's impressive library. She attended the Brooklyn Institute of Arts and Sciences, Tufts College, Columbia University, and Baylor University. A 1902 visit to the theater, where she saw the famed actress Eleanora Duse, inspired her to become a poet, and she spent the next years perfecting her art, publishing her first volume of poems, A Dome of Many-Coloured Glass, *in 1912. About the same time she met Ada Dwyer Russell, the woman who would become her lifelong com-*
panion and editor. Greatly influenced by the imagist movement, which rejected sentimentality in favor of precision in images and language, Lowell traveled to Europe to befriend the movement's leading practitioners and returned to become its champion in the United States. Her books of poetry include Sword Blades and Poppy Seed *(1914),* Men, Women and Ghosts *(1916), and the posthumously published* What's O'Clock, *which was awarded the Pulitzer Prize in 1926.*

PATTERNS   [1915]

I walk down the garden paths,
And all the daffodils
Are blowing, and the bright blue squills.
I walk down the patterned garden paths
In my stiff, brocaded gown.   5
With my powdered hair and jewelled fan,
I too am a rare
Pattern. As I wander down
The garden paths.

My dress is richly figured,   10
And the train
Makes a pink and silver stain
On the gravel, and the thrift
Of the borders.
Just a plate of current fashion,   15
Tripping by in high-heeled, ribboned shoes.
Not a softness anywhere about me,
Only whalebone and brocade.

And I sink on a seat in the shade
Of a lime tree. For my passion 20
Wars against the stiff brocade.
The daffodils and squills
Flutter in the breeze
As they please.
And I weep; 25
For the lime tree is in blossom
And one small flower has dropped upon my bosom.

And the plashing of waterdrops
In the marble fountain
Comes down the garden paths. 30
The dripping never stops.
Underneath my stiffened gown
Is the softness of a woman bathing in a marble basin,
A basin in the midst of hedges grown
So thick, she cannot see her lover hiding, 35
But she guesses he is near,
And the sliding of the water
Seems the stroking of a dear
Hand upon her.
What is Summer in a fine brocaded gown! 40
I should like to see it lying in a heap upon the ground.
All the pink and silver crumpled up on the ground.

I would be the pink and silver as I ran along the paths,
And he would stumble after,
Bewildered by my laughter. 45
I should see the sun flashing from his sword-hilt and the buckles on his shoes.
I would choose
To lead him in a maze along the patterned paths,
A bright and laughing maze for my heavy-booted lover.
Till he caught me in the shade, 50
And the buttons of his waistcoat bruised my body as he clasped me,
Aching, melting, unafraid.
With the shadows of the leaves and the sundrops,
And the plopping of the waterdrops,
All about us in the open afternoon— 55
I am very like to swoon
With the weight of this brocade,
For the sun sifts through the shade.

Underneath the fallen blossom
In my bosom 60
Is a letter I have hid.
It was brought to me this morning by a rider from the Duke.

"Madam, we regret to inform you that Lord Hartwell
Died in action Thursday se'ennight."
As I read it in the white, morning sunlight,   65
The letters squirmed like snakes.
"Any answer, Madam," said my footman.
"No," I told him.
"See that the messenger takes some refreshment.
No, no answer."   70
And I walked into the garden,
Up and down the patterned paths,
In my stiff, correct brocade.
The blue and yellow flowers stood up proudly in the sun,
Each one.   75
I stood upright too,
Held rigid to the pattern
By the stiffness of my gown;
Up and down I walked,
Up and down.   80

In a month he would have been my husband.
In a month, here, underneath this lime,
We would have broken the pattern;
He for me, and I for him,
He as Colonel, I as Lady,   85
On this shady seat.
He had a whim
That sunlight carried blessing.
And I answered, "It shall be as you have said."
Now he is dead.   90

In Summer and in Winter I shall walk
Up and down
The patterned garden paths
In my stiff, brocaded gown.
The squills and daffodils   95
Will give place to pillared roses, and to asters, and to snow.
I shall go
Up and down,
In my gown.
Gorgeously arrayed,   100
Boned and stayed.
And the softness of my body will be guarded from embrace
By each button, hook, and lace.
For the man who should loose me is dead,
Fighting with the Duke in Flanders,   105
In a pattern called a war.
Christ! What are patterns for?

➤ QUESTIONS FOR READING AND WRITING

1. Describe the setting of this poem. Do you think it's an appropriate setting for the news the speaker is told? Explain.
2. After receiving the news of her lover's death, the speaker says, "I stood upright too, / Held rigid to the pattern / By the stiffness of my gown." What do you think she means?
3. She later says, "the softness of my body will be guarded from embrace / By each button, hook, and lace. / For the man who should loose me is dead." In what ways would he have "loosed" her?
4. How would you answer the question at the end of the poem: "What are patterns for?"
5. Compare this poem to Emily Dickinson's "After Great Pain, a Formal Feeling Comes" on page 153.

ARCHIBALD MACLEISH (1892–1982)

Born in Glencoe, Illinois, Archibald MacLeish attended Yale University as an undergraduate, where he published poems in the Yale Review, *though he later earned a law degree from Harvard University. In 1923, he abandoned his lucrative law career and moved to Paris with his young family to pursue writing. In Paris, he came into contact with many of the greatest poets of the age including Ezra Pound and T. S. Eliot, who greatly influenced his work. In 1932, after returning to the United States, he won the first of his three Pulitzer Prizes for* Conquistador *(1932), an epic poem about Cortez's sixteenth-century expedition to Mexico. In 1939, MacLeish was appointed Librarian of Congress, and during World War II, held a number of important political posts including assistant secretary of state. In his later years he won two more Pulitzer Prizes, the first for his* New and Collected Poems 1917–1952 *(1952), and the second for his verse drama* J. B. *(1958), a modern retelling of the story of Job. In his later years, MacLeish taught at Harvard before retiring to Amherst, Massachusetts. "Ars Poetica" is Latin for "the art of poetry."*

ARS POETICA   [1926]

A poem should be palpable and mute
As a globed fruit,

Dumb
As old medallions to the thumb,

Silent as the sleeve-worn stone
Of casement ledges where the moss has grown—   5

A poem should be wordless
As the flight of birds.

A poem should be motionless in time
As the moon climbs,   10

Leaving, as the moon releases
Twig by twig the night-entangled trees,

Leaving, as the moon behind the winter leaves,
Memory by memory the mind—

A poem should be motionless in time   15
As the moon climbs.

A poem should be equal to:
Not true.

For all the history of grief
An empty doorway and a maple leaf.   20

For love
The leaning grasses and two lights above the sea—

A poem should not mean
But be.

> ## ► QUESTIONS FOR READING AND WRITING

1. Summarize each of the three things that the speaker says "a poem should be."
2. Do you agree with this definition? Explain.
3. Compare MacLeish's definition of poetry with Marianne Moore's on page 220.

CHRISTOPHER MARLOWE

(1564–1593)

Christopher Marlowe was a contemporary of Shakespeare and one of the most successful playwrights and poets of the Elizabethan era, but his career was cut short when he was murdered in a tavern brawl. His major plays include Tamburlaine the Great *(1587),* Dr. Faustus *(1588), and* Edward II *(1592). Walter Raleigh's response to "The Passionate Shepherd to His Love" appears on page 232.*

THE PASSIONATE SHEPHERD TO HIS LOVE

[1599]

Come live with me, and be my love,
And we will all the pleasures prove,
That valleys, groves, hills and fields,
Woods, or steepy mountain yields.

And we will sit upon the rocks,   5
Seeing the shepherds feed their flocks,
By shallow rivers, to whose falls
Melodious birds sing madrigals.

And I will make thee beds of roses,
And a thousand fragrant posies,   10
A cap of flowers, and a kirtle°
Embroidered all with leaves of myrtle;

A gown made of the finest wool,
Which from our pretty lambs we pull,
Fair lined slippers for the cold,   15
With buckles of the purest gold;

A belt of straw and ivy buds,
With coral clasps and amber studs,
And if these pleasures may thee move,
Come live with me, and be my love.   20

The shepherds' swains° shall dance and sing
For thy delight each May morning.
If these delights thy mind may move,
Then live with me, and be my love.

¹¹**kirtle** a long gown   ²¹**swains** boy servants

➤ QUESTIONS FOR READING AND WRITING

1. What does the shepherd want? What does he offer?
2. Do you think he is being realistic? Explain.
3. Compare this poem with Walter Raleigh's "The Nymph's Reply to the Shepherd" on page 232.

ANDREW MARVELL (1621–1678)

Andrew Marvell was born in the town of Hull, England and attended Cambridge University, graduating in 1638. During the English civil war, he held posts as a tutor for the family of an important general on the Parliamentary side, and as a secretary to the poet John Milton. During the war, in 1659, Marvell was elected to Parliament and served, even after the Restoration, as a well-regarded member until his death. Marvell, who was known during his lifetime only for the few satires he published, was recognized as an important lyric poet after his death, when his Miscellaneous Poems *was published in 1681. "To His Coy Mistress" is widely considered one of the greatest English love poems.*

To His Coy Mistress   [1641]

Had we but world enough, and time,
This coyness, lady, were no crime.
We would sit down, and think which way
To walk, and pass our long love's day.
Thou by the Indian Ganges' side   5
Shouldst rubies find: I by the tide
Of Humber° would complain. I would
Love you ten years before the Flood,
And you should, if you please, refuse
Till the conversion of the Jews.°   10
My vegetable love° should grow
Vaster than empires, and more slow.
An hundred years should go to praise
Thine eyes, and on thy forehead gaze;
Two hundred to adore each breast,   15
But thirty thousand to the rest;
An age at least to every part,
And the last age should show your heart.
For, lady, you deserve this state,
Nor would I love at lower rate.   20
　　But at my back I always hear
Time's wingèd chariot hurrying near;

---

⁷**Humber** the river that runs through Marvell's native town, Hull   ¹⁰**the conversion of the Jews** supposedly to occur at the end of time   ¹¹**vegetable love** growing slowly

And yonder all before us lie
Deserts of vast eternity.
Thy beauty shall no more be found;   25
Nor, in thy marble vault, shall sound
My echoing song; then worms shall try
That long-preserved virginity,
And your quaint honor turn to dust,
And into ashes all my lust.   30
The grave's a fine and private place,
But none, I think, do there embrace.
    Now therefore, while the youthful hue
Sits on thy skin like morning dew
And while thy willing soul transpires°   35
At every pore with instant fires,
Now let us sport us while we may;
And now, like amorous birds of prey,
Rather at once our time devour
Than languish in his slow-chapped° power.   40
Let us roll all our strength and all
Our sweetness up into one ball,
And tear our pleasures with rough strife
Through the iron gates of life.
Thus, though we cannot make our sun   45
Stand still, yet we will make him run.

³⁵**transpires** breathes   ⁴⁰**slow-chapped** devouring slowly

▶ QUESTIONS FOR READING AND WRITING

1. What does the speaker in the poem want? Why does he think he should have it?
2. The poem is divided into three parts. Discuss the speaker's logic as he moves through each of these parts.
3. What images does the speaker use to dramatize his points?
4. Do you find his argument sincere or convincing? Explain.
5. Do you find any of the language exaggerated? Explain.
6. How do you think Ella in Judy Grahan's "Ella, in a Square Apron, Along Highway 80" (see p. 178) would respond to this argument?

CLAUDE MCKAY (1889–1948)

Claude McKay was born to peasant farmers in Sunny Ville, Jamaica. Encouraged by his older brother, who was a schoolteacher, he turned to writing poetry when he was just a boy. He won an award for his first volume of poetry, Songs of Jamaica, *published in London in 1912. The award money allowed McKay to travel to the United States, where he studied for a time at the Tuskegee Institute and at Kansas State University before settling in New York City. Energized by the racism he encountered, McKay continued to write poetry, much of it political, as he became active in a number of social causes. In the 1920s, together with writers such as Langston Hughes and Zora Neale Hurston, McKay became one of the leading figures of the movement known as the Harlem Renaissance.* Home to Harlem, *his 1928 novel about a black soldier's return home*

following World War I, was a tremendous commercial success. His other works include two novels, Banjo: A Story Without a Plot *(1929) and* Banana Bottom *(1933), and an autobiography,* A Long Way from Home *(1937).*

AMERICA   [1921]

Although she feeds me bread of bitterness,
And sinks into my throat her tiger's tooth,
Stealing my breath of life, I will confess
I love this cultured hell that tests my youth!
Her vigor flows like tides into my blood,   5
Giving me strength erect against her hate.
Her bigness sweeps my being like a flood.
Yet as a rebel fronts a king in state,
I stand within her walls with not a shred
Of terror, malice, not a word of jeer.   10
Darkly I gaze into the days ahead,
And see her might and granite wonders there,
Beneath the touch of Time's unerring hand,
Like priceless treasures sinking in the sand.

► QUESTIONS FOR READING AND WRITING

1. Despite the abuse he experiences, the speaker says, "I love this cultured hell." Why?
2. What does he mean when he says that he sees America "like priceless treasures sinking in the sand"?

EDNA ST. VINCENT MILLAY

(1892–1950)

Edna St. Vincent Millay was born in Rockland, Maine, and began writing poetry as a child. After graduating from Vassar College in 1917, she moved to New York City, where she quickly became a noted figure in the bustling arts scene of Greenwich Village. She published her first book of poetry, the acclaimed Renascence and Other Poems, *that same year. In 1923, she won the Pulitzer Prize for* The Harp Weaver and Other Poems. *Her later poetry, which became increasingly political, never received the same acclaim as her early work, and, after 1940, when she suffered a nervous breakdown, she wrote very little. She died in 1950, feeling that she had been largely forgotten. After her death, the publication of her collected poems in 1956 restored her position as one of the most accomplished poets of the century.*

LAMENT   [1921]

Listen, children:
Your father is dead.
From his old coats
I'll make you little jackets;
I'll make you little trousers   5
From his old pants.
There'll be in his pockets
Things he used to put there,
Keys and pennies
Covered with tobacco;   10
Dan shall have the pennies
To save in his bank;
Anne shall have the keys
To make a pretty noise with.
Life must go on,   15
And the dead be forgotten;
Life must go on,
Though good men die;
Anne, eat your breakfast;
Dan, take your medicine;   20
Life must go on;
I forget just why.

➤ *QUESTIONS FOR READING AND WRITING*

1. What is your reaction to the first two lines? To what extent does your own experience affect your response to this poem?
2. What is the tone of the poem? What does the last line, "I forget just why," tell you about the speaker's real feelings?
3. Compare this poem to Seamus Heaney's "Mid-Term Break" on page 184.

IF I SHOULD LEARN, IN SOME QUITE CASUAL WAY [1917]

If I should learn, in some quite casual way,
That you were gone, not to return again—
Read from the back-page of a paper, say,
Held by a neighbor in a subway train,
How at the corner of this avenue   5
And such a street (so are the papers filled)
A hurrying man, who happened to be you,
At noon today had happened to be killed—
I should not cry aloud—I could not cry
Aloud, or wring my hands in such a place—   10
I should but watch the station lights rush by
With a more careful interest on my face;
Or raise my eyes and read with greater care
Where to store furs and how to treat the hair.

➤ *QUESTIONS FOR READING AND WRITING*

1. Who is the "you" the speaker addresses? Do you think you would respond as the speaker suggests she would in this circumstance? Explain.
2. How does the location affect her response? Do you think it would be different if she were elsewhere?

WHAT LIPS MY LIPS HAVE KISSED, AND WHERE, AND WHY [1923]

What lips my lips have kissed, and where, and why,
I have forgotten, and what arms have lain
Under my head till morning; but the rain
Is full of ghosts tonight, that tap and sigh
Upon the glass and listen for reply,   5
And in my heart there stirs a quiet pain
For unremembered lads that not again
Will turn to me at midnight with a cry.
Thus in the winter stands the lonely tree,
Nor knows what birds have vanished one by one,   10
Yet knows its boughs more silent than before:
I cannot say what loves have come and gone,
I only know that summer sang in me
A little while, that in me sings no more.

► *QUESTIONS FOR READING AND WRITING*

1. How would you respond to the title "What Lips My Lips Have Kissed, and Where, and Why"?
2. What do you think the speaker means when she says, "I only know that summer sang in me / A little while, that in me sings no more"?

JOHN MILTON (1608–1674)

Born in London, John Milton was the son of a London notary who converted from Roman Catholicism to Protestantism. His father was determined that Milton receive the best possible education, enrolling him in St. Paul's School and hiring private tutors. Milton was an enthusiastic student throughout his youth—he later blamed his blindness on his habit, formed when he was a boy, of reading late into the night. After graduating from Cambridge University in 1629, Milton, supported by his father, traveled to mainland Europe, and began writing poetry, including his well-known "Lycidas" (1638), *an elegy for a college friend. When the English civil war broke out, Milton returned home to fight for the Puritan cause, writing a series of deeply felt essays in its support throughout the war, as well as treatises about divorce (Milton had married unhappily) and education. During the Commonwealth (1649–1660) Milton served as Latin secretary to Oliver Cromwell, handling correspondence with foreign governments, while writing spirited defences of Cromwell's government. Milton, his eyes weakened by so much writing, went blind in the early 1650s, and he was forced to dictate his work to secretaries (among them the poet Andrew Marvell). With the restoration of Charles II in 1660, Milton was imprisoned for a time, and barely managed to escape death. Forced into obscurity and disillusioned by the failure of the cause for which he had given so much of his life, Milton composed* Paradise Lost (1667)—*an epic poem about the fall of Adam and Eve and the hope of redemption—which is generally considered the greatest epic poem in English. In his final years, Milton composed one other epic about the temptation of Christ,* Paradise Regained (1671), *and a verse drama,* Samson Agonistes *(1671).*

HOW SOON HATH TIME   [1645]

How soon hath Time, the subtle thief of youth,
  Stol'n on his wing my three and twentieth year!
  My hasting days fly on with full career,
  But my late spring no bud or blossom shew'th.°

---

⁴**shew'th** shows

Perhaps my semblance might deceive the truth,   5
  That I to manhood am arrived so near,
  And inward ripeness doth much less appear,
  That some more timely-happy spirits endu'th.°
Yet be it less or more, or soon or slow,
  It shall be still in strictest measure even°   10
  To that same lot, however mean or high,
Toward which Time leads me, and the will of Heaven;
  All is, if I have grace to use it so,
  As ever in my great Taskmaster's eye.

⁸**endu'th** endows   ¹⁰**even** equal

> ## QUESTIONS FOR READING AND WRITING

1. Unlike many poems that consider the passage of time from the perspective of old age, the speaker in this one is relatively young. Do you think that matters? Do you think he felt the same 30 years later? Explain.
2. Compare this poem to Shakespeare's sonnet "That Time of Year Thou Mayst in Me Behold" on page 249.

WHEN I CONSIDER HOW MY LIGHT IS SPENT   [1652]

When I consider how my light is spent,
  Ere half my days in this dark world and wide,
  And that one talent which is death to hide
  Lodged with me useless, though my soul more bent
To serve therewith my Maker, and present   5
  My true account, lest he returning chide,
  "Doth God exact day-labor, light denied?"
  I fondly° ask; but Patience to prevent
That murmur, soon replies, "God doth not need
  Either man's work or his own gifts; who best   10
  Bear his mild yoke, they serve him best. His state
Is kingly. Thousands at his bidding speed
  And post o'er land and ocean without rest:
  They also serve who only stand and wait."

⁸**fondly** foolishly

> ## QUESTIONS FOR READING AND WRITING

1. This poem was written with reference to the poet's blindness. How does he reconcile his blindness with his place and usefulness in the world?
2. Compare this poem with Marge Piercy's "To Be of Use" on page 229.

JANICE MIRIKITANI (b. 1938)

*Like many Japanese Americans of her genera-
tion, Janice Mirikitani was incarcerated with
her family in an internment camp during
World War II. She was educated at UCLA
and the University of California at Berkeley,
where she first developed her interests in the
arts, both from a creative and administrative
perspective. During her career, she has managed numerous social and arts programs,
public and private, including San Francisco's
famous Glide Foundation. She has published
three collections of poetry:* Awake in the River
(1978), Shedding Silence *(1987), and* We,
the Dangerous *(1994).*

FOR MY FATHER

[1987]

He came over the ocean
carrying Mt. Fuji on
his back/Tule Lake on his chest
hacked through the brush
of deserts   5
and made them grow
strawberries

we stole berries
from the stem
we could not afford them   10
for breakfast

his eyes held
nothing
as he whipped us
for stealing.   15

the desert had dried
his soul.

wordless
he sold
the rich,   20
full berries
to hakujin°

---

²² **hakujin** white people

whose children
pointed at our eyes

they ate fresh   25
strawberries
on corn flakes.

Father,
i wanted to scream
at your silence.   30
Your strength
was a stranger
i could never touch.

iron
in your eyes   35
to shield
the pain
to shield desert-like wind
from patches
of strawberries   40
grown
from
tears.

➤ QUESTIONS FOR READING AND WRITING

1. The speaker says that her father "came over the ocean / carrying Mt. Fuji on his back." What do you think she means?
2. Later in the poem, she addresses her father directly and says, "Your strength / was a stranger / I could never touch." What do you think she is saying about their relationship? What has she been missing?
3. Have you ever had this kind of response to a parent or authority figure in your life? Explain.

MARIANNE MOORE (1887–1972)

Marianne Moore was born in Kirkwood, Missouri. In 1894, she moved with her mother and brother (she never knew her father) to Pennsylvania, where she later attended Bryn Mawr University. Following graduation in 1910, she taught business courses at the U.S. Indian School in Carlisle, Pennsylvania. The family then moved to Brooklyn, where Moore lived for the rest of her life, becoming a beloved figure (and devoted Brooklyn Dodger's fan) in

her old age. By 1915, she was publishing her first poems, already displaying the wit,
verbal skill, and metrical dexterity that later made her famous. Her first volume of
poetry, Poems *(1921), was published by her friends (the poet H. D. among them) with-*
out her knowledge, and Moore soon found herself with a devoted audience including
the poets T. S. Eliot and William Carlos Williams. From 1921 to 1925, Moore edited the
Dial, *one of the most important arts journals of the day. Her publications include*
Selected Poems *(1935),* Pangolin, and Other Verse *(1936),* Nevertheless *(1944), and*
Collected Poems *(1951), for which she was awarded a Pulitzer Prize. In 1967, she pub-*
lished what is now considered the definitive edition of her poems, The Complete
Poems of Marianne Moore.

POETRY [1921]

I, too, dislike it: there are things that are important beyond
      all this fiddle.
   Reading it, however, with a perfect contempt for it, one
      discovers in
   it after all, a place for the genuine.   5
      Hands that can grasp, eyes
      that can dilate, hair that can rise
         if it must, these things are important not because a

high-sounding interpretation can be put upon them but be-
      cause they are   10
useful. When they become so derivative as to become
      unintelligible,
   the same thing may be said for all of us, that we
      do not admire what
      we cannot understand: the bat   15
        holding on upside down or in quest of something to

eat, elephants pushing, a wild horse taking a roll, a tireless
      wolf under
   a tree, the immovable critic twitching his skin like a horse
      that feels a flea, the base-   20
   ball fan, the statistician—
   nor is it valid
      to discriminate against "business documents and

schoolbooks"; all these phenomena are important. One
      must make a distinction   25
   however: when dragged into prominence by half poets,
      the result is not poetry,
   nor till the poets among us can be
      "literalists of
      the imagination"—above   30
        insolence and triviality and can present

for inspection, "imaginary gardens with real toads in them,"
    shall we have
it. In the meantime, if you demand on the one hand,
the raw material of poetry in   35
    all its rawness and
    that which is on the other hand
        genuine, you are interested in poetry.

➤ QUESTIONS FOR READING AND WRITING

1. At the beginning of the poem, the speaker says, "I, too, dislike it." What assumption is she making about her readers? Do you think she is correct in her assumption? Explain.
2. To what extent can poetry be described as "'imaginary gardens with real toads in them'"?
3. This poem is printed here as it first appeared. In a later 1967 version, it was reduced to its first two sentences. Which version do you prefer? Why?
4. How would you define *poetry*?

PAT MORA (b. 1942)

Pat Mora was born in El Paso, Texas. Her father was an ophthalmologist and her mother was a homemaker. Mora earned her bachelor's degree from Texas Western College in 1963, and a master's degree in 1967 from the University of Texas at El Paso. She taught for many years at both the high school and university levels, but now devotes herself completely to her poetry. Chants, *her first volume of verse, was published in 1984, and she has since published three additional collections:* Borders *(1986),* Communion *(1991), and* Holy Water *(1995). "For a variety of complex reasons," she told* Contemporary Authors, *"anthologized American literature does not reflect the ethnic diversity of the United States. I write, in part, because Hispanic perspectives need to be part of our literary heritage; I want to be part of that validation process. I also write because I am fascinated by the pleasure and power of words."*

IMMIGRANTS   [1986]

wrap their babies in the American flag,
feed them mashed hot dogs and apple pie,
name them Bill and Daisy,
buy them blonde dolls that blink blue
eyes or a football and tiny cleats   5
before the baby can even walk,

speak to them in thick English,
        hallo, babee, hallo,
whisper in Spanish or Polish
when the babies sleep, whisper   10
in a dark parent bed, that dark
parent fear, "Will they like
our boy, our girl, our fine American
boy, our fine American girl?"

➤ QUESTIONS FOR READING AND WRITING

1. To whom is the speaker saying, "wrap their babies in the American flag"?
2. What does she mean by "that dark parent fear"?
3. Compare this poem to Sherman Alexies' "On the Amtrak from Boston to New York City" on page 116.

PABLO NERUDA (1904–1973)

Pablo Neruda was born in Chile and is considered one of the greatest Spanish-American poets. Neruda's poetry often mixes his views on political oppression with passionate lyrics about romantic love. He was awarded the Nobel Prize for Literature in 1971.

ODE TO MY SOCKS   [1971]

Translated by Robert Bly

Maru Mori brought me
a pair
of socks
which she knitted herself
with her sheep-herder's hands,   5
two socks as soft
as rabbits.
I slipped my feet
into them

as though into   10
two
cases
knitted
with threads of
twilight   15
and goatskin.
Violent socks,
my feet were
two fish made
of wool,   20
two long sharks
seablue, shot
through
by one golden thread,
two immense blackbirds,   25
two cannons,
my feet
were honored
in this way
by   30
these
heavenly
socks.
They were
so handsome   35
for the first time
my feet seemed to me
unacceptable
like two decrepit
firemen, firemen   40
unworthy
of that woven
fire,
of those glowing
socks.   45

Nevertheless
I resisted
the sharp temptation
to save them somewhere
as students   50
keep
fireflies,

as learned men
collect
sacred texts,   55
I resisted
the mad impulse
to put them
in a golden
cage   60
and each day give them
birdseed
and pieces of pink melon.
Like explorers
in the jungle who hand   65
over the very rare
green deer
to the spit
and eat it
with remorse,   70
I stretched out
my feet
and pulled on
the
magnificent   75
socks
and
then my shoes.

The moral
of my ode is this:
beauty is twice   80
beauty
and what is good is doubly
good
when it is a matter of two socks   85
made of wool
in winter.

➤ QUESTIONS FOR READING AND WRITING

1. Do you think socks are an appropriate subject for a poem? Explain.
2. What does the speaker mean by "beauty is twice beauty"?

SHARON OLDS (b. 1942)

Born in San Francisco, California, Sharon Olds graduated from Stanford University in 1964 and earned a doctorate from Columbia University in 1972. She published her first book of poetry, Satan Says, *in 1980, but it was not until her second,* The Dead and the Living, *which won the National Book Critics Circle Award in 1985, that her reputation as an important voice was firmly established. Her poetry, which is often intensely personal, is noted for its candor and power. Her latest book of poems,* Blood, Tin, and Straw, *was published in 1999. She teaches creative writing at New York University.*

35/10

[1984]

Brushing out my daughter's dark
silken hair before the mirror
I see the grey gleaming on my head,
the silver-haired servant behind her. Why is it
just as we begin to go   5
they begin to arrive, the fold in my neck
clarifying as the fine bones of her
hips sharpen? As my skin shows
its dry pitting, she opens like a small
pale flower on the tip of a cactus;   10
as my last chances to bear a child
are falling through my body, the duds among them,
her full purse of eggs, round and
firm as hard-boiled yolks, is about
to snap its clasp. I brush her tangled   15
fragrant hair at bedtime. It's an old
story—the oldest we have on our planet—
the story of replacement.

▶ QUESTIONS FOR READING AND WRITING

1. What does the title of the poem refer to? How do the numbers "35/10" match the specific comparisons of the poem?
2. In what way is it "an old / story—the oldest we have on our planet"? How does it play itself out in your own life?
3. Compare this poem to Julia Alvarez's "Dusting" on page 118.

SEX WITHOUT LOVE [1984]

How do they do it, the ones who make love
without love? Beautiful as dancers,
gliding over each other like ice-skaters
over the ice, fingers hooked
inside each other's bodies, faces   5
red as steak, wine, wet as the
children at birth whose mothers are going to
give them away. How do they come to the
come to the come to the God come to the
still waters, and not love   10
the one who came there with them, light
rising slowly as steam off their joined
skin? These are the true religious,
the purists, the pros, the ones who will not
accept a false Messiah, love the   15
priest instead of the God. They do not
mistake the lover for their own pleasure,
they are like great runners: they know they are alone
with the road surface, the cold, the wind,
the fit of their shoes, their over-all cardio-   20
vascular health—just factors, like the partner
in the bed, and not the truth, which is the
single body alone in the universe
against its own best time.

➤ QUESTIONS FOR READING AND WRITING

1. What is the tone of this poem?
2. In what way do the lovers glide "over each other like ice-skaters / over the ice"?
3. What is the purpose of the stammered "come to the" in lines 8 and 9?

WILFRED OWEN (1893–1918)

Born in the Shropshire region of England, Wilfred Owen spent two years studying to be a clergyman before becoming disillusioned with the Anglican church. In 1914, World War I broke out. Owen spent a year debating whether or not his Christian beliefs allowed him to fight. In 1915, he decided to enlist. He became a commander, and in 1916 was stationed with the Lancashire Fusiliers in the trenches in France. In 1917, Owen suffered a nervous breakdown and was sent to an army hospital in Scotland to

recover. He spent 14 months at the hospital, where, befriended by the poet Sigfried Sassoon, he turned to writing poetry. Shipped back to the front, he was killed in action at Sambre Canal, France, only one week before the end of the war. Only four of Owen's poems were published during his lifetime. The rest were collected and published by Sassoon in 1920. Sassoon said of Owen, "My trench sketches were like rockets, set up to illuminate the darkness. . . . It was Owen who revealed how, out of realistic horror and scorn, poetry might be made." The last two lines (and title) of "Dulce et Decorum Est" are taken from an ode by Horace, a great Roman poet. They can be translated as: "It is sweet and fitting to die for one's country."

Dulce et Decorum Est   [1920]

Bent double, like old beggars under sacks,
Knock-kneed, coughing like hags, we cursed through sludge,
Till on the haunting flares we turned our backs
And towards our distant rest began to trudge.
Men marched asleep. Many had lost their boots   5
But limped on, blood-shod. All went lame; all blind;
Drunk with fatigue; deaf even to the hoots
Of tired, outstripped Five-Nines that dropped behind.

Gas! GAS! Quick, boys!—An ecstasy of fumbling,
Fitting the clumsy helmets just in time;   10
But someone still was yelling out and stumbling
And flound'ring like a man in fire or lime . . .
Dim, through the misty panes and thick green light,
As under a green sea, I saw him drowning.
In all my dreams, before my helpless sight,   15
He plunges at me, guttering, choking, drowning.

If in some smothering dreams you too could pace
Behind the wagon that we flung him in,
And watch the white eyes writhing in his face,
His hanging face, like a devil's sick of sin;   20
If you could hear, at every jolt, the blood
Come gargling from the froth-corrupted lungs,

Obscene as cancer, bitter as the cud
Of vile, incurable sores on innocent tongues,—
My friend, you would not tell with such high zest   25
To children ardent for some desperate glory.
The old Lie: *Dulce et decorum est*
Pro patria mori.

► QUESTIONS FOR READING AND WRITING

1. Who is the speaker in this poem? What is the setting?
2. When he says at the beginning of the last stanza, "If in some smoldering dreams you too could pace. . .," "You" seems to refer to us—the readers. What does he assume about "us"? What does he assume would change our view?
3. Why does he call the Latin saying that is the title of this poem "The old Lie"?

LINDA PASTAN (b.1932)

Linda Pastan was born in New York City and has degrees from Radcliffe College and Brandeis University. Her books of poetry include A Perfect Circle of Sun *(1971),* Five Stages of Grief *(1978),* PM/AM *(1982), which was nominated for the American Book Award,* Imperfect Paradise *(1988), and* Heroes in Disguise *(1991). She has been honored with grants from the National Endowment for the Arts and by being named Poet Laureate of the State of Maryland.*

MARKS   [1978]

My husband gives me an A
for last night's supper,
an incomplete for my ironing,
a B plus in bed.
My son says I am average,   5
an average mother, but if
I put my mind to it
I could improve.
My daughter believes
in Pass/Fail and tells me   10
I pass. Wait 'til they learn
I'm dropping out.

➤ QUESTIONS FOR READING AND WRITING

1. What kind relationship does the speaker have with her family?
2. What does she mean by "Wait 'til they learn / I'm dropping out"?
3. How does the speaker compare with the mothers in Julia Alvarez's "Dusting" (p. 118) or Sharon Olds's "35/10" (p. 225)?

MARGE PIERCY (b. 1936)

Born in Detroit, Michigan, to a working-class family, Marge Piercy earned a bachelor's degree at the University of Michigan in 1957 and a master's degree at Northwestern University in 1958. Piercy began writing poems as a result of her involvement in the antiwar movement of the 1960s. In 1969, in reaction to what she considered the misogyny of many activists, she changed her focus to the growing women's movement. She has published many volumes of poetry, beginning with Breaking Camp *in 1968, and many novels. Her most recent* City of Darkness, City of Light: A Novel *appeared in 1996. Much of her work is political, and she has expressed a desire for her writing to be "useful." She has written, "To find ourselves spoken for in art gives dignity to our pain, our anger, our lust, our losses. We can hear what we hope for and what we most fear in the small release of cadenced utterance."*

TO BE OF USE   [1973]

The people I love the best
jump into work head first
without dallying in the shallows
and swim off with sure strokes almost out of sight.
They seem to become natives of that element,   5
the black sleek heads of seals
bouncing like half-submerged balls.

I love people who harness themselves, an ox to a heavy cart,
who pull like water buffalo, with massive patience,
who strain in the mud and the muck to move things forward,   10
who do what has to be done, again and again.

I want to be with people who submerge
in the task, who go into the fields to harvest
and work in a row and pass the bags along,

who are not parlor generals and field deserters   15
but move in common rhythm
when the food must come in or the fire be put out.

The work of the world is common as mud.
Botched, it smears the hands, crumbles to dust.
But the thing worth doing well done   20
has a shape that satisfies, clean and evident.
Greek amphoras for wine or oil,
Hopi vases that held corn, are put in museums
but you know they were made to be used.
The pitcher cries for water to carry   25
and a person for work that is real.

➤ QUESTIONS FOR READING AND WRITING

1. Do you think it's important "to be of use"? Why?
2. The speaker says that Greek amphoras and Hopi vases "are put in museums / but you know they were made to be used." What does she mean?
3. Compare this poem to John Milton's "When I Consider How My Light Is
   Spent" on page 217.

SYLVIA PLATH (1932–1963)

*Encouraged by her mother, Sylvia Plath began
writing poetry as a precocious child in Boston,
publishing her first poem in the* Boston
Traveller *when she was only 8 years old. That
same year her father died, an event that
haunted her for the rest of her life. Like the pro-
tagonist in her autobiographical novel* The Bell
Jar *(1963), she was a star student at Smith
College, became a guest editor of a fashion
magazine, and moved for a short time to New
York City. When she returned home, she suffered the first of her serious mental breakdowns
and attempted suicide. She was institutional-
ized for over a year and received electric shock treatments. When she returned to Smith
she again excelled, winning a Fulbright Scholarship to England after her final year.
While studying at Cambridge University she met and fell in love with the English poet
Ted Hughes. Married in 1956, the couple eventually settled in the English countryside
and produced two children. The marriage was a difficult one, and the couple separated
in 1962. Once again Plath entered a severe depression, committing suicide in 1963. Her
greatest work dates to the tortured final years of her life, when she was able to channel
her energies into highly personal, ironic, and often terrifying poems. Her* Collected
Poems, *edited by Ted Hughes, appeared in 1981 and was awarded the Pulitzer Prize.*

MIRROR   [1963]

I am silver and exact. I have no preconceptions.
Whatever I see I swallow immediately
Just as it is, unmisted by love or dislike.
I am not cruel, only truthful—
The eye of a little god, four-cornered.   5
Most of the time I meditate on the opposite wall.
It is pink, with speckles. I have looked at it so long
I think it is a part of my heart. But it flickers.
Faces and darkness separate us over and over.

Now I am a lake. A woman bends over me,   10
Searching my reaches for what she really is.
Then she turns to those liars, the candles or the moon.
I see her back, and reflect it faithfully.
She rewards me with tears and an agitation of hands.
I am important to her. She comes and goes.   15
Each morning it is her face that replaces the darkness.
In me she has drowned a young girl, and in me an old woman
Rises toward her day after day, like a terrible fish.

▶ QUESTIONS FOR READING AND WRITING

1. Who is the speaker in this poem?
2. To what extent is the mirror honest? In what way are "the candles or the moon" liars?
3. Who and what is being mirrored? In what way does it rise to the surface "like a terrible fish"?

WALTER RALEIGH (1552–1618)

Walter Raleigh is best known as an adventurer, explorer, and adviser to Queen Elizabeth I. He organized expeditions to North America, founded a settlement in Virginia, and introduced tobacco to Europe. Involved in political intrigue for much of his career, he was imprisoned for 13 years in the Tower of London and was eventually executed by James I. "The Nymph's Reply to the Shepherd" was written in response to Christopher Marlowe's "The Passionate Shepherd to His Love" on page 210.

THE NYMPH'S REPLY TO THE SHEPHERD   [1600]

If all the world and love were young,
And truth in every shepherd's tongue,
These pretty pleasures might me move
To live with thee and be thy love.

Time drives the flocks from field to fold   5
When rivers rage and rocks grow cold,
And Philomel° becometh dumb;
The rest complains of cares to come.

The flowers do fade, and wanton fields
To wayward winter reckoning yields;   10
A honey tongue, a heart of gall,
Is fancy's spring, but sorrow's fall.

Thy gowns, thy shoes, thy bed of roses,
Thy cap, thy kirtle,° and thy posies
Soon break, soon winter, soon forgotten—   15
In folly ripe, in season rotten.

Thy belt of straw and ivy buds,
Thy coral clasps and amber studs,
All these in me no means can move
To come to thee and be thy love.   20

But could youth last and love still breed,
Had joys no date nor age no need,
Then these delights my mind might move
To live with thee and be thy love.

⁷ **Philomel** nightingale bird   ¹⁴ **kirtle** a long gown

► *QUESTIONS FOR READING AND WRITING*

1. Do you agree with this reply to "The Passionate Shepherd to His Love"
   (p. 210)? Explain.
2. Why doesn't the speaker give the shepherd what he wants? How does her
   vision of reality differ from his? What reality does she recognize that he
   does not?
3. How would you imagine this speaker might respond to the argument in
   Andrew Marvell's "To His Coy Mistress" (p. 211)?

ADRIENNE RICH (b. 1929)

Adrienne Rich's most recent books of poetry are Dark Fields of the Republic *(Poems 1991–1995) and* Midnight Salvage *(Poems 1995–1998). A new selection of her essays,* Arts of the Possible: Essays and Conversations, *and a new volume of poems,* Fox *(Poems 1998–2000), will be published in 2001. She has recently been the recipient of the Dorothea Tanning Prize and of the Lannan Foundaton Lifetime Achievement Award. She lives in California.*

RAPE   [1973]

There is a cop who is both prowler and father:
he comes from your block, grew up with your brothers,
had certain ideals.

You hardly know him in his boots and silver badge,
on horseback, one hand touching his gun.   5

You hardly know him but you have to get to know him:
he has access to machinery that could kill you.
He and his stallion clop like warlords among the trash,
his ideals stand in the air, a frozen cloud
from between his unsmiling lips.   10

And so, when the time comes, you have to turn to him,
the maniac's sperm still greasing your thighs,
your mind whirling like crazy. You have to confess
to him, you are guilty of the crime
of having been forced.   15

And you see his blue eyes, the blue eyes of all the family
whom you used to know, grow narrow and glisten,
his hand types out the details
and he wants them all
but the hysteria in your voice pleases him best.   20

You hardly know him but now he thinks he knows you:
he has taken down your worst moment
on a machine and filed it in a file.
He knows, or thinks he knows, how much you imagined;
he knows, or thinks he knows, what you secretly wanted.   25

He has access to machinery that could get you put away;
and if, in the sickening light of the precinct,
your details sound like a portrait of your confessor,
will you swallow, will you deny them, will you lie your way home?   30

DIVING INTO THE WRECK   [1972]

First having read the book of myths,
and loaded the camera,
and checked the edge of the knife-blade,
I put on
the body-armor of black rubber   5
the absurd flippers
the grave and awkward mask.
I am having to do this
not like Cousteau° with his
assiduous team   10
aboard the sun-flooded schooner
but here alone.

There is a ladder.
The ladder is always there
hanging innocently   15
close to the side of the schooner.
We know what it is for,
we who have used it.
Otherwise
it is a piece of maritime floss   20
some sundry equipment.

I go down.
Rung after rung and still
the oxygen immerses me
the blue light   25
the clear atoms
of our human air.
I go down.
My flippers cripple me,
I crawl like an insect down the ladder   30
and there is no one
to tell me when the ocean
will begin.

First the air is blue and then
it is bluer and then green and then   35
black I am blacking out and yet

⁹ **Cousteau** Jacques-Yves Cousteau (1910–1997), famous underwater explorer

my mask is powerful
it pumps my blood with power
the sea is another story
the sea is not a question of power   40
I have to learn alone
to turn my body without force
in the deep element.

And now: it is easy to forget
what I came for   45
among so many who have always
lived here
swaying their crenellated fans
between the reefs
and besides   50
you breathe differently down here.

I came to explore the wreck.
The words are purposes.
The words are maps.
I came to see the damage that was done   55
and the treasures that prevail.
I stroke the beam of my lamp
slowly along the flank
of something more permanent
than fish or weed   60

the thing I came for:
the wreck and not the story of the wreck
the thing itself and not the myth
the drowned face always staring
toward the sun   65
the evidence of damage
worn by salt and sway into this threadbare beauty
the ribs of the disaster
curving their assertion
among the tentative haunters.   70

This is the place.
And I am here, the mermaid whose dark hair
streams black, the merman in his armored body.
We circle silently
about the wreck   75
we dive into the hold.
I am she: I am he

whose drowned face sleeps with open eyes
whose breasts still bear the stress
whose silver, copper, vermeil cargo lies   80

obscurely inside barrels
half-wedged and left to rot
we are the half-destroyed instruments
that once held to a course
the water-eaten log   85
the fouled compass

We are, I am, you are
by cowardice or courage
the one who find our way
back to this scene   90
carrying a knife, a camera
a book of myths
in which
our names do not appear.

ALBERTO RIOS (b. 1952)

*Alberto Rios is a native of Nogales, Arizona,
and is the product of Mexican-American and
British parents. His books of poetry include*
Whispering to Fool the Wind *(1981), for
which he won the Walt Whitman Award,* The
Live Orchard Woman *(1990), and* Pig
Cookies and Other Stories *(1995). He teaches
at Arizona State University.*

THE PURPOSE OF ALTAR BOYS   [1982]

Tonio told me at catechism
the big part of the eye
admits good, and the little
black part is for seeing
evil—his mother told him   5
who was a widow and so
an authority on such things.
That's why at night
the black part gets bigger.
That's why kids can't go out   10
at night, and at night
girls take off their clothes
and walk around their

bedrooms or jump on their
beds or wear only sandals   15
and stand in their windows.
I was the altar boy
who knew about these things,
whose mission on some Sundays
was to remind people of   20
the night before as they
knelt for Holy Communion.
To keep Christ from falling
I held the metal plate
under chins, while on the thick   25
red carpet of the altar
I dragged my feet
and waited for the precise
moment: plate to chin
I delivered without expression   30
the Holy Electric Shock,
the kind that produces
a really large swallowing
and makes people think.
I thought of it as justice.   35
But on other Sundays the fire
in my eyes was different,
my mission somehow changed.
I would hold the metal plate
a little too hard   40
against those certain same
nervous chins, and I,
I would look
with authority down
the tops of white dresses.   45

➤ QUESTIONS FOR READING AND WRITING

1. Who is the speaker? What is the tone of the poem?
2. What does he mean in lines 19 to 21 that his "mission on some Sundays /
   was to remind people of / the night before"?
3. He says that on other Sundays his mission changed. How so?

EDWIN ARLINGTON ROBINSON (1869–1935)

*Born into a wealthy New England family, Edwin Arlington Robinson was raised in
Gardiner, Maine, a small town that later served as the model for "Tilbury Town," the
setting for many of his most famous poems. Encouraged by a neighbor, he developed an
interest in poetry and wrote numerous original poems, as well as diligently translating*

the great Greek and Roman poets. He spent two years at Harvard University, and after failing to get his poems published he decided to print copies of his first collection, The Torrent and the Night Before *(1896), himself. He mailed copies to publishers and received some favorable responses, though some found his subject matter bleak. Encouraged, he published* The Children of the Night *(1896), which contained many of what were to become his best-known Tilbury poems (including "Richard Cory"). The collection was considered a failure, and Robinson descended into poverty and alcoholism. In 1902, in a stroke of luck, President Theodore Roosevelt stumbled onto a copy of* The Children of the Night *and was taken with it, saying, "I am not sure I understand . . . . but I'm entirely sure that I like it." Roosevelt found Robinson a post with very few duties in the customs office in New York City, and Robinson was free to devote himself to his poetry. He stepped down from the post following the success of his 1910 collection,* The Town Down the River. *In 1921, Robinson was awarded the first Pulitzer Prize for poetry for his* Collected Poems, *and was awarded two more for* The Man Who Died Twice *(1924) and* Tristam *(1927). After Robinson's death in 1935, Robert Frost, who listed Robinson as one of his greatest influences, wrote of him and his often unhappy life: "His theme was unhappiness itself, but his skill was as happy as it was playful. There is that comforting thought for those who suffered to see him suffer."*

RICHARD CORY   [1896]

Whenever Richard Cory went down town,
We people on the pavement looked at him:
He was a gentleman from sole to crown,
Clean favored, and imperially slim.

And he was always quietly arrayed,   5
And he was always human when he talked;
But still he fluttered pulses when he said,
"Good-morning," and he glittered when he walked.

And he was rich—yes, richer than a king—
And admirably schooled in every grace: 10
In fine, we thought that he was everything
To make us wish that we were in his place.

So on we worked, and waited for the light,
And went without the meat, and cursed the bread;
And Richard Cory, one calm summer night,   15
Went home and put a bullet through his head.

➤ QUESTIONS FOR READING AND WRITING

1. Who is the speaker in this poem?
2. Who are "we"? Who is Richard Cory to us? What lines in the poem indicate these things?
3. What effect does the last line have on you? Were you surprised? Why?

MR. FLOOD'S PARTY   [1896]

Old Eben Flood, climbing alone one night
Over the hill between the town below
And the forsaken upland hermitage
That held as much as he should ever know
On earth again of home, paused warily.   5
The road was his with not a native near;
And Eben, having leisure, said aloud,
For no man else in Tilbury Town to hear:

"Well, Mr. Flood, we have the harvest moon
Again, and we may not have many more;   10
The bird is on the wing, the poet says,
And you and I have said it here before.
Drink to the bird." He raised up to the light
The jug that he had gone so far to fill,
And answered huskily: "Well, Mr. Flood,   15
Since you propose it, I believe I will."

Alone, as if enduring to the end
A valiant armor of scarred hopes outworn,
He stood there in the middle of the road
Like Roland's ghost winding a silent horn.   20
Below him, in the town among the trees,
Where friends of other days had honored him,
A phantom salutation of the dead
Rang thinly till old Eben's eyes were dim.

Then, as a mother lays her sleeping child   25
Down tenderly, fearing it may awake,
He set the jug down slowly at his feet
With trembling care, knowing that most things break;
And only when assured that on firm earth
It stood, as the uncertain lives of men   30
Assuredly did not, he paced away,
And with his hand extended paused again:

"Well, Mr. Flood, we have not met like this
In a long time; and many a change has come
To both of us, I fear, since last it was   35
We had a drop together. Welcome home!"

Convivially returning with himself,
Again he raised the jug up to the light;
And with an acquiescent quaver said:
"Well, Mr. Flood, if you insist, I might.   40

"Only a very little, Mr. Flood—
For auld lang syne. No more, sir; that will do."
So, for the time, apparently it did,
And Eben evidently thought so too;
For soon amid the silver loneliness   45
Of night he lifted up his voice and sang,
Secure, with only two moons listening,
Until the whole harmonious landscape rang—

"For auld lang syne." The weary throat gave out,
The last word wavered, and the song was done,   50
He raised again the jug regretfully
And shook his head, and was again alone.
There was not much that was ahead of him,
And there was nothing in the town below—
Where strangers would have shut the many doors   55
That many friends had opened long ago.

► QUESTIONS FOR READING AND WRITING

1. Who is the audience for Mr. Flood's oration?
2. Why do you think "strangers would have shut the many doors / That many friends had opened long ago"?
3. Does this poem remind you of anyone you know or of people you've seen or met? Explain.

THEODORE ROETHKE (1908–1963)

Theodore Roethke was a native of Saginaw, Michigan, where his father owned a greenhouse. The poem "My Papa's Waltz" is taken from his second volume of poems, The Lost Son *(1948). During the course of a long career, he won two National Book Awards, and in 1954 received the Pulitzer Prize for his book of poems* The Waking: Poems 1933–1953.

MY PAPA'S WALTZ   [1942]

The whiskey on your breath
Could make a small boy dizzy;
 But I hung on like death:
Such waltzing was not easy.

We romped until the pans   5
Slid from the kitchen shelf;
My mother's countenance
Could not unfrown itself.

The hand that held my wrist
Was battered on one knuckle;   10
At every step you missed
My right ear scraped a buckle.

You beat time on my head
With a palm caked hard by dirt,
Then waltzed me off to bed   15
Still clinging to your shirt.

▶ QUESTIONS FOR READING AND WRITING

1. To what extent is your response to this poem affected by your own experience?

2. What is the mother's response to the dancing? Why?

3. How does this father compare with the fathers in Robert Hayden's "Those Winter Sundays" on page 13 or Janice Mirikitani's "For My Father" on page 218.

ELEGY FOR JANE   [1953]

My Student, Thrown by a Horse

I remember the neckcurls, limp and damp as tendrils;
And her quick look, a sidelong pickerel smile;
And how, once startled into talk, the light syllables leaped for her,
And she balanced in the delight of her thought,
A wren, happy, tail into the wind,   5
Her song trembling the twigs and small branches.
The shade sang with her;
The leaves, their whispers turned to kissing;
And the mold sang in the bleached valleys under the rose.

Oh, when she was sad, she cast herself down into such a pure depth,   10
Even a father could not find her:
Scraping her cheek against straw;
Stirring the clearest water.

My sparrow, you are not here,
Waiting like a fern, making a spiny shadow.   15
The sides of wet stones cannot console me,
Nor the moss, wound with the last light.

If only I could nudge you from this sleep,
My maimed darling, my skittery pigeon.
Over this damp grave I speak the words of my love: 20
I, with no rights in this matter,
Neither father nor lover.

▶ QUESTIONS FOR READING AND WRITING

1. To what extent does your own experience influence your response to this poem?
2. What does the speaker mean when she says "I, with no rights in this matter, / Neither father nor lover"?
3. Compare this poem to Seamus Heaney's "Mid-Term Break" on page 184 or Edna St. Vincent Millay's "Lament" on page 214.

CARL SANDBURG (1878–1967)

Born in Galesburg, Illinois, to Swedish immigrant parents, Carl Sandburg quit school at 13 and worked for a number of years at a series of low-paying jobs, even spending time as a hobo riding trains around the Midwest. Following his service in the army during the Spanish-American War (1898), Sandburg returned to Galesburg and worked his way through Lombard (now Knox) College. He left without a degree but with a sense that he wanted to be a poet, publishing his first (and largely forgotten) collection of poetry In Reckless Ecstasy *in 1904. For the next four years, Sandburg again worked at a number of odd jobs, until he married and eventually settled into a job as a reporter for the* Chicago Daily News. *In 1916, he published* Chicago Poems *and soon became one of the leading members of the Chicago Group, which included such famous writers as Theodore Dreiser, Ben Hecht, and Edgar Lee Masters. Beginning in the 1920s, Sandburg began touring the country with his guitar and giving readings of his poetry, a practice he continued until he died. In addition to his numerous volumes of free-verse poems, Sandburg published a monumental six-volume biography of Abraham Lincoln, one of his personal heroes, that won the Pulitzer Prize for history in 1940.*

GRASS   [1918]

Pile the bodies high at Austerlitz and Waterloo.
Shovel them under and let me work—
        I am the grass; I cover all.

And pile them high at Gettysburg
And pile them high at Ypres and Verdun.   5
Shovel them under and let me work.
Two years, ten years, and passengers ask the conductor:
        What place is this?
        Where are we now?

        I am the grass.   10
        Let me work.

▶ QUESTIONS FOR READING AND WRITING

1. What do "Austerlitz," "Waterloo," "Gettysburg," "Ypres," and "Verdun" refer to?
2. Why would the passengers ask the conductor, "What place is this?" Does it matter? Explain.

ANNE SEXTON (1928–1974)

Born and raised in New England, Anne Sexton attended Garland Junior College and was married at the age of 20. She suffered the first of many mental breakdowns following the birth of her first child in 1954. After a breakdown following the birth of her second child, she began writing poetry at the suggestion of a therapist. To Bedlam and Part Way Back, *her first book of poems, was published in 1960. Her 1967 volume,* Live or Die, *was awarded the Pulitzer Prize. Though she became extraordinarily successful, Sexton continually struggled with depression. Following her divorce, she committed suicide in 1974. Like her contemporary Sylvia Plath, Sexton's powerful and often startling work has been characterized as confessional poetry, in which deeply personal topics once considered taboo in modern poetry—mental illness, religious guilt, therapy—are openly discussed.*

CINDERELLA   [1970]

You always read about it:
the plumber with twelve children
who wins the Irish Sweepstakes.
From toilets to riches.
That story.   5

Or the nursemaid,
some luscious sweet from Denmark
who captures the oldest son's heart.
From diapers to Dior.
That story.   10

Or a milkman who serves the wealthy,
eggs, cream, butter, yogurt, milk,
the white truck like an ambulance
who goes into real estate
and makes a pile.   15
From homogenized to martinis at lunch.

Or the charwoman
who is on the bus when it cracks up
and collects enough from the insurance.
From mops to Bonwit Teller.   20
That story.

Once
the wife of a rich man was on her deathbed
and she said to her daughter Cinderella:
Be devout. Be good. Then I will smile   25
down from heaven in the seam of a cloud.
The man took another wife who had
two daughters, pretty enough
but with hearts like blackjacks.
Cinderella was their maid.   30
She slept on the sooty hearth each night
and walked around looking like Al Jolson.
Her father brought presents home from town,
jewels and gowns for the other women
but the twig of a tree for Cinderella.   35
She planted that twig on her mother's grave
and it grew to a tree where a white dove sat.
Whenever she wished for anything the dove
would drop it like an egg upon the ground.
The bird is important, my dears, so heed him.   40

Next came the ball, as you all know.
It was a marriage market.
The prince was looking for a wife.

All but Cinderella were preparing
and gussying up for the big event.   45
Cinderella begged to go too.
Her stepmother threw a dish of lentils
into the cinders and said: Pick them
up in an hour and you shall go.
The white dove brought all his friends;   50
all the warm wings of the fatherland came,
and picked up the lentils in a jiffy.
No, Cinderella, said the stepmother,
you have no clothes and cannot dance.
That's the way with stepmothers.   55

Cinderella went to the tree at the grave
and cried forth like a gospel singer:
Mama! Mama! My turtledove,
send me to the prince's ball!
The bird dropped down a golden dress   60
and delicate little gold slippers.
Rather a large package for a simple bird.
So she went. Which is no surprise.
Her stepmother and sisters didn't
recognize her without her cinder face   65
and the prince took her hand on the spot
and danced with no other the whole day.

As nightfall came she thought she'd better
get home. The prince walked her home
and she disappeared into the pigeon house   70
and although the prince took an axe and broke
it open she was gone. Back to her cinders.
These events repeated themselves for three days.
However on the third day the prince
covered the palace steps with cobbler's wax   75
and Cinderella's gold shoe stuck upon it.
Now he would find whom the shoe fit
and find his strange dancing girl for keeps.
He went to their house and the two sisters
were delighted because they had lovely feet.   80
The eldest went into a room to try the slipper on
but her big toe got in the way so she simply
sliced it off and put on the slipper.
The prince rode away with her until the white dove
told him to look at the blood pouring forth.   85
That is the way with amputations.
They don't just heal up like a wish.
The other sister cut off her heel
but the blood told as blood will.
The prince was getting tired.   90

He began to feel like a shoe salesman.
But he gave it one last try.
This time Cinderella fit into the shoe
like a love letter into its envelope.

At the wedding ceremony   95
the two sisters came to curry favor
and the white dove pecked their eyes out.
Two hollow spots were left
like soup spoons.

Cinderella and the prince   100
lived, they say, happily ever after,
like two dolls in a museum case
never bothered by diapers or dust,
never arguing over the timing of an egg,
never telling the same story twice,   105
never getting a middle-aged spread,
their darling smiles pasted on for eternity
Regular Bobbsey Twins.
That story.

► QUESTIONS FOR READING AND WRITING

1. Compare this version of Cinderella with the version you know.
2. Who is the speaker in this version? How does the speaker's "voice" differ from that of the narrator in the fairy tale? What words or phrases exemplify that difference? How are you affected by the repetition of the phrase "That story"?
3. The last stanza is a variation on the usual ending of a fairy tale. What is its tone? To what extent does it emphasize the tone of the entire poem?

PAIN FOR A DAUGHTER   [1966]

Blind with love, my daughter
has cried nightly for horses,
those long-necked marchers and churners
that she has mastered, any and all,
reigning them in like a circus hand—   5
the excitable muscles and the ripe neck;
tending this summer, a pony and a foal.
She who is too squeamish to pull
a thorn from the dog's paw,
watched her pony blossom with distemper,   10
the underside of the jaw swelling
like an enormous grape.
Gritting her teeth with love,
she drained the boil and scoured it

with hydrogen peroxide until pus   15
ran like milk on the barn floor.

Blind with loss all winter,
in dungarees, a ski jacket and a hard hat,
she visits the neighbor's stable,
our acreage not zoned for barns;   20
they who own the flaming horses
and the swan-whipped thoroughbred
that she tugs at and cajoles,
thinking it will burn like a furnace
under her small-hipped English seat.   25

Blind with pain she limps home.
The thoroughbred has stood on her foot.
He rested there like a building.
He grew into her foot until they were one.
The marks of the horseshoe printed   30
into her flesh, the tips of her toes
ripped off like pieces of leather,
three toenails swirled like shells
and left to float in blood in her riding boot.

Blind with fear, she sits on the toilet,   35
her foot balanced over the washbasin,
her father, hydrogen peroxide in hand,
performing the rites of the cleansing.
She bites on a towel, sucked in breath,
sucked in and arched against the pain,   40
her eyes glancing off me where
I stand at the door, eyes locked
on the ceiling, eyes of a stranger,
and then she cries . . .
Oh my God, help me!   45
Where a child would have cried *Mama!*
Where a child would have believed *Mama!*
she bit the towel and called on God
and I saw her life stretch out . . .
I saw her torn in childbirth,   50
and I saw her, at that moment,
in her own death and I knew that she
knew.

➤ QUESTIONS FOR READING AND WRITING

1. Why do you think the speaker places so much importance on her daughter crying out, "Oh my God, help me!" instead of her mother's name?
2. What does the speaker mean when she says "I knew that she knew"?
3. Compare this poem with Sharon Olds's "35/10" on page 225.

WILLIAM SHAKESPEARE (1564–1616)

Though William Shakespeare is the most famous writer ever to have written in English, details of his life are surprisingly sketchy. It is known that he was born in the town of Stratford-on-Avon, where he probably attended the local grammar school, and that he married Anne Hathaway in 1582. By 1592, he was an actor and playwright in London, associated with the Lord Chamberlain's Men, the most successful acting troupe of the time. In 1593 and 1594, he published two long mythological poems, Venus and Adonis *and* The Rape of Lucrece. *His astonishing sequence of sonnets, some of the most beautiful poetry ever created, were published in 1609, though they were probably written from 1592 to 1594, when the theaters were shut because of the plague. By 1597, he was able to buy a large house in Stratford and apparently retired there in 1610. His works for the theater, which were not published until after his death, number 13 comedies (including* A Midsummer's Night Dream, Twelfth Night, *and* The Merchant of Venice*), ten tragedies (including* Romeo and Juliet, Macbeth, Julius Caesar, Othello, *and* Hamlet*), ten history plays, and four romances (including* The Tempest*). Ben Jonson, a playwright who was Shakespeare's contemporary and rival, wrote of him, "He was not of an age, but for all time!"*

SHALL I COMPARE THEE TO A SUMMER'S DAY? (SONNET NO. 18)   [1609]

Shall I compare thee to a summer's day?
Thou art more lovely and more temperate.
Rough winds do shake the darling buds of May,
And summer's lease hath all too short a date.
Sometime too hot the eye of heaven shines,   5
And often is his gold complexion dimm'd;
And every fair from fair sometime declines,
By chance or nature's changing course untrimm'd;
But thy eternal summer shall not fade
Nor lose possession of that fair thou ow'st;   10
Nor shall Death brag thou wand'rest in his shade,
When in eternal lines to time thou grow'st.
So long as men can breathe or eyes can see,
So long lives this, and this gives life to thee.

➤ QUESTIONS FOR READING AND WRITING

1. Do you think he should compare his beloved to a summer's day? Why or why not?

2. Compare this sonnet to "My Mistress' Eyes Are Nothing Like the Sun" below.
3. In many of Shakespeare's sonnets, a dilemma is presented in the first eight lines— followed by a turning point and solution in the next six. To what extent is that the case here?

WHEN TO THE SESSIONS OF SWEET SILENT THOUGHT (SONNNET NO. 30)   [1609]

When to the sessions° of sweet silent thought
I summon° up remembrance of things past,
I sigh the lack of many a thing I sought,
And with old woes new wail my dear time's waste:
Then can I drown an eye (un-used to flow)   5
For precious friends hid in death's dateless° night,
And weep afresh love's long since canceled° woe,
And moan th' expense° of many a vanished sight.
Then can I grieve at grievances foregone,
And heavily from woe to woe tell o'er   10
The sad account of fore-bemoanèd moan,
Which I new pay, as if not paid before.
But if the while I think on thee (dear friend)
All losses are restored, and sorrows end.

¹ **sessions** court sessions   ² **summon** as in a legal summons   ⁶ **dateless** endless   ⁷ **canceled** as in paid-up debt

➤ QUESTIONS FOR READING AND WRITING

1. What does the speaker mean by "weep afresh love's long since canceled woe"?
2. Compare this poem to Elizabeth Gaffney's "Losses that Turn Up in Dreams" on page 173 or Shakespeare's "When in Disgrace with Fortune and Men's Eyes" on page 72.

THAT TIME OF YEAR THOU MAYST IN ME BEHOLD (SONNET NO. 73)   [1609]

That time of year thou mayst in me behold
When yellow leaves, or none, or few, do hang
Upon those boughs which shake against the cold,
Bare ruin'd choirs, where late the sweet birds sang.
In me thou see'st the twilight of such day   5
As after sunset fadeth in the west,

Which by and by black night doth take away,
Death's second self, that seals up all in rest.
In me thou see'st the glowing of such fire
That on the ashes of his youth doth lie,   10
As the death-bed whereon it must expire,
Consum'd with that which it was nourish'd by.
This thou perceiv'st, which makes thy love more strong,
To love that well which thou must leave ere long.

➤ QUESTIONS FOR READING AND WRITING

1. What "time of year" is this? Why do you think it seems to matter so much to the speaker?
2. What does the speaker mean when he says, "Consum'd by that which it was nourish'd by"?
3. Compare this poem to John Donne's "A Valediction: Forbidding Mourning" on page 158.

LET ME NOT TO THE MARRIAGE OF TRUE MINDS (SONNET NO. 116)   [1609]

Let me not to the marriage of true minds
Admit impediments.° Love is not love
Which alters when it alteration finds,
Or bends with the remover to remove.
Oh, no, it is an ever-fixed mark   5
That looks on tempests and is never shaken:
It is the star to every wand'ring bark,°
Whose worth's unknown, although his height be taken.
Love's not Time's fool, though rosy lips and cheeks
Within his bending sickle's compass come;   10
Love alters not with his brief hours and weeks,
But bears° it out even to the edge of doom.°
If this be error and upon me proved,
I never writ, nor no man ever loved.

² **impediments** hindrances   ⁷**bark** ship   ¹²**bears** lasts   **doom** judgment day

➤ QUESTIONS FOR READING AND WRITING

1. Do you think there are "impediments" to "the marriage of true minds"? Explain.
2. Do you think this speaker is being realistic? Explain.
3. Compare this sonnet with Marilyn Hacker's "Sonnet Ending with a Film Subtitle" on page 179.

MY MISTRESS' EYES ARE NOTHING LIKE THE SUN (SONNET NO. 130)   [1609]

My mistress' eyes are nothing like the sun;
Coral is far more red than her lips' red;
If snow be white, why then her breasts are dun;
If hairs be wires, black wires grow on her head.
I have seen roses damasked,° red and white,   5
But no such roses see I in her cheeks;
And in some perfumes is there more delight
Than in the breath that from my mistress reeks.
I love to hear her speak, yet well I know
That music hath a far more pleasing sound;   10
I grant I never saw a goddess go;°
My mistress, when she walks, treads on the ground.
And yet, by heaven, I think my love as rare
As any she belied with false compare.

⁵ **damasked** of mingled red and white   ¹¹ **go** walk

▶ QUESTIONS FOR READING AND WRITING

1. According to the speaker, his mistress's eyes, lips, breasts, hair, cheeks, breath, voice, and walk don't stand up to nature very well. Do you think he is insulting her? Explain.
2. In what way do the last two lines reverse the first ten?
3. To what extent is this poem about the use of language?

WHEN MY LOVE SWEARS THAT SHE IS MADE OF TRUTH (SONNET NO. 138)   [1609]

When my love swears that she is made of truth
I do believe her, though I know she lies,
That she might think me some untutor'd youth,
Unlearned in the world's false subtleties.
Thus vainly thinking that she thinks me young,   5
Although she knows my days are past the best,
Simply I credit her false-speaking tongue;
On both sides thus is simple truth suppress'd.
But wherefore says she not she is unjust?
And wherefore say not I that I am old?   10
O, love's best habit is in seeming trust,
And age in love loves not to have years told.
    Therefore I lie with her, and she with me,
    And in our faults by lies we flattered be.

➤ *QUESTIONS FOR READING AND WRITING*

1. If the speaker knows his love "lies," why do you think he believes her?
2. Do you agree that "love's best habit is in seeming trust"? Why or why not?
3. Compare this sonnet with "My Mistress' Eyes Are Nothing Like the Sun" on page 251.

CHARLES SIMIC (b. 1938)

Charles Simic was born in Yugoslavia and immigrated with his family to Chicago when he was 11 years old. He was educated at New York University, and his collection of poems The World Doesn't End *was awarded the Pulitzer Prize in 1990. He teaches at the University of New Hampshire.*

THE PLEASURES OF READING
[1993]

On his deathbed my father is reading
The memoirs of Casanova.
I'm watching the night fall,
A few windows being lit across the street.
In one of them a young woman is reading   5
Close to the glass.
She hasn't looked up in a long while,
Even with the darkness coming.

While there's still a bit of light
I want her to lift her head,   10
So I can see her face,
Which I have already imagined,
But her book must be full of suspense.
And besides, it's so quiet,
Every time she turns a page   15
I can hear my father turn one, too,
As if they were reading the same book

➤ *QUESTIONS FOR READING AND WRITING*

1. What are the pleasures of reading for you? Do you think that is an appropriate title for this poem?
2. What do you think the speaker means when he says, "As if they were reading the same book"? Are they? Explain.
3. Compare this poem with Wallace Stevens's "The House Was Quiet and the World Was Calm" on page 258.

CATHY SONG (b. 1955)

Cathy Song was born in Honolulu, Hawaii, to a Korean father and a Chinese mother. She graduated from Wellesley College in 1975, and received a master's degree from Boston College in 1981. She currently lives in Hawaii, when she is not teaching creative writing on the mainland. Her first book, The Picture Bride, *from which "The Youngest Daughter" is taken, was published in 1983.* Frameless Windows, Squares of Light, *her second, was published in 1991. Her latest book of poems,* School Figures, *appeared in 1994.*

THE YOUNGEST DAUGHTER   [1983]

The sky has been dark
for many years.
My skin has become as damp
and pale as rice paper
and feels the way   5
mother's used to before the drying sun
parched it out there in the fields.

Lately, when I touch my eyelids,
my hands react as if
I had just touched something   10
hot enough to burn.
My skin, aspirin colored,
tingles with migraine. Mother
has been massaging the left side of my face
especially in the evenings   15
when the pain flares up.

This morning
her breathing was graveled,
her voice gruff with affection
when I wheeled her into the bath.   20
She was in a good humor,
making jokes about her great breasts,
floating in the milky water
like two walruses,
flaccid and whiskered around the nipples.   25
I scrubbed them with a sour taste
in my mouth, thinking:
six children and an old man
have sucked from these brown nipples.

I was almost tender   30
when I came to the blue bruises
that freckle her body,
places where she has been injecting insulin
for thirty years. I soaped her slowly,
she sighed deeply, her eyes closed.   35
It seems it has always
been like this: the two of us
in this sunless room,
the splashing of the bathwater.

In the afternoons   40
when she has rested,
she prepares our ritual of tea and rice,
garnished with a shred of gingered fish,
a slice of pickled turnip,
a token for my white body.   45
We eat in the familiar silence.
She knows I am not to be trusted,
even now planning my escape.
As I toast to her health
with the tea she has poured,   50
a thousand cranes curtain the window,
fly up in a sudden breeze.

▶ QUESTIONS FOR READING AND WRITING

1. How would you describe the relationship between the speaker and her mother? What lines in the poem support your view?
2. What does she mean by "She knows I am not to be trusted, / even now planning my escape"?
3. Compare this poem to Julia Alvarez's "Dusting" on page 118 and Sharon Olds's "35/10" on page 225.

WOLE SOYINKA (b. 1934)

Wole Soyinka (pronounced "Woh-leh Shaw-yin-ka"), the pen name of Akinwanda Oluwole, was born in Isara, Nigeria. In a memoir, Ake: The Years of Childhood *(1981), Soyinka has written movingly about his early childhood, where he was influenced both by the Christianity of his parents and the traditional tribal culture of his grandfather. While attending the University of Ibadan in Nigeria, he began publishing his first poems in Nigerian literary magazines. He soon transferred to the University of Leeds in England, graduating in 1959. He worked as a script reader for the Royal Court Theatre in London, which produced his play* The Swamp Dwellers *in 1955, and returned to Nigeria in 1960 following its independence. While teaching at a number of Nigerian universities he continued to write, and during this period produced some of his most important works including the plays* The Lion and the Jewel *(1962),* The Strong Breed *(1963), and* The Dance of the Forests *(1964). In 1965, following the publication of his first novel,* The Interpreters *(1965), he suffered the first of many arrests by the Nigerian police for political reasons. From 1967 to 1969, during the Nigerian-Biafran war, he was held mostly in solitary confinement, and though he was not permitted to read or write, he managed to keep a journal on fragments of packages and toilet paper, and between the lines of books he secretly obtained. After his release in 1969, he fled Nigeria, returning in 1975 following a change in the political climate. In 1986, he was awarded the Nobel Prize for literature. He fled Nigeria again in 1994 to avoid arrest and was convicted of treason in absentia; a change in the political climate allowed him to return from exile in 1998.*

TELEPHONE CONVERSATION   [1960]

The price seemed reasonable, location
Indifferent. The landlady swore she lived
Off premises. Nothing remained
But self-confession. "Madam," I warned,
"I hate a wasted journey—I am African."   5
Silence. Silenced transmission of
Pressurized good-breeding. Voice, when it came,
Lipstick coated, long gold-rolled
Cigarette-holder pipped. Caught I was, foully.
"HOW DARK?" . . . I had not misheard. . . . "ARE YOU LIGHT   10
OR VERY DARK?" Button B. Button A. Stench
Of rancid breath of public hide-and-speak.
Red booth. Red pillar-box. Red double-tiered

Omnibus squelching tar. It *was* real! Shamed
By ill-mannered silence, surrender   15
Pushed dumbfoundment to beg simplification.
Considerate she was, varying the emphasis—
"ARE YOU DARK? OR VERY LIGHT?" Revelation came.
"You mean—like plain or milk chocolate?"
Her assent was clinical, crushing in its light   20
Impersonality. Rapidly, wave-length adjusted.
I chose. "West African sepia"—and as afterthought,
"Down in my passport." Silence for spectroscopic
Flight of fancy, till truthfulness clanged her accent
Hard on the mouthpiece. "WHAT'S THAT?" conceding   25
"DON'T KNOW WHAT THAT IS." "Like brunette."
"THAT'S DARK, ISN'T IT?" "Not altogether.
Facially, I am brunette, but, madam, you should see
The rest of me. Palm of my hand, soles of my feet
Are a peroxide blonde. Friction, caused—   30
Foolishly, madam—by sitting down, has turned
My bottom raven black—One moment madam!"—sensing
Her receiver rearing on the thunderclap
About my ears—"Madam," I pleaded, "wouldn't you rather
See for yourself?"   35

► QUESTIONS FOR READING AND WRITING

1. Who is the speaker in this poem? What are the circumstances of the call?
2. Whom is he speaking to? Describe her. What lines in the poem characterize her?
3. What does the speaker mean at the end of the poem by "wouldn't you rather / See for yourself?"

WILLIAM STAFFORD (1914–1993)

*William Stafford grew up in Kansas, earned a
doctorate from Iowa State University, and for
many years taught at Lewis and Clark College
in Portland, Oregon. The rural regions he lived
in are central to his poetry; he spent much of
his time hunting, camping, and fishing, and he
often wrote about the relationship between
humans and animals. His collection of poems,*
Traveling Through the Dark, *from which the
poem below is taken, received the National
Book Award in 1963.*

TRAVELING THROUGH THE DARK

[1960]

Traveling through the dark I found a deer
dead on the edge of the Wilson River road.
It is usually best to roll them into the canyon:
that road is narrow; to swerve might make more dead.

By glow of the tail-light I stumbled back of the car   5
and stood by the heap, a doe, a recent killing;
she had stiffened already, almost cold.
I dragged her off; she was large in the belly.

My fingers touching her side brought me the reason—
her side was warm; her fawn lay there waiting,   10
alive, still, never to be born.
Beside that mountain road I hesitated.

The car aimed ahead its lowered parking lights;
under the hood purred the steady engine.
I stood in the glare of the warm exhaust turning red;   15
around our group I could hear the wilderness listen.

I thought hard for us all—my only swerving—
then pushed her over the edge into the river.

➤ QUESTIONS FOR READING AND WRITING

1. Do you think "Traveling Through the Dark" is an appropriate title for this poem? Explain.
2. What does the speaker mean when he says, "I thought hard for us all—my only swerving"?
3. Compare this poem to James Wright's "A Blessing" on page 273.

WALLACE STEVENS (1879–1955)

Wallace Stevens was born in Reading, Pennsylvania, and attended Harvard University and New York Law School before practicing law and eventually becoming the vice president of a Connecticut insurance company. Harmonium, *his first collection of poems, appeared in 1923. His second collection,* Ideas of Order, *appeared in 1936. Not well-known to the general public for most of his career, he received the Bollingen Prize in 1950 and was awarded a Pulitzer Prize in 1955.*

THE SNOW MAN

[1923]

One must have a mind of winter
To regard the frost and the boughs
Of the pine-trees crusted with snow;

And have been cold a long time
To behold the junipers shagged with ice,   5
The spruces rough in the distant glitter

Of the January sun; and not to think
Of any misery in the sound of the wind,
In the sound of a few leaves,

Which is the sound of the land   10
Full of the same wind
That is blowing in the same bare place

For the listener, who listens in the snow,
And, nothing himself, beholds
Nothing that is not there and the nothing that is.   15

➤ QUESTIONS FOR READING AND WRITING

1. What do you think the speaker means when he says, "One must have a mind of winter/ To regard the frost . . ."?
2. Compare this poem to Emily Dickinson's "There's a Certain Slant of Light" on page 154.

THE HOUSE WAS QUIET AND THE WORLD WAS CALM

[1947]

The house was quiet and the world was calm.
The reader became the book; and summer night

Was like the conscious being of the book.
The house was quiet and the world was calm.

The words were spoken as if there was no book,   5
Except that the reader leaned above the page,

Wanted to lean, wanted much most to be
The scholar to whom his book is true, to whom

The summer night is like a perfection of thought.
The house was quiet because it had to be.   10

The quiet was part of the meaning, part of the mind:
The access of perfection to the page.

And the world was calm. The truth in a calm world,
In which there is no other meaning, itself

Is calm, itself is summer and night, itself   15
Is the reader leaning late and reading there.

➤ *QUESTIONS FOR READING AND WRITING*

1. Who is the speaker and what is he doing? To what extent does your own experience affect your response to this poem?
2. Compare this poem to Charles Simic's "The Pleasures of Reading" on page 252.

ALFRED, LORD TENNYSON

(1809–1892)

The most popular poet in England during his lifetime, Alfred, Tennyson began writing poetry during his difficult childhood as one of 12 children of an alcoholic minister in Lincolnshire, England. While attending Cambridge University, he published a volume of poetry he had written with his brother Charles. The success of this venture led to his involvement with a group of undergraduates known as the "Apostles," who encouraged him to pursue poetry as a vocation. Returning home without a degree due to financial hardships, Tennyson continued to write and publish for the following 20 years, but it was not until the publication of In Memoriam *in 1850, a sequence of remarkable elegiac poems written following the death of his great friend Arthur Hallam, that he achieved a major success. In that same year, he was appointed Poet Laureate, and spent the rest of his life as one of England's most recognizable and successful literary figures. Some of his longer poetry, which is often criticized for its sentimentality, has gone out of fashion, but many of his shorter poems retain their original power.*

ULYSSES°   [1833]

It little profits that an idle king,
By this still hearth, among these barren crags,
Matched with an aged wife, I mete and dole
Unequal laws unto a savage race,
That hoard, and sleep, and feed, and know not me.   5
I cannot rest from travel; I will drink
Life to the lees. All times I have enjoyed
Greatly, have suffered greatly, both with those
That loved me, and alone; on shore, and when

Ulysses Ulysses (Odysseus) is the hero of Homer's *The Odyssey*. As the speaker in this poem, he is now an old man, many years after his adventures.

Through scudding drifts the rainy Hyades   10
Vexed the dim sea. I am become a name;
For always roaming with a hungry heart
Much have I seen and known—cities of men
And manners,° climates, councils, governments,
Myself not least, but honored of them all—   15
And drunk delight of battle with my peers,
Far on the ringing plains of windy Troy.
I am a part of all that I have met;
Yet all experience is an arch wherethrough
Gleams that untraveled world whose margin fades   20
Forever and forever when I move.
How dull it is to pause, to make an end,
To rust unburnished, not to shine in use!
As though to breathe were life! Life piled on life
Were all too little, and of one to me   25
Little remains; but every hour is saved
From that eternal silence, something more,
A bringer of new things; and vile it were
For some three suns to store and hoard myself,
And this grey spirit yearning in desire   30
To follow knowledge like a sinking star,
Beyond the utmost bound of human thought.
    This is my son, mine own Telemachus,
To whom I leave the scepter and the isle,
Well-loved of me, discerning to fulfill   35
This labor, by slow prudence to make mild
A rugged people, and through soft degrees
Subdue them to the useful and the good.
Most blameless is he, centered in the sphere
Of common duties, decent° not to fail   40
In offices° of tenderness, and pay
Meet° adoration to my household gods,
When I am gone. He works his work, I mine.
There lies the port; the vessel puffs her sail;
    There gloom the dark, broad seas. My mariners,   45
Souls that have toiled, and wrought, and thought with me,
That ever with a frolic welcome took
The thunder and the sunshine, and opposed
Free hearts, free foreheads—you and I are old;
Old age hath yet his honor and his toil.   50
Death closes all; but something ere the end,
Some work of noble note, may yet be done,

¹⁴ **manners** customs   ⁴⁰ **decent** proper   ⁴¹ **offices** duties   ⁴² **meet** appropriate

Not unbecoming men that strove with gods.
The lights begin to twinkle from the rocks;
The long day wanes; the low moon climbs; the deep   55
Moans round with many voices. Come, my friends,
'Tis not too late to seek a newer world.
Push off, and sitting well in order smite
The sounding furrows; for my purpose holds
To sail beyond the sunset, and the baths   60
Of all the western stars, until I die.
It may be that the gulfs will wash us down;
It may be we shall touch the Happy Isles,
And see the great Achilles, whom we knew.
Though much is taken, much abides; and though   65
We are not now that strength which in old days
Moved earth and heaven, that which we are, we are,
One equal temper of heroic hearts,
Made weak by time and fate, but strong in will
To strive, to seek, to find, and not to yield.   70

➤ QUESTIONS FOR READING AND WRITING

1. Who is the speaker in this poem? What is his history? Does it matter? Explain.
2. What is he struggling with now? Do you think he has accepted his fate? Explain.
3. Compare this poem with Marge Piercy's "To Be of Use" on page 229 or John Milton's "When I Consider How My Light Is Spent" on page 217.

DYLAN THOMAS (1914–1953)

Dylan Thomas was born in Swansea, Wales, a region of England with its own linguistic and cultural heritage. Though he began publishing his work when he was only 20, Thomas struggled throughout his life to make ends meet, first as a reporter in London, and later, when he was better established, by writing screenplays and short stories from his home in Wales. Beginning in the late 1940s, Thomas became internationally famous for his poetry readings both in person and on the radio, making numerous recordings and touring both in England and the United States. In 1953, Thomas, who was well-known for his drinking, died following a drinking binge in New York City. The influence of the Welsh language can be clearly felt throughout his works, particularly in his remarkable radio play Under Milk Wood *(1954), which depicts a day in the life of the inhabitants of a Welsh village.*

THE FORCE THAT THROUGH THE GREEN FUSE DRIVES THE FLOWER [1934]

The force that through the green fuse drives the flower
Drives my green age; that blasts the roots of trees
Is my destroyer.
And I am dumb to tell the crooked rose
My youth is bent by the same wintry fever.   5

The force that drives the water through the rocks
Drives my red blood; that dries the mouthing streams
Turns mine to wax.
And I am dumb to mouth unto my veins
How at the mountain spring the same mouth sucks.   10

The hand that whirls the water in the pool
Stirs the quicksand; that ropes the blowing wind
Hauls my shroud sail.
And I am dumb to tell the hanging man
How of my clay is made the hangman's lime.   15

The lips of time leech to the fountain head;
Love drips and gathers, but the fallen blood
Shall calm her sores.
And I am dumb to tell a weather's wind
How time has ticked a heaven round the stars.   20

And I am dumb to tell the lover's tomb
How at my sheet goes the same crooked worm.

▶ QUESTIONS FOR READING AND WRITING

1. Who is the speaker in this poem? To what is he comparing himself? What
   is "the force" that he is subject to?
2. What is he "dumb to tell the crooked rose"? Why is he "dumb" to communicate the "force" they share in common with so many aspects of nature?

DO NOT GO GENTLE INTO THAT GOOD NIGHT   [1952]

Do not go gentle into that good night,
Old age should burn and rave at close of day;
Rage, rage against the dying of the light.

Though wise men at their end know dark is right,
Because their words had forked no lightning they   5
Do not go gentle into that good night.

Good men, the last wave by, crying how bright
Their frail deeds might have danced in a green bay,
Rage, rage against the dying of the light.

Wild men who caught and sang the sun in flight,   10
And learn, too late, they grieved it on its way,
Do not go gentle into that good night.

Grave men, near death, who see with blinding sight
Blind eyes could blaze like meteors and be gay,
Rage, rage against the dying of the light.   15

And you, my father, there on the sad height,
Curse, bless, me now with your fierce tears, I pray.
Do not go gentle into that good night.
Rage, rage against the dying of the light.

► QUESTIONS FOR READING AND WRITING

1. Who is the speaker in this poem? To what extent do you think that influences his attitude toward this death?
2. Were you surprised by the advice of this poem? Why?
3. If "wise men . . . know that dark is right" why do you think the speaker wants his father to rage against it?

JEAN TOOMER (1894–1967)

One of the important figures of the Harlem Renaissance, Jean Toomer was born in Washington D.C. Toomer, who was of mixed racial heritage, was raised in the house of his grandfather, who had been governor of Louisiana during Reconstruction. After attending a series of universities without taking a degree, he worked at a series of odd jobs while reading and writing, as he wrote later, "at all possible times." In 1921, Toomer held a position for a few months as principal of a technical institute in Sparta, Georgia, traveling to the Deep South for the first time in his life. The experience inspired him to write his great masterpiece Cane *(1923), an experimental novel made up of the poems, songs, and stories he encountered among the African-Americans of the region. The novel established Toomer's reputation, and throughout the twenties his work appeared in many of the leading African-American and avante-*

garde journals of the day. In the late 1920s, Toomer became involved with the teachings of a Russian mystic, and eventually stopped writing. He was largely forgotten until the republication of Cane *in 1969 reawakened interest in his life and works.*

REAPERS [1923]

Black reapers with the sound of steel on stones
Are sharpening scythes. I see them place the hones
In their hip-pockets as a thing that's done,
And start their silent swinging, one by one.

Black horses drive a mower through the weeds,   5
And there, a field rat, started squealing bleeds,
His belly close to ground. I see the blade,
Blood-stained, continue cutting weeds and shade.

➤ QUESTIONS FOR READING AND WRITING

1. How does the poem's rhythm and rhyme scheme affect your response?
2. Describe the images in the poem. How do they emphasize the plight of the reapers?

JOHN UPDIKE (b. 1932)

John Updike was born in Shillington, Pennsylvania. His father was a teacher, and his mother a writer. After graduating from Harvard University in 1954, Updike spent two years in England, where he studied at the Ruskin School of Drawing and Fine Art. After returning to the United States in 1955, he worked as a reporter for the New Yorker, *leaving the magazine two years later to become a full-time writer. Though he is an accomplished critic, essayist, and poet, Updike is best known for his novels, which include* The Centaur *(1963),* Couples *(1968),* S. *(1988), and* Rabbit is Rich, *which was awarded the Pulitzer Prize in 1982. His novel* The Witches of Eastwick *(1984) was turned into a film starring Susan Sarandon and Jack Nicholson in 1987. His latest novel,* Gertrude and Cladius, *was published in 2000. Michiko Kakutani, a long-time critic for the* New York Times, *has said of Updike's fiction: "His heroes over the years, have all suffered from 'the tension and guilt of being human.' Torn between vestigial spiritual yearnings and the new imperatives of self-fulfillment, they hunger for salvation even as they submit to importunate demands of the flesh."*

THE MOSQUITO

[1963]

On the fine wire of her whine she walked,
Unseen in the ominous bedroom dark.
A traitor to her camouflage, she talked
A thirsty blue streak distinct as a spark.

I was to her a fragrant lake of blood   5
From which she had to sip a drop or die.
A reservoir, a lavish field of food,
I lay awake, unconscious of my size.

We seemed fair-matched opponents. Soft she dropped
Down like an anchor on her thread of song.   10
Her nose sank thankfully in; then I slapped
At the sting on my arm, cunning and strong.

A cunning, strong Gargantua, I struck
This lover pinned in the feast of my flesh,
Lulled by my blood, relaxed, half-sated, stuck   15
Engrossed in the gross rivers of myself.

Success! Without a cry the creature died,
Became a fleck of fluff upon the sheet.
The small welt of remorse subsides as side
By side we, murderer and murdered, sleep.   20

➤ QUESTIONS FOR READING AND WRITING

1. To what extent can you connect this poem to your own experience? Do you think the images the speaker uses capture the experience? How many of your senses are evoked? Which images do you think work best?
2. What is the setting for this encounter? Who wins?
3. Compare this poem to John Donne's "The Flea" on page 156.

WALT WHITMAN (1819-1892)

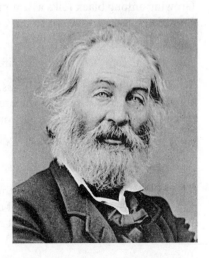

Walt Whitman was born on an impoverished farm near the town of Huntington on Long Island, New York, and moved with his family to the then-independent city of Brooklyn. For many years, he worked in the printing trade, taking occasional writing jobs, until he landed a position as an editor of a Brooklyn newspaper. During this period he wrote a largely forgotten novel, Franklin Evans *(1842), a tract against the evils of drink. Dismissed from his editorial position because of his politics, and after his own attempt at starting a paper failed,*

Whitman supported himself working as a carpenter and contractor, while he wrote in his spare time. In 1855, he published his own book of poetry Leaves of Grass, *a collection of 12 poems (including* Song of Myself*), which Whitman continually expanded and revised throughout his life, publishing a final "death bed" edition in 1892. His work as a volunteer nurse during the Civil War inspired his next collection of verse,* Drum Taps *(1865), as well as his famous elegy for Abraham Lincoln, "When Lilacs Last in the Dooryard Bloom'd." As he grew older,* Leaves of Grass, *which was largely ignored when it was first published, grew more popular and, because of its sexual frankness, more controversial. At one point, Whitman was dismissed from his post as a government clerk, when the book was labeled immoral. Whitman spent his later years as a revered figure in Camden, New Jersey, where he was the center of a devoted band of disciples and visited by many writers from around the world. His strikingly original poetry, with its boldness of form, scope, and subject matter, has influenced generations of poets. The first selection is taken from* Song of Myself *(1855), Whitman's longest—it runs over two thousand lines—and perhaps greatest poem.*

SONG OF MYSELF
6   [1855]

A child said *What is the grass?* fetching it to me with full hands;
How could I answer the child? I do not know what it is any more than he.

I guess it must be the flag of my disposition, out of hopeful green stuff woven.

Or I guess it is the handkerchief of the Lord,
A scented gift and remembrancer designedly dropped,   5
Bearing the owner's name someway in the corners, that we may see and remark,
        and say *Whose?*

Or I guess the grass is itself a child, the produced babe of the vegetation.

Or I guess it is a uniform hieroglyphic,
And it means, Sprouting alike in broad zones and narrow zones,
Growing among black folks as among white,   10
Kanuck, Tuckahoe, Congressman, Cuff, I give them the same,
        I receive them the same.

And now it seems to me the beautiful uncut hair of graves.

Tenderly will I use you curling grass,
It may be you transpire from the breasts of young men,
It may be if I had known them I would have loved them,   15
It may be you are from old people, or from offspring taken soon out of their
        mothers' laps,
And here you are the mothers' laps.

This grass is very dark to be from the white heads of old mothers,
Darker than the colorless beards of old men,
Dark to come from under the faint red roofs of mouths.   20

O I perceive after all so many uttering tongues,
And I perceive they do not come from the roofs of mouths for nothing.

I wish I could translate the hints about the dead young men and women,
And the hints about old men and mothers, and the offspring taken soon out of
    their laps.

What do you think has become of the young and old men?   25
And what do you think has become of the women and children?

They are alive and well somewhere,
The smallest sprout shows there is really no death,
And if ever there was it led forward life, and does not wait at the end to arrest it,
And ceased the moment life appeared.   30

All goes onward and outward, nothing collapses,
And to die is different from what anyone supposed, and luckier.

➤ QUESTIONS FOR READING AND WRITING

1. Who is the speaker in this poem? How does he experience the world? Do
   you experience the world this way? Explain.
2. What do you think he means by "To die is different from what anyone supposed, and luckier"? Does the rest of this poem support that? Explain.

A NOISELESS PATIENT SPIDER   [1876]

A noiseless patient spider,
I mark'd where on a little promontory it stood isolated,
Mark'd how to explore the vacant vast surrounding,
It launch'd forth filament, filament, filament, out of itself,
Ever unreeling them, ever tirelessly speeding them.   5

And you O my soul where you stand,
Surrounded, detached, in measureless oceans of space,
Ceaselessly musing, venturing, throwing, seeking the spheres to
    connect them,
Till the bridge you will need be form'd, till the ductile anchor
    hold,
Till the gossamer thread you fling catch somewhere, O my soul.   10

➤ QUESTIONS FOR READING AND WRITING

1. In what way does the activity and patience of the spider provide a
   metaphor for the speaker's quest?
2. Compare this poem to Marge Piercy's "To Be of Use" on page 229 or John
   Milton's "When I Consider How My Light is Spent" on page 217.

WILLIAM CARLOS WILLIAMS

(1883–1961)

William Carlos Williams was born in Rutherford, New Jersey. While attending high school in New York City, where he focused most of his energies on math and science, he first discovered his love for writing poetry. He skipped a traditional college education at his parents' insistence and went directly to medical school at the University of Pennsylvania. While completing his studies, he came into contact with Ezra Pound, then a graduate student, who would become his lifelong friend and critic, and Hilda Doolitle (the poet H. D.). Pound and H. D. introduced Williams to the imagist movement, which rejected rigid and ordered poetry in favor of simple phrases and an embrace of the ordinary. Over the next 40 years, though he practiced medicine full time, Williams wrote volumes of poetry, often finding inspiration in the stories of his patients, jotting poems on prescription pads or, between appointments, turning to a typewriter he kept in his office. His publications include: Collected Poems *(1934);* Later Collected Poems *(1950); a five-volume poem about a nearby city in New Jersey,* Paterson *(1946–1958); a collection of experimental plays,* Many Loves and Other Plays *(1961); a series of novels; and numerous short stories and essays. His final book of poems,* Pictures from Brueghel and Other Poems, *was awarded the Pulitzer Prize in 1963. With his innovative use of free verse, his embrace of American speech, and insistence on the importance of the commonplace, Williams profoundly influenced the course of American poetry.*

At the Ball Game   [1923]

The crowd at the ball game
is moved uniformly

by a spirit of uselessness
which delights them—

all the exciting detail   5
of the chase

and the escape, the error
the flash of genius—

all to no end save beauty
the eternal—   10

So in detail they, the crowd,
are beautiful

for this
to be warned against

saluted and defied—   15
It is alive, venomous

it smiles grimly
its words cut—

The flashy female with her
mother, gets it—   20

The Jew gets it straight—it
is deadly, terrifying—

It is the Inquisition, the
Revolution

It is the beauty itself   25
that lives

day by day in them
idly—

This is
the power of their faces   30

It is summer, it is the solstice
the crowd is

cheering, the crowd is laughing
in detail

permanently, seriously   35
without thought

➤ QUESTIONS FOR READING AND WRITING

1. The setting of this poem is a baseball game. Is this a poem about baseball?
   Explain.
2. What do you think the references to "the flashy female," "the Jew," "the
   Inquisition," and "the Revolution" mean?
3. What does the speaker mean by "The crowd is laughing / in detail / permanently, seriously / without thought"?

THIS IS JUST TO SAY   [1934]

I have eaten
the plums
that were in
the icebox

and which
you were proabably   5
saving
for breakfast

Forgive me
they were delicious   10
so sweet
and so cold

► *QUESTIONS FOR READING AND WRITING*

1. The title is the first line of the poem. Do you this arrangement is effective?
   Explain.
2. Compare this poem to Helen Chassin's "The Word *Plum*" on page 62.

WILLIAM WORDSWORTH

(1770–1850)

*William Wordsworth was born in
Cockermouth on the northern tip of England's
Lake District and spent much of his childhood
exploring the natural sights of this region,
which later served as the setting for many of his
greatest poems. In 1791, after attending
Cambridge University he traveled to France,
where he became a supporter of the French
Revolution and met and fell in love with a
French woman, Annette Vallon, with whom he
had a daughter. Due to the political situation,
Wordsworth was forced to flee France, and the
couple never married. Together with his sister Dorothy, an accomplished writer herself and later his editor, Wordsworth settled first in a rent-free cottage in Dorsetshire,
and then moved to Somersetshire to be near his friend, the poet Samuel Taylor
Coleridge. In 1798, the two men collaborated to produce* Lyrical Ballads *(which
Wordsworth revised in 1800), a collection of poetry credited with bringing the
Romantic movement to England. The enormously influential volume was a commercial success, and Wordsworth and his sister were able to live comfortably for the rest of
their lives. In 1843, he was appointed Poet Laureate. Today, Wordsworth is best
remembered for his deeply felt depiction of the English countryside and of the customs
and common speech of its people.*

COMPOSED UPON WESTMINSTER BRIDGE   [1807]

Earth has not anything to show more fair:
Dull would he be of soul who could pass by